"John Wilsey takes the concept of A rod if ever there was one—and helps us to think deeply about it. Both historian and theologian, Wilsey's larger goal is to help American Christians think historically and Christianly about our national identity. Rather than pushing us either to embrace or reject the view of America as exceptional, he argues persuasively that there are expressions of exceptionalism that the Christian can affirm, as well as aspects that the faithful believer must renounce. His book helps us to discern between the two. Any thinking Christian who aspires to patriotism without idolatry would benefit from reading this fine work."

Robert Tracy McKenzie, professor and chair, department of history, Wheaton College

"Distinguished by rich historical details and astute theoretical insights, John Wilsey liberates academic discussions of American exceptionalism and civil religion from their ivory-tower confines and presents them anew to a broad audience. Positioning himself as both an unapologetic American citizen and Christian, Wilsey skillfully describes, defines and critiques these interlocking categories. This book will be of great interest not only to scholars, but also to all people of good will who cherish American diversity alongside the worthy pursuit of establishing a broad and inclusive consensus."

Arthur Remillard, associate professor of religious studies, St. Francis University, author of *Southern Civil Religions*

"This unsparing recitation of manifest destiny, Indian removal, slavery, Cold War dualism and pervasive jingoism should give all American Christians pause. John Wilsey, in offering an alternative model for Christian engagement with the state, moves the conversation toward a higher ideal of global and kingdom citizenship."

David Swartz, assistant professor of history, Asbury Theological Seminary, author of *Moral Minority*

"Nations are what we make them. Inherently, they are neither godly, nor wicked. Most are both. John D. Wilsey demonstrates this and much more. Deeply thought and engagingly written, this book delves into religious claims about American exceptionalism with passion and compassion. Through the twists and turns, Wilsey offers entirely new ways to be faithfully Christian while participating in the life of the nation."

Edward J. Blum, professor of history, San Diego State University

"In an age that appears as confused as ever about the connections between the kingdom of Christ and American identity, *American Exceptionalism and Civil Religion* is vital reading. John Wilsey has charted the complex course of a historical idea, American exceptionalism, in a way that is fair and nuanced, yet honest and timely. Combining far-reaching interaction with the most current scholarship and careful theological reflection, Wilsey tells this story in a way that will be accessible to a broad audience. I am delighted to recommend it widely and enthusiastically!"

Matthew J. Hall, vice president for academic services, The Southern Baptist Theological Seminary

"Wilsey provides the most up-to-date history of the concept of American exceptionalism available and shows an astute understanding of its relationship to civil religion. He argues for the adaptation of a pluralistic exceptionalism based on the nation's continuing struggle for and commitment to equality, freedom and justice, rejecting the frequently invoked model that frames America as an innocent nation chosen and commissioned by God."

Anne M. Blankenship, assistant professor, department of history, philosophy and religious studies, North Dakota State University

"John Wilsey has delivered a provocative and much-needed account of the promise and perils of American exceptionalism. Few other writers possess the combination of historical and theological insight required to produce a book of this kind."

Thomas S. Kidd, professor of history, Baylor University, author of *George Whitefield*

AMERICAN
EXCEPTIONALISM
AND CIVIL RELIGION

REASSESSING THE
HISTORY OF AN IDEA

JOHN D. WILSEY
FOREWORD BY JOHN FEA

IVP Academic

An imprint of InterVarsity Press
Downers Grove, Illinois

InterVarsity Press
P.O. Box 1400, Downers Grove, IL 60515-1426
ivpress.com
email@ivpress.com

InterVarsity Press® is the book-publishing division of InterVarsity Christian Fellowship/USA®, a movement of students and faculty active on campus at hundreds of universities, colleges and schools of nursing in the United States of America, and a member movement of the International Fellowship of Evangelical Students. For information about local and regional activities, visit intervarsity.org.

Scripture quotations, unless otherwise noted, are from The Holy Bible, English Standard Version, copyright © 2001 by Crossway Bibles, a division of Good News Publishers. Used by permission. All rights reserved.

While any stories in this book are true, some names and identifying information may have been changed to protect the privacy of individuals.

Cover design: Cindy Kiple
Interior design: Beth McGill

Images: Lincoln Memorial: © baumsaway/iStockphoto

ISBN 978-0-8308-4094-6 (print)
ISBN 978-0-8308-9929-6 (digital)

Printed in the United States of America ∞

Library of Congress Cataloging-in-Publication Data
Wilsey, John D.
 American exceptionalism and civil religion : reassessing the history of an idea / John D. Wilsey ; foreword by John Fea.
  pages cm
 Includes bibliographical references and index.
 ISBN 978-0-8308-4094-6 (pbk. : alk. paper)
 1. Christianity and politics—United States. 2. Exceptionalism—United States. 3. Nationalism—United States.
 4. United States—Religion. I. Title.
 BR115.P7W4945 2015
 261.70973—dc23

                                                                                    2015027566

P 23 22 21 20 19 18 17 16 15 14 13 12 11 10 9 8 7 6 5 4 3 2 1

Y 34 33 32 31 30 29 28 27 26 25 24 23 22 21 20 19 18 17 16 15

To Mandy, Caroline and Sally

Ad vitam aeternam

Contents

Foreword

John Fea

Is the United States an exceptional nation? Of course it is. The United States was the first nation to be built on the ideas that would come to define the Western world—freedom, democracy and the celebration of individual rights. The United States' commitment to religious freedom, the exportation of its capitalist economy around the world and its long-lasting experiment in ordered liberty make it unlike any other nation. Though not everyone may like the way the United States has used its exceptional status over the course of the last two centuries, it is hard to deny that it has been, and continues to be, extraordinary.

But if we were to approach this question from a theological rather than a historical perspective, the answer becomes more difficult. Does God have a special plan for the United States of America? Is God always on the side of American democracy or the free market? Is America a "city on a hill"? A new Israel? Many citizens and leaders of the United States have answered yes to all of these questions. But are they correct?

I first began to think deeply about these questions when I started teaching in the history department at Messiah College in fall 2002. Messiah is an embracing evangelical college near Harrisburg, Pennsylvania, with roots in Anabaptism, a Christian tradition that has always warned the church about the dangers of aligning too closely with the state. The school does not fly an American flag on campus, a reminder that the kingdom of God is more important than any nation-state—even the USA. Though I do not worship in an Anabaptist congregation, I have come to appreciate the school's commitment to never letting its allegiance to the United States trump its loyalty to the higher purposes of God's work among the people of all nations.

I do not know if John Wilsey would feel comfortable working at an institution that does not fly an American flag. As he explains in the introduction to this book, he is an ardent patriot. But if I understand his argument in the pages that follow, I think he would agree with my Anabaptist friends that Christians in the United States commit idolatry when they exalt the nation over the kingdom of God.

I first met John a few years ago at a talk I was giving at the Virginia Book Festival. At the time he was an associate pastor at a Baptist church in Charlottesville and was putting the finishing touches on his excellent *One Nation Under God? An Evangelical Critique of Christian America*. Shortly after that first meeting, John moved to Houston and joined the faculty of Southwestern Baptist Theological Seminary. Today he teaches history, theology and apologetics to seminarians, undergraduates and inmates in one of the largest maximum security prisons. I have seen John live out his vocation in a number of settings, from professor and author to husband, father and Baptist preacher. I know that he loves his country, but I also know that he loves his God more. I can think of few scholars better equipped to offer a nuanced historical and theological understanding of American exceptionalism and its relationship to civil religion.

John Fea
Messiah College

Acknowledgments

I OWE MANY THANKS TO FAMILY, friends, and colleagues that words do not have the force to convey. My editors, Brannon Ellis and Andy LePeau, have been tremendously helpful in shepherding me through the process of producing this book. Phillip L. Sinitiere, Bruce L. Etter, Edward J. Blum, Heath Carter and Arthur Remillard each pored over every word of the manuscript. Phil and I spent many hours discussing the flow of the book, and I have lost track of the number of valuable insights and contributions he offered. Bruce and I also spent many hours together discussing the prose, and his expertise in helping me frame my ideas more clearly was invaluable. I so appreciate Ed's wisdom, creativity and enormous base of knowledge. Heath's critiques challenged me toward precision and to avoid blind spots. And as an expert on civil religion, Art provided many helpful suggestions.

My friend and colleague Stephen O. Presley at Southwestern Seminary walked with me through the entire writing process. I remember the day I went into his office and asked him to look over the first draft of my book proposal before I gave it to Brannon Ellis. His encouragement and enthusiastic support have meant the world to me. All my friends and colleagues at the Houston campus of Southwestern Seminary provided me with rich conversations about exceptionalism and helped me to sharpen my thinking, particularly Benjamin Phillips, Miles Mullin and my dean, J. Denny Autrey.

John Fea has been truly an inspiration to me. He is learned, gracious and patient. I am honored to call him a friend and mentor. We were having breakfast one morning at the 2012 Conference on Faith and History meeting at Gordon College, and he specifically encouraged me to write this book. John is a great teacher and scholar, and he is also one of the classiest people I know. Many thanks also to James W. Ceaser and Raymond Haberski Jr. Both of them provided me with insights and encouragement at critical times during the project, and I truly cannot thank them enough.

My students at Southwestern have consistently helped me shape my thinking, particularly those at Southwestern's Darrington extension campus. The Darrington Unit is a maximum security prison, and the students enrolled there are studying in a fully accredited bachelor of science degree program in biblical studies. The Darrington students, as well as my traditional students at the Houston campus, always challenge my thinking. Discussing ideas with them remains a source of great pleasure and profit. I owe a special word of thanks to Darrington students Jake Strickland, Jason Karch and Jason Gibson. They tirelessly combed the manuscript to help me produce the subject and author indexes. Their contributions were invaluable.

Most importantly, my dear wife, Mandy, has been the greatest encourager imaginable. She read every word of every draft of the manuscript, and gave me insights and wisdom that no one else could. She has been my most engaged interlocutor and most stalwart friend. And my little children, Caroline and Sally, continually checked in to see how I was progressing. "Daddy, how is your book coming?" was a question I was greeted with from sweet and pure voices almost every day for the past two years.

With such indispensable and wise family and friends, it goes without saying that all errors contained herein are my own.

Introduction

Exceptionalism and Civil Religion

The American is a new man, who acts upon new principles; he must therefore entertain new ideas and form new opinions. From involuntary idleness, servile dependence, penury, and useless voluntary labour, he has passed to toils of a very different nature, rewarded by ample subsistence. This is an American.

J. Hector St. John de Crèvecoeur, 1782

An American said to me at Bern: "The trouble is that we are all eaten by the fear of being less American than our neighbor."

Jean Paul Sartre, 1947

Writing an essay titled "True Americanism" in 1894, Theodore Roosevelt attempted to help his readers separate authentic from sham patriotism. At the time of his writing, Roosevelt was serving as US Civil Service Commissioner, appointed to that position by then-President Benjamin Harrison. Young Roosevelt had yet to become nationally famous for charging up Kettle and San Juan Hills as the colonel of the Rough Riders in the Spanish American War, or to become the twenty-sixth president of the United States. Still, even before filling the national stage as only Roosevelt could—and considering the spirit of the nation in the 1890s—few could match Roosevelt's patriotic zeal or flair in articulating the meaning of being a "real American."

One of the ways in which Roosevelt defined "true Americanism" was to describe what it did not mean. For example, it did not mean being unpatriotic. He actually could not envision a time in the near future when the general population would abandon patriotism. Perhaps, Roosevelt mused, that time would come in a couple thousand years, about the same time when "people will look down upon and disregard monogamic marriage."[1] No, citizens would not altogether flee from patriotic fervor, but they might succumb to what Roosevelt described as "that flaccid habit of mind which its possessors style cosmopolitanism."[2] Their patriotism might weaken and abate to the extent that they become worthless to their country, and "silly and undesirable"[3] citizens. Indeed, such a prospect was deeply alarming to Roosevelt throughout his life. A hallmark of Roosevelt's career was his dedication to preventing the citizenry from losing its sense of gratitude for the blessing and responsibility entailed by American citizenship.

Much has changed in how Americans have defined patriotism since the 1890s. Today, many consider the idea of "true Americanism" to be sorely naive, outdated, jingoistic and boorish. Given the events and lessons learned by Americans in the twelve decades that have passed since Roosevelt served under Harrison, the act of associating love of country with such ideological and national-

Figure I.1. Theodore Roosevelt as colonel of the 1st US Volunteer Regiment (Rough Riders)

istic certainty does not resonate with them like it once did. But fervent patriotism and sincere love for country animated by a sense of uniqueness has not departed from American culture, despite the fact that Americans have grown wiser about their own limits, particularly since the Vietnam War and the Watergate scandal. The idea that America is a unique nation—an exceptional nation—set apart and qualitatively different from, even superior to, the rest of the world is alive and well. A casual Google search of the term *American exceptionalism* yields almost nine million results at this writing in November 2013, and almost half a million results if the search is narrowed to the exact phrase. CNN recently reported that a Gallup poll conducted in 2010 found that 80 percent of participants agreed that America possessed "a unique character" making it "the greatest country in the world."[4]

None other than the Russian president, Vladimir Putin, gave his own perspective in a *New York Times* editorial on American exceptionalism during the Syrian crisis in the fall of 2013. In his piece, he took issue with President Obama's claim of American exceptionalism, a claim Obama made in part to justify a possible punitive American strike on Syrian forces for its alleged use of chemical weapons against rebels in its civil war. Putin, a staunch supporter of the Syrian regime, chided Obama for his considering America exceptional and for using the notion to justify a military strike against Syria, saying, "It is extremely dangerous to encourage people to see themselves as exceptional, whatever the motivation."[5] Perhaps Putin did not realize the gravity of what he was doing, but he was interposing his perspective into an old and multifaceted tradition of how Americans self-identify and understand their own meaning in space and time. To be charitable to Putin, it is probable that he did not understand or appreciate that the term *exceptionalism* is an enormously important term and concept to Americans. The fact that a Russian president scolded an American president for using the term *exceptionalism* was, to many, an affront to American honor itself,[6] something as inconceivable as an Eastern dandy lecturing a Texan cowboy as to why his Western saddle looked silly with a horn, and was not fit for seating a rider on horseback. And yet, Putin's admonition to President

Obama only underscores the persistence and emotional power of the idea of American exceptionalism.

The fact is that Americans have always seen themselves as exceptional. Americans have not always used the term *exceptionalism* to describe the stark uniqueness of America as a land and a nation. However, the idea that Americans are a people specially chosen by God and given a destiny to fulfill by him has endured since colonial days. John Winthrop, the first governor of the Massachusetts Bay Colony, told his fellow sojourners to America in 1630 that they were about to establish what would become "a Citty upon a Hill, the eies of all people [being] uppon us."[7] While Winthrop was thinking of himself as an Englishman and not as an American per se, he did have in mind that the colony he was helping to establish in America would set an example of righteousness and God-blessedness that would make Englishmen back home desirous of moral, civil and theological reform.

During the French and Indian War (1754–1763), American colonists saw their struggle against Catholic France in millennial terms, thinking themselves to be God's instrument in bringing chastisement to the forces of the Antichrist represented by the French in America. In the Revolutionary War, many believed God had brought the American colonists out from the British yoke, much as he had brought Israel out from the yoke of Pharaoh. The Great Seal of the United States, designed by Charles Thomson and adopted by the Congress of the Confederation in 1782, depicts a scene that characterizes how Americans saw themselves in exceptional terms from their national beginnings. The reverse of the Great Seal, seen on the one-dollar note, includes a depiction of a pyramid with the eye of providence at its apex. Surrounding the depiction are two Latin phrases: *Annuit Coeptis*, meaning that God "approves our undertaking," and *Novus Ordo Seclorum*, meaning "a new order for the ages."

The nineteenth century witnessed the territorial growth of the United States beyond the natural boundary of the Mississippi River set by the Treaty of Paris in 1783. Alexis de Tocqueville, a Frenchman traveling around America and reporting on his observations in the 1830s, was the first to apply the term *exceptional* to America in his two-volume work,

Democracy in America. John L. O'Sullivan, editor of the *United States Magazine and Democratic Review,* coined the term *manifest destiny* in 1845, and used it to explain God's unique mission for America. That mission was to civilize and democratize the North American continent through the acquisition of territory westward to the Pacific Ocean. During the Civil War (1861–1865), Abraham Lincoln introduced one of the most important developments of how Americans self-identified. He offered the powerful imagery of renewal and rebirth out of the ashes of war to the concept of American exceptionalism. This he did, in part, by pointing to the sacrifices of soldiers who had fallen in the field. He personified the theme of sacrifice in his own death as a victim of the war, cut down at virtually the moment of his having saved the Union and ended slavery. And US territorial expansion into the Caribbean and Pacific at the end of the nineteenth century continued to feed the concept of exceptionalism.

At the outset of the twentieth century, Woodrow Wilson infused his vision of messianism that extended from the Western to the Eastern hemisphere after Americans helped win World War I (1914–1918). American victory in World War II (1939–1945) seemed to confirm Wilson's vision of America saving the world from tyranny and destruction. During the subsequent Cold War, especially during the 1950s, America saw itself as a bulwark of Western civilization centered on belief in God and ranged against the atheistic worldwide Soviet threat. And in the twenty-first century, most Americans continue to believe that their nation is indispensable and exceptional. This is so much the case that, despite all the setbacks in its foreign wars since 1950, the disillusionment in its leaders since Watergate, and the secularization of its public spaces since prayer was outlawed in schools in 1962, the concept of exceptionalism remains the guiding paradigm in self-identification for most Americans.

This is a book about American exceptionalism as an aspect of civil religion in America. The topic interests me because I am a patriotic American—I love my country and am thankful to God that America is my home. I am also thankful to those who have sacrificed their lives, and to those whose loved ones' lives were lost, so that I may enjoy the blessings of America. But as a Christian—a member of a multiethnic community of faith that transcends nationality—I affirm that any nation that uses God talk to self-identify must be prepared to accept scrutiny.

Some may object to the use of the term *exceptionalism*. In the minds of many, the word conjures up attitudes of superiority, historical providentialism, racism, warmongering and idolatry. As I hope to show in the following pages, I understand and sympathize with many people's discomfort with the term. Certainly in the eyes of people outside America's borders, *American exceptionalism* is often an offensive notion—Putin is definitely a case in point. But this is the term in common use, and no other word captures the civil religious potency of American patriotism like *exceptionalism*. Our task is to understand its meaning by defining it historically and religiously as precisely as possible. We can even try and make the term useful, especially for those who may not be satisfied with it. One thing seems certain—neither the word nor the civil religion it enlivens is going away.

The questions being raised in the pages of this book are of a fundamental nature. What is the meaning of American exceptionalism? What are the origins of the term? Does the idea entail theological commitments? If so, what are they, and how do they relate to the Christian faith? Does the concept of American exceptionalism conflict with Christianity at any point? Can a Christian adopt the concept of American exceptionalism? Are American churches faithful to Christ as their first love (Revelation 2:4) if they embrace American exceptionalism? Or is the idea of American exceptionalism free from any religious commitments?

In this book, I will argue that a high view of American exceptionalism is, at significant points, at odds with the Christian gospel. Exceptionalism does not necessarily come into conflict with Christianity. But when expressed and understood in strongly providential terms, it involves at least five theological themes imported from Protestant Christian theology and applied to America: (1) chosen nation, (2) divine commission, (3) innocence, (4) sacred land and (5) glory. When exceptionalism relies on these themes, then the idea is in conflict with the Christian gospel. This kind of exceptionalism should be rejected because it potentially makes America an object of worship, bestowing a transcendent status upon it. And it sets America up as a necessary player in redemption history. From a biblical standpoint, this soteriological form of American exceptionalism paves the way toward heterodoxy at best, heresy and idolatry at worst.

However, American exceptionalism does not necessarily carry this salvifically charged meaning, even though the idea still ought to be considered as an aspect of civil religion. American exceptionalism can carry a more limited political/cultural meaning. That is, America strives to serve as a communal paragon of justice, freedom and equality among nations. Civil religion and American exceptionalism, when understood politically/culturally rather than salvifically, can serve as a beacon pointing to justice, natural rights and the ethical well-being of the nation and the world. In short, when American exceptionalism calls for a God-ordained empire, then it leads to idolatry and injustice. When American exceptionalism points to moral and civil example, then it leads to compassion, justice and general human flourishing. Throughout the work, I am referring to the former as *closed* and the latter as *open* American exceptionalism.

In the pages that follow, I will try to show that American exceptionalism is not a monolithic concept to be either totally rejected or devotedly embraced. It is not a signpost with only one side. As an element of civil religion, exceptionalism is a coin with two sides. Closed exceptionalism, as one side of the coin, must be faced down to avoid idolatry; open exceptionalism must be faced up to foster human flourishing. The closed side is exclusive; the open side is inclusive. The closed side limits freedom to some; the open side expands it to all. The closed side is self-satisfied, because it is based on determinism. The open side is never satisfied, because it is reaching for an ideal based on natural law and rights theory as well as historical contingency. The closed side denies America can do wrong; the open side acknowledges America's flaws and endeavors toward improvement. The Christian gospel chastens closed exceptionalism, to keep the nation from becoming an object of worship. Open exceptionalism chastens sectarianism, encouraging the advance of religious freedom.

Precision in language is necessary if I am to argue this thesis without ambiguity or equivocation. To repeat, the argument of the book is this: exceptionalism is an aspect of American civil religion. Closed American exceptionalism entails the five theological commitments I listed above, each conflicting with the Christian gospel and potentially leading to idolatry, so it must be discarded. But open American exceptionalism—while it remains a part of civil religion—serves as a benefit to the nation, to religion and to the world by fostering a civic engagement informed by freedom, equality and justice.

CIVIL RELIGION IN AMERICA

Civil religion is a set of practices, symbols and beliefs distinct from traditional religion, yet providing a universal values paradigm around which the citizenry can unite. Unity is key to understanding civil religion. Peter Gardella, in his book-length treatment of American civil religion, wrote that religion in general—and civil religion in particular—is composed of "systems of symbols, actions, and ideas that purport to bind together groups of people."[8] The modern notion of civil religion was introduced to the Western mind by Jean Jacques Rousseau in the eighteenth century,[9] but Robert Bellah's 1967 seminal essay, "Civil Religion in America," provides the paradigmatic understanding of civil religion for the purposes of this work. Bellah looked at John F. Kennedy's 1961 inaugural address, noting that the president made several references to America's special relationship and responsibility to God. Bellah also noted that Kennedy's references were not in conflict with his Catholic Christianity—he made no references to Jesus Christ, the Bible or to church tradition. Kennedy was appealing to his religiously diverse audience to unify around certain religious affirmations as members of the same political community. Bellah said that when Kennedy spoke, "his only reference was to the concept of God, a word that almost all Americans can accept," and "there are . . . certain common elements of religious orientation that the great majority of Americans share."[10] In other words, there are definite religious themes that have existed in the American mind that have continuously formed American culture, identity and engagement with the world since the inception of the nation at its founding in the eighteenth century, and also of the protonation at the planting of the colonies in the seventeenth century. Bellah said these themes "still provide a religious dimension for the whole fabric of American life,"[11] and although he wrote nearly fifty years ago, Bellah's thesis still holds today. Furthermore, Bellah continues to be correct in his assertion that civil religion is so elemental in America that its sources, beliefs, symbols and practices must be understood as much as those of any traditional religion.

While not everyone has agreed with Bellah's particular conception of civil religion, it is rare to find anyone who denies that some form, or forms, of American civil religion exists. Civil religion does not have to consist of a system of strict theological dogmas. Because American civil religion has always been a cultural and a political construct, it is malleable, shaped by the circumstances of the times and the conceptions of its leaders.[12] Even in America, where religion and the state are supposed to exist in separate spheres of authority, Americans share a unifying body of affirmations and traditions that animate their conceptions of themselves. And rather than being a hindrance to civil religion, religious freedom and disestablishment actually form fertile ground for its growth. Since there is no state church, a civil religion arises to fill the role that an established religion might have played in society.

Like a traditional religion, American civil religion is made up of a body of scriptures, symbols, sources and traditions. When it comes to sources, civil religion in America has drawn from at least three intellectual wells in various degrees and at various times in its history—Protestant Christian theology, Enlightenment philosophy and Roman civil religion. Raymond Haberski noted a special irony in the fact that the roots of civil religion have been in both theology and philosophy—"The nation lives with a misbegotten confidence born from a union of religion and reason."[13] From Protestant Christian theology has arisen monotheism, national salvation through divine chosenness and a God-ordained mission to expand. Notions of individual freedom, natural rights and equality have derived from the liberalism, empiricism and common-sense realism of the English and Scottish Enlightenment. The Roman model has provided Americans with images and ideas that foster loyalty to the *patria*, despite the fact that members of a plurality of ethnicities and religions people the *patria*. Gardella asserted that "the Roman model has become more prevalent"[14] in American civil religion since World War II. As we will see, civil religion in America is at its best when it relies most on political and social values—like freedom and justice—and least on revealed religion.

The values of civil religion have found articulation in an authoritative canon, a collection of "scriptures" that have come to define the American nation and character. Bellah wrote that the Revolution is the historical framework of one set of scriptures, and the Civil War is another framework, one that succeeds and completes those scriptures of the Revolution. The scriptures of the Revolution—the Declaration of Independence, the Constitution and the Bill of Rights—express the original beliefs of the civil religion, in addition to serving as the national founding documents. Thus, in the revolutionary period, America became what Gordon Wood called "an ideological people."[15] The Revolution, according to Bellah, serves as something akin to the Exodus of Israel from Egypt, and George Washington is analogous to Moses leading the people out of slavery. Bellah wrote, "Europe is Egypt; America, the promised land. God has led his people to establish a new sort of social order that shall be a light unto all the nations."[16]

Furthermore, since 1865, the Civil War has served as the central turning point in the history of the nation and in the nation's civil religion. Bellah regarded Abraham Lincoln, the great president who saved the Union and freed the slaves, as "our greatest, perhaps our only, civil theologian."[17] Through the speeches of Lincoln, the notion of the rebirth of the nation after the trauma of the Civil War became inculcated into the civil religion. Lincoln's Gettysburg Address and Second Inaugural Address serve as a sort of "New Testament" to the "Old Testament" of the Declaration and the Constitution. As Bellah described it, "The earlier symbolism of the civil religion has been the Hebraic without in any specific sense being Jewish. The Gettysburg symbolism ('. . . those who here gave their lives, that that nation might live') is Christian without having anything to do with the Christian church."[18] Lincoln's articulation of civil religion thus harks back to Judeo-Christianity. Nevertheless, Lincoln shaped American civil religion into a form suited to his contemporary context, much as Kennedy did in his 1961 inaugural address. So, in contrast to revealed religion, civil religion in America has been purely a construct of its leaders and its people.

Civil religion also finds expression in meaningful symbols, both tangible and intangible. For example, powerful tangible symbols of civil religion are American national cemeteries. There is no more stark imagery of ultimate sacrifice on behalf of the *patria* than that found in a national cemetery. Lincoln gave his famous Gettysburg Address to dedicate the national cemetery adjacent to where the titanic battle of Gettysburg was fought. Other national cemeteries sprang up all over the nation, many adjacent to the sites of other great battles of the Civil War, like the one near the Kennesaw battlefield in Georgia. My grandfather was born and raised in the town of Kennesaw in 1913, and he spent much of his childhood combing the Kennesaw Mountain battlefield for souvenirs years before the National Park Service began preserving it. He even gave little tours around the battlefield as a boy. He used to tell us about taking Northern visitors to see the federal cemetery at Kennesaw, and delightedly announcing to his chagrined charges that in Kennesaw they had "more dead Yankees than live Southerners." The greatest of the national cemeteries, and perhaps the most hallowed ground in the nation, is located at Arlington National Cemetery at the former plantation of Robert E. and Martha C. Lee. Soldiers, sailors, Marines and airmen from every war fought since the Civil War are buried at Arlington, as are John F. and Robert F. Kennedy. The Tomb of the Unknown Soldier contains the remains of American fighting men "known but to God" from World War I, World War II and Korea. The Tomb is guarded every single day and night by the watchful eye of the sentinel on post, and one does not violate the sanctity of that hallowed place without experiencing the public shame that attends the sentinel's unmistakably strenuous chastisement and warning. As a teenager, I witnessed firsthand the sentinel guarding the Tomb confront a hapless tourist who had crossed under the cordon to get a better photo. The sentinel's performance of his duty in that moment was unforgettable to me as an onlooker. I can only imagine the emotional, mental (and physiological) effect it had on the tourist!

The national cemeteries across the land, serving as the final resting places of those who have sacrificed their lives on behalf of the nation and its ideals, are poignant symbols of what Lincoln expressed in the Gettysburg Address. On Memorial Day, the president of the United States traditionally lays a wreath at the Tomb of the Unknowns, and elected officials all over the country pay tribute to those who died that the nation might live. Conrad Cherry called the Memorial Day ceremony "a modern cult of the dead."[19] Cherry noted that the celebration of Memorial Day affirms the civil religious tenets that God has delivered to the United States a destiny, and sacrifice for the attainment of that destiny is required.

Memorial Day, Veterans Day and Presidents' Day are each holidays in which Americans celebrate the sacrificial deaths of those who have gone forth to serve the nation. More recently, Martin Luther King Jr. Day was established as a national holiday to celebrate the meaning of King's life, and to remember his martyrdom on April 4, 1968. As Lincoln embodies much of the meaning of the civil religion, King is also a powerful civil religious symbol. King represents the dream of an entire race of Americans to share in the promise of individual freedom, equality and dignity as promised in the civil religious canon, a dream that, in many ways, still remains elusive. Still, these holidays also serve as symbols—something like liturgical symbols because Americans habitually observe them as part of a civil religious calendar. But this liturgy is cultural and political; it is not a liturgy pointing to salvation.

Civil religion in America has thrived in part because religious freedom and disestablishment of church and state have meant that no particular sect will define the nation's identity or actions. Whereas the civil religions of many European countries at various times were articulated by the state churches, civil religion in America took on its own identity distinct from any traditional religion. Because of disestablishment,

American churches have not served as the sources of civil religion in America. Nevertheless, in many ways, churches have served as agents of the civil religion to support it and advance it. American clergy do not serve in political offices as an extension of their ecclesial role, but they have historically served as mouthpieces for the civil religion in various ways. Alexis de Tocqueville observed in the early nineteenth century that the American Catholic churches were emblematic of this reality. He was fascinated by how Catholic clergy could teach and embody the dogmas of the faith in their ecclesial role while at the same time advance democratic ideals in the political community. When it came to revealed religion, Catholics came under the authority of Rome. But when it came to citizenship, Catholics respected the freedom of the individual conscience in line with disestablishment. And this reality extended beyond the Catholic clergy. Tocqueville observed that "each sect adores the Deity in its own peculiar manner, but all sects preach the same moral law in the name of God."[20] Here we have in Tocqueville's observation an example of how civil religion did not necessarily come into conflict with revealed religion. But this balance has not always existed between revealed and civil religion.

Many American churches, particularly Protestant churches, have encouraged civil religion, because it often has been indebted to Christianity for many of its affirmations. Churches and civil religion often have had a symbiotic relationship in American history—clergy and churchgoers have supported civil religion where it seemed to comport with Christianity. Bellah stated, "[The civil religion] borrowed selectively from the religious tradition in such a way that the average American saw no conflict between the two,"[21] so the national interest and interests of religious people have frequently been understood to be one and the same.

But problems arise when civil religion becomes excessively indebted to revealed religion. Civil religion then can become counterproductive. For example, in supporting civil religion, many churches have vacated their place in society and left it for civil religion to replace the church with the nation. For example, it is the church's role, regardless of denomination, to serve as both a preserving agent and witness to the gospel in the culture (Matthew 5:13-16). But in some respect, churches have been content to allow the nation itself to step into that role via the civil religion. Largely, it is America that has become, in place of churches, the preserving agent of world culture, and America the beacon of light to the suffering and oppressed of the world. And rather than the Bible serving as the testimony of God pointing the way to eternal life through Jesus Christ, the civil religious canon serves to point toward an earthly salvation rooted in Americanistic notions of freedom and opportunity. As Cherry stated, "Lacking special endorsement by the state, the American churches gave up the functions normally associated with the universal church. But where the churches moved out, the nation moved in."[22]

Christian churches have often cooperated with this phenomenon conflating the ideology of the nation with the gospel. Patriotic services, displays of and pledges to the US flag, songs celebrating the virtues of America sung during services—these and other related demonstrations in many churches are examples of how Christians have cooperated with civil religion to identify the American nation as God's answer to human suffering in the world. More disturbingly, many churches have stood by in the interest of a civil religious concept of "law and order" while great injustices were perpetrated by the state. King wrote to warn white clergy of this reality in his "Letter from a Birmingham Jail" in 1963. And Christians' devotion to a civil religion that hijacks Christian theology is in part what the present study seeks to critique.

Still, civil religion has not always been a bad thing. It is not necessary for civil religion to borrow heavily from revealed religion or revere the nation or its heroes as gods. Nor is violence a necessary civil religious value. When civil religion leans too heavily on the theology of revealed religion, it should be rejected. But when civil religion is confined to a cultural/political set of universal values, it can serve to unify the nation around those values transcending time and circumstance: the rights to life, liberty and property, religious freedom, equality, rule of law, individual dignity and justice.

While America looks to no established church for guidance on objective ideals such as these, Americans have always been a uniquely religious people.[23] In general, they do not hesitate to accept the idea that God is the source of their fundamental values. Tocqueville observed this fact when he wrote, "I do not know whether all Americans have a sincere faith in their religion—for who can search the human heart?—but I am certain that they hold it to be indispensable to the maintenance of the republican institutions. This opinion . . . belongs to the whole nation and to every rank of society."[24] Bellah affirmed the same assertion. Civil religion has the potential to unify Americans around a common set of values, symbols, beliefs and purposes. Indeed, in a republic with no established church to partner with the state to advance justice, civil religion can play a vital role in the articulation of justice in the republic. Bellah stated that civil religion "inevitably pushes toward the symbolization of an ultimate order of existence in which republican values and virtues make sense."[25]

In the final analysis, civil religion (and exceptionalism as a belief associated with it) can go in one of two ways—it can move toward deifying the nation, or it can present a just model of civil government and community for which to strive. In deifying the nation, civil religion through exceptionalism appropriates Christian theological assertions for its own uses. In effect, it takes the form of revealed religion. America then engages its citizens and the world as God's agent that can do no wrong.

But another manifestation of civil religion, a cultural/political manifestation, is what Seymour Martin Lipset called "the American creed."[26] According to Lipset, there are five features of this creed, and together they make America exceptional—"liberty, egalitarianism, individualism, populism, and laissez-faire."[27] Richard Hughes located the essence of the American creed in words of the Declaration of Independence—"We hold these truths to be self-evident, that all men are created equal, that they are endowed by their Creator with certain inalienable rights. . . ."[28] And Gardella identified four values defining American civil religion: "Personal freedom . . . political democracy, world peace, and cultural . . . tolerance."[29]

Lipset, Hughes and Gardella each pointed to a set of beliefs in natural rights, individual freedom and equality. This way of conceiving of civil religion is certainly preferable to the other. One is a national construct strictly confined to this world. The other is a faith system of salvation. One is a supple, malleable political idea fashioned by those who shape it, yet guided by universal and just concepts. The other consists in a binding set of absolutes, absolutes that are not open to question or dissent. One complements a revealed religion such as Christianity. The other hijacks Christian theology and thus is fit neither for sound American patriotism nor for religious devotion—it is, as Christ said, salt that "has lost its taste. ... It is no longer good for anything except to be thrown out and trampled under people's feet" (Matthew 5:13).

AMERICANS AND EXCEPTIONALISM

This discussion on civil religion leads us directly to laying out the contours of exceptionalism. American exceptionalism is part of a civil religious belief system. And as an aspect of civil religion, exceptionalism can either deify the nation or present a just political model to emulate. Closed American exceptionalism serves to deify the nation. Open American exceptionalism serves to present a worthy example for the nation to pursue.

Where does this term, *exceptionalism*, originate? The origins of the word are fascinating in their diversity. Alexis de Tocqueville was likely the first person to use it in reference to America. Here is how he did so:

> In spite of the ocean that intervenes, I cannot consent to separate America from Europe. I consider the people of the United States as that portion of the English people who are commissioned to explore the forests of the New World, while the rest of the nation, enjoying more leisure and less harassed by the drudgery of life, may devote their energies to thought and enlarge in all directions the empire of mind.
>
> *The position of the Americans is therefore quite exceptional*, and it may be believed that no democratic people will ever be placed in a similar one. Their strictly Puritanical origin, their exclusively commercial habits, even the country they inhabit, which seems to divert their minds from the pursuit of science, literature, and the arts, the proximity of Europe, which allows them to neglect these pursuits without relapsing into barbarism, a thousand special causes, of which I have only been able to point out the

most important, have singularly concurred to fix the mind of the American upon purely practical objects. His passions, his wants, his education, and everything about him seem to unite in drawing the native of the United States earthward; his religion alone bids him turn, from time to time, a transient and distracted glance to heaven. Let us cease, then, to view all democratic nations under the example of the American people, and attempt to survey them at length with their own features.[30]

Tocqueville was noting some distinctions here between the physical and social conditions in Europe with those in America, and their ramifications. Americans, formerly Europeans, planted a European-style civilization in North America, and in doing so, became a more practical and entrepreneurial people than their cousins in England. What was exceptional about America? According to Tocqueville, (1) Americans found their origins in Puritan theology, (2) the civilization they built displaced a wilderness, and (3) their pursuits were directed more toward making the most of life here on earth rather than on religious or philosophical speculation or on the arts and sciences. What this meant for the English nation in general is that the portion of Englishmen who settled in America were going to be focused on taming the wilderness and building civilization in North America, while that portion that remained in the old country would devote their time to more intellectual and artistic pursuits. Because of the physical conditions in which the American nation found itself, no society on earth can be compared to it, no matter how free, because no society shared the same circumstances of origin and geography that Americans had. As a result, no people were as interested in that which was useful—and less interested in speculative or aesthetic intellectual pursuits for their own sake—than Americans.

Throughout his work, Tocqueville was impressed with the liberal traditions and state of equality existing in America, despite the existence of slavery in the American South. But this is the only time Tocqueville explicitly described America as "exceptional," and his meaning is somewhat prosaic compared to how Americans of later generations understood the term.

So, the term *exceptionalism*, when applied to America, likely originated in the writings of Tocqueville. Then in the 1920s, the term was used again in reference to America, this time by the Comintern of Soviet Russia. Marxist philosophy of history, drawing in part from German philosopher G. W. F. Hegel, taught that history was in the process of moving from feudalism to capitalism and finally to communism. The proletariat would inevitably displace the forces of capital in violent revolution. This had taken place in Russia, and ultimately would take place in every corner of the world. But in America, the world movement toward communism was apparently stymied by the blazing success of capitalism. The American Communist Party under the leadership of Jay Lovestone faced obstacles in organizing during the economic boom experienced in America prior to 1929. Daniel Rodgers wrote that the American party leaders were "branded with the heresy of 'exceptionalism,' . . . [and] were ejected from the party and a rival cadre installed in their place."[31] To Stalin, Lovestone and his colleagues were making excuses for their failures to organize a strong communist party in America by asserting that economic conditions there were not yet ripe for revolution. Thus Stalin and others in the Soviet Union used the appellation of *exceptionalism* to describe America in a Marxist historical context.

Given these origins of the term, it would not seem possible that it could have had much future in the American self-identification or in the rhetoric of American nationalism. Even Tocqueville's use of the word was ordinary. There was nothing normative or transcendent in Tocqueville's meaning. But the idea of exceptionalism—the civil religious idea that America was, as Lincoln described it in his 1862 Annual Message to Congress, "the last best hope of earth"[32]—had existed in America for a long time. The idea had manifested itself in various ways in America's history, but notions of specialness and divine destiny can be traced back to colonial beginnings.

How has American exceptionalism been defined in contemporary discourse? Interestingly enough, the term has not been applied outside of the academic field of social science for very long. James Ceaser noted that only in the past few years has the term truly taken off—"exceptionalism has gone viral,"[33] he said. After 2000, Hugh Heclo observed that the appearance of the term *exceptionalism* in books published since 1800 was roughly as frequent as that of the term *patriotism* in American writings during the First World War.[34] Thus, it may be safe to suggest that *exceptionalism* has largely replaced *patriotism* as a word expressing American conceptions of national devotion. That is not surprising, since exceptionalism became the rallying cry of both Newt Gingrich and Mitt Romney in their presidential campaigns during 2011 and 2012.

Ceaser distinguished between two contemporary articulations of exceptionalism: "different" and "special."[35] Exceptionalism as "difference" refers to comparison between America and other countries, and certainly America is distinguished from other countries. "America on many important features (including size of government, the number per capita of voluntary associations, rates of private philanthropic activity, and commitment to personal freedom) is a statistical outlier."[36] So, Ceaser's exceptionalism as "difference" appears to mean something close to what Tocqueville meant. That is, America is exceptional but not necessarily in any normative way, or even by any qualitative standard (superior, better, in other words).

But for Ceaser, exceptionalism can also take the meaning of "special." Exceptionalism as "special" is a reference not only to America as an outlier, but as an outlier because it has a normative, or transcendent, status. America is special because a higher power has bestowed on it a particular task. And, Ceaser wrote, "the task is not undertaken for enjoyment or profit, but to fulfill a larger purpose on the stage of world history."[37] This form of exceptionalism goes beyond a social scientific meaning. Exceptionalism as "special" implies divine chosenness.

Heclo asserted that exceptionalism should be understood in three contexts, that of condition, mission and character.[38] Heclo's exceptionalism as "condition" is similar to Ceaser's "difference." American geography is the obvious physical feature setting the nation apart from others, especially the fact of its isolation from Europe and Asia and the bounty of its yield in natural resources. The historical timing of the American founding is unique, America being the only country founded before the

Industrial Revolution, but after the Enlightenment. Heclo suggested that this had something to do with the failure of communism to take firm hold in America. Then there are the sociopolitical components of equality, pluralism and voluntarism that exist uniquely in America. But none of these distinctions, while noteworthy, point to any transcendent purpose or identity.

That is where exceptionalism as "mission" enters the discourse. Providentialism is a salient feature of exceptionalism as mission. The nation's mission takes on four manifestations, according to Heclo: divine favor, divine judgment, moral example and world redeemer. This last element in exceptionalism as mission is particularly dangerous, because, as Heclo wrote, "it denotes a faith in human perfectibility that is undermined by the stark reality that every advance in human achievement at any level always brings with it the possibility of both greater good *and* greater evil."[39]

Lastly for Heclo, there is exceptionalism of "character." He described this aspect of exceptionalism as "what Americans are like when they are most being themselves."[40] In other words, Americans are individualistic, practical and optimistic, principled when it comes to freedom and equality, communal, and theistically moral. These features of the American nation set it apart from other nations qualitatively. And though Heclo acknowledged that "exceptionalism as character" may be somewhat subjective, nevertheless, this is the meaning that he regarded as most important. But because of the highly subjective—and historically selective—aspect of Heclo's "exceptionalism as character," this part of his definition of the term is that which requires the most precise articulation.

The ways in which Ceaser and Heclo analyzed and defined exceptionalism are helpful. What both of these scholars' studies demonstrate is that exceptionalism is indeed a two-sided coin—closed and open. Closed exceptionalism is unrealistic and unchristian because it locates life's ultimate purpose and meaning in America itself as the millennial fulfillment of the human experience. But open exceptionalism finds its expression in the American creed of individual freedom, natural rights, justice and equality.

In his final speech before his assassination, Martin Luther King Jr. said,

> All we say to America is, "Be true to what you said on paper." If I lived in China or even Russia, or any totalitarian country, maybe I could understand some of these illegal injunctions. Maybe I could understand the denial of certain basic First Amendment privileges, because they hadn't committed themselves to that over there. But somewhere I read of the freedom of assembly. Somewhere I read of the freedom of speech. Somewhere I read of the freedom of press. Somewhere I read that the greatness of America is the right to protest for right. And so just as I say, we aren't going to let dogs or water hoses turn us around, we aren't going to let any injunction turn us around. We are going on.[41]

King pointed to the moral examples of justice and equality that America professed in its civil religious canon. In open exceptionalism, America presents itself to the world as a beacon of hope to the oppressed. Admittedly, America is not a perfect model, but the conception of liberty and equality expressed in its creed are seen as an ideal to be strived toward and ultimately achieved. Open exceptionalism thus acknowledges Lipset's conception of exceptionalism as a "two-edged phenomenon."[42] While America may be the most future-oriented, optimistic and freedom-loving nation, it also has one of the highest rates of crime and incarceration, and wealth is more unevenly distributed there than in the rest of the developed world. Lipset wrote, "The positive and negative are frequently opposite sides of the same coin."[43] But this acknowledgment of both strengths and weaknesses, virtues and flaws, does not reveal weakness but strength. The realism in open exceptionalism is part of what makes it an authentic form of patriotism.

EXCEPTIONALISM AS AN ASPECT OF CIVIL RELIGION

How, then, is exceptionalism an aspect of civil religion and why is it important? Every conception of civil religion serves as a paradigm that brings meaning to the American nation and unifies it around a moral vision. And every conception of exceptionalism is a central value of American civil religion. But like civil religion, exceptionalism can either be dangerous or helpful depending on how it is articulated and understood. Civil religion has the tendency to make the nation out to be God, just as closed exceptionalism has the same tendency by misappropriating theological assertions from the Christian tradition. But civil religion can have the great value of unifying the nation around a universal set of liberal ideals, as open exceptionalism does as well.

Furthermore, it is important to stress that exceptionalism is an aspect of civil religion in order that Christianity not be asked to pay for the sins of closed exceptionalism. In other words, closed exceptionalism is not a feature of Christianity, because Christianity does not teach that nation-states are the expressions of God's kingdom. Also, open exceptionalism is not an aspect of Christianity, at least not directly. Christianity does not articulate an explicit, developed theory of natural rights, equality of opportunity or political freedom. These ideas, as applied in America, developed from within a broad Christian/Western intellectual and cultural framework, but they are largely part of the secular, and mostly English, Enlightenment.[44] Nevertheless, these ideas are largely consistent with Christian teaching in the Bible on the dignity and value of the individual person before God and within community. But open exceptionalism does not favor one particular faith system over another—not even the Christian religion. Inherent in open American exceptionalism is the right of freedom of religion, that the individual answers only to God for the content of her faith, and the state has no authority to compel in matters of religious faith and practice. Again, when either the closed or open brand of exceptionalism is at issue, it cannot be overemphasized that neither of these is an aspect of Christianity. Both conceptions of exceptionalism are aspects of civil religion.

Sidney Mead, in writing on the American civil religion, spoke of the symbiotic role of Christianity and civil religion in the life of the nation. He asserted that Christianity, as a revealed religion, reminds the civil religion that the nation is not a god. Civil religion, as a cultural/political construct, stresses the need for religious pluralism and liberty of conscience against the tendencies of revealed religion to factionalize and curtail religious freedom. He wrote, "Our final concern, then, is to assure ourselves that our attitude toward the nation does not become idolatrous; that the state does not become God. . . . All men, and all sects, must understand 'that they correct one another, and that a limit under the sun, shall curb them all. Each tells the other that he is not God.'"[45] While Mead was referring to civil religion and revealed religious sects, the same could be applied to exceptionalism. The Christian tradition chastens closed exceptionalism, to keep the nation from becoming an object of worship. And open exceptionalism chastens the sectarian tendencies of the Christian tradition (or any religion, for that matter), to prevent the curtailment of religious freedom. So while a patriotic American can love her country and be devoted to it above all others, she can remain a faithful and authentic Christian by not ascribing to her country that which is not its due. And while a faithful Christian can hold her conviction that Christ is the Truth and the gospel is the power of salvation, she can remember that salvation is not up to her; that in America, persons should acknowledge that ultimately everyone bears responsibility for the content of their beliefs.

This work is divided into eight chapters. The first and second chapters will give a historical overview of exceptionalism. These chapters will trace the development of exceptionalism from the seventeenth to the nineteenth century. In every stage of development, exceptionalism has carried theological meaning and implications. Chapters three through seven will identify five theological aspects of closed exceptionalism and identify how these components are connected to one another within the rubric of American civil religion.

Chapter three will address the theological theme of chosen nation. Since the Puritans established the New England colonies, divine election, or chosenness, has been a continuous theme in closed exceptionalism. National election entails God-given mission, and I will write about this theme in chapter four. The chosen and commissioned nation, in the closed exceptionalist framework, is morally regenerate—in chapter five, I lay out this important theological theme. In chapter six, we will consider the physical place the American nation occupies. The dominion mandate of Genesis 1 figures prominently here, and we will look at this biblical notion in detail as it relates to exceptionalism. Chapter seven will examine the idea of the glory of America, especially as it was expressed in Christian school and homeschool curriculum in the 1990s and 2000s. How did American exceptionalism figure in Christian curricula during this period? We will consider this question, as well as what it means to think historically.

The final chapter will restate the argument of the book—that closed exceptionalism is theologically and practically incompatible with the Christian faith. What are we to do with the concept of American exceptionalism? It is not necessary to do away with the concept entirely. An open exceptionalist model for civic engagement contributes to human flourishing by setting up the American creed as an ideal to be pursued. In this way, Christianity chastens closed exceptionalism by barring the path to idolatry. And this model encourages justice, equality and the individual right of conscience. Thus, Christians who affirm open exceptionalism can live as patriotic citizens of the United States without compromising their distinct witness as believers in Christ.

FOR FURTHER READING

Gardella, Peter. *American Civil Religion: What Americans Hold Sacred*. Oxford: Oxford University Press, 2014.

Haberski, Raymond. *God and War: American Civil Religion Since 1945*. New Brunswick: Rutgers University Press, 2012.

Lipset, Seymour Martin. *American Exceptionalism: A Double-Edged Sword*. New York: W. W. Norton, 1996.

Madsen, Deborah L. *American Exceptionalism*. Jackson, MS: University Press of Mississippi, 1998.

Remillard, Arthur. *Southern Civil Religions: Imagining the Good Society in the Post-Reconstruction Era*. Athens: University of Georgia Press, 2011.

Schuck, Peter H., and James Q. Wilson, eds. *Understanding America: The Anatomy of an Exceptional Nation*. New York: Public Affairs, 2008.

1

The Origins of American Exceptionalism

Anglo-Americans . . . conceive a high opinion of their superiority and are not very remote from believing themselves to be a distinct species of mankind.

ALEXIS DE TOCQUEVILLE, 1835

In MAY 1856, THE ADMINISTRATION of President Franklin Pierce extended diplomatic recognition to the newly established government of the Republic of Nicaragua. This would seem a rather ordinary turn of events, except for the fact that the government of the new republic was headed by an American by the name of William Walker (1824–1860). Walker's followers dubbed him "the grey-eyed man of destiny."[1] He was one of several "filibusters," a term used to describe American soldiers of fortune in the 1850s who attempted to seize lands in Central America and the Caribbean through revolution and subsequently transform them into slaveholding states modeled after those of the South. Walker, with a private army of sixty men, intervened in a Nicaraguan civil war and successfully took over its government in 1855. As president of Nicaragua, Walker repudiated an 1824 edict emancipating slaves, intending to set up a new slave republic south of the Rio Grande. He also encouraged Americans to settle there as colonists in the same way Americans were invited by Mexico to settle in Texas in the 1820s.

But Walker was not of a mind to win friends in his new position. In addition to making powerful enemies all over Central America, Walker managed to alienate one of his chief American benefactors, Cornelius Vanderbilt. He seized control of Vanderbilt's steamship assets and handed them over to his cronies. After being defeated in battle by a coalition of Central American forces, Walker was able to flee to the United States.

Figure 1.1. William Walker, the "grey-eyed man of destiny"

And when he rolled the dice on another filibustering expedition in 1860, this time in Honduras, he was captured by the British navy, handed over to Honduran authorities, and executed by firing squad. If you are seized by curiosity, you can go to Trujillo on the northern coast of Honduras to see his grave.

Why on earth would anyone attempt such rash adventures? Walker's motives were animated by the cause of "manifest destiny," the idea that God by his providence had ordained that the United States would overspread the North American continent, and perhaps beyond. Walker sought to establish the institution of slavery in Nicaragua, as well as the English language, and fiscal policies that would attract and develop a white population in Central America. Walker hoped these policies would prepare the way for the United States to ultimately annex Nicaragua, in the same way it annexed Texas in 1845.

The story of the swashbuckling "man of destiny" William Walker, as bizarre as it seems to those of us on this side of sanity, is an example of what closed exceptionalism could lead to in the mid-nineteenth century. During the early national period, that is, the period from the ratification of the Constitution until the opening of the Civil War (1789–1861), closed American exceptionalism largely took shape. By the time the Southern states seceded from the Union in 1861, much of the American populace had accepted closed exceptionalism in the form of manifest destiny. By the end of the Civil War, slavery and secession were dead and another articulation of exceptionalism was championed—namely, the open exceptionalism of Abraham Lincoln. Thus, by 1865, the two forms of American exceptionalism, closed and open, were formed and continued to develop as the decades of the American experience progressed.

What are the origins of American exceptionalism? Where did the idea that America served as an exception to the norm of nations everywhere else in the world come from? How, why and when did closed and open exceptionalism develop, and who would be among their most persuasive spokesmen? These questions are the subject of this chapter.

Imagine for a moment that the idea of American exceptionalism is a tree. The tree's root system is intricate and deep. The trunk of the tree splits into two near the ground, becoming a multistem tree, like a maple. One trunk develops its own branch system independent of the other, but they both originate from the same root system. Closed and open exceptionalism are like this multistem maple tree. They are two trunks forming the same tree arising from the same root system.

There are four main root systems of the tree of American exceptionalism. These root systems are theological, political, exegetical and historiographical. Out of these root systems grows one tree, American exceptionalism, which separated into two trunks, closed and open, during the nineteenth century. Territorial expansion and the spread of slavery shaped and nourished the trunk of closed exceptionalism. That of open exceptionalism was bent and twisted by opposition to slavery and pruned by Abraham Lincoln during the Civil War, preparing it for growth and development into contemporary times.

THEOLOGICAL ROOTS

As an aspect of civil religion, exceptionalism entails distinct theological elements. Exceptionalism in general consists of an invocation to God; closed exceptionalism entails God's special favor on the nation. Both closed and open exceptionalism acknowledge divine providence, although in differing ways. American exceptionalism's theological roots are found in the Puritan worldview, and in particular, those Puritans who settled and flourished in the New England colonies during the seventeenth and eighteenth centuries.

It is important to acknowledge here that the Puritans represent but one religious group among several in the colonial period. Religious diversity within the Christian tradition in the British North American colonies was a given, since a variety of religious groups were involved in most of the thirteen colonies' founding. And as the Great Awakening got underway in the early to middle 1700s, that diversity became even more pronounced as evangelical groups such as the Baptists and Presbyterians became more populous. But the Puritans were perhaps the most influential intellectual group during the colonial period. In 1835, Tocqueville went as far as to say that "I see the destiny of America embodied in the first Puritan who landed on these shores, just as the whole human race was represented by the first man."[2] Through the enormous volume of Puritan writings in the form of sermons, books, pamphlets, newspapers, letters and so on, Puritan thought spread from New England to the Middle and Southern Colonies as well as to the western hinterlands. George McKenna wrote that the Puritans were, more than any other religious group, behind "an emerging sense of American nationhood, a realization that America was something more than a patchwork of villages, towns, and regions."[3]

The history of the Puritans in England and America, while fascinating, is beyond the scope of this study. Suffice it to say here that many Puritans in England, after failing to reform the state church from within, migrated to America and established colonies in what became known as New England in the first part of the 1600s. Their theological positions were defined largely by Calvinism, and they sought to integrate theology into a worldview encompassing every aspect of life and thought.[4] McKenna noted that Puritan thought provided what became a coherent framework or scaffolding around which American self-identification was constructed. It is my contention that three theological ideas in particular shaped that framework: the Puritan understanding of covenant, typology and millennialism.

Covenant. Central to the Puritan worldview was the concept of the covenant, an earnestly solemn communal arrangement between the people and God. The Old Testament provided the model for a covenant community, specifically that covenant that existed between the children of Israel and Yahweh, mediated by the law of Moses. In short, the people of the covenant community committed themselves wholly to God's care, trusting in him for protection, provision and blessing. Their responsibility as God's covenantal people was to obey his commandments and walk faithfully in his ways. In response to the people's faithfulness, God would bless them and establish them in the land, and demonstrate his own faithfulness to them by exalting them before other peoples as they humbled themselves before him. John Winthrop, the first governor of the Massachusetts Bay Colony, articulated this covenant concept in his famous treatise, "A Model of Christian Charity." According to Winthrop, if the people were faithful to obey God's commandments, then God would "please to heare us, and bring us in peace to the place wee desire, [and] hath hee ratified this Covenant and sealed our Commission."[5] If, however, they became unfaithful to their identity as God's covenant people, then God was certain to punish them, to "surely breake out in wrathe against us, be revenged of such a perjured people and make us knowe the price of the breache of such a Covenant."[6]

The covenant as a structural theme in the Puritan conception of culture was articulated brilliantly in the literary genre known as the jeremiad. Preachers and writers employed this unique style of literature to shake the people awake and out of their spiritual and ethical lethargy and call them to repentance from their sin and to return to faithfulness to God.

Unlike most of us in contemporary times, when some calamity befalls a group of people, the Puritans' first thought was not to assign some natural explanation to it. When a hurricane devastates a community in our times, for example, most of our thoughts go to things like climate change, lack of wind shear, or elevated surface temperature of the ocean when we attempt to explain its course, its strength and why it happened in the first place. But the Puritans' first thought after experiencing a crisis was simply God's meticulous providence. This view of providence has in mind that every single thing that happens (or does not happen), down to the minutest of details, is directly attributable to God's intentional activity in his world. A famine, a disease, a drought or an Indian raid—the Puritans habitually thought God used natural events like these to directly respond to their backsliding, their sinful neglect of their covenant with him.

During the second half of the 1600s, the jeremiad arose as an inimitable Puritan—and by extension, American—literary genre. It took on new efficacy in the wake of the disaster of King Philip's War (1675–1678), in which the Puritan colonists and their Indian allies fought against the Wampanoag tribe under Metacom (King Philip to the English). Both sides were devastated. The native population was reduced from a quarter of all inhabitants in New England to a tenth, and one in sixteen English settlers were killed.[7] Larry Witham wrote, "After King Philip was killed in August 1676, and his severed head stuck on a pike in Plymouth, ministers poured out their Jeremiah-like interpretations through the printing presses."[8] The first drop in a flood of jeremiads was likely Michael Wigglesworth's 1662 poem, "God's Controversy with New England," written in response to a drought. Jonathan Mitchel wrote "Nehemiah on the Wall in Troublesome Times," a 1667 election-day sermon. In 1670, Samuel Danforth preached his "Brief Recognition of New England's Errand into the Wilderness," which provided one of the first lists of Puritan sins. And in 1702, Cotton Mather published his monumental *Magnalia Christi Americana*, which was a providential history of the New England colonies. Witham called *Magnalia* "a sustained jeremiad."[9]

This Puritan conception of covenant entailed a special calling on them as God's chosen people with a divinely ordained mission. Even though they believed they existed as the people of God, they were always cognizant of the enormous responsibility that came with that privileged position. As they read the Old Testament, they saw not only the ancient Israelites existing in covenant relationship to God; they saw themselves.

Typology. In the Christian tradition of biblical interpretation, typology has served as a consistent method in demonstrating the symbiotic relationship of the Old Testament and the New. Christian biblical interpreters have recognized for millennia that the key to the harmony between the Old and New Testaments is the person and work of Jesus Christ. Christ made the Old Testament meaningful. Thus, for example, the Israelite exodus from Egypt served as a type, a foreshadowing, of the antitype, namely, the Christian's passage from death to life made possible by the atoning sacrifice of Christ on the cross. David as the king of Israel served as a type of Christ, who is at once the eternal King of the Jews and the King of kings who will personally come to reign at his second advent. The return of the captives from Babylon in the late sixth century served as a type of salvation, which is the work of Christ alone. And there are many, many others.

Sacvan Bercovitch identified the significance of the Puritan practice of seeing themselves and their experience as colonists in New England in typological terms. The Puritans extended the hermeneutical method of typology from mere biblical interpretation to a providential interpretation of secular history as well. They were not the first to do this—this practice dates back to the earliest centuries of the church—but they consistently saw themselves as key players in salvation history. Scripture served as a benchmark for the interpretation of God's work in both sacred and secular history, since God's activities had not ceased with the death of the apostolic generation. Bercovitch wrote, "In effect, they incorporated Bible history into the American experience—they substituted a regional for a biblical past, consecrated the American present as a movement from promise to fulfillment, and translated fulfillment from its meaning within the closed system of sacred history into a metaphor for limitless secular improvement."[10] He also said, "It became the task of typology to define the course of the church ('spiritual Israel') and of the exemplary Christian life."[11] By employing this literal-historical interpretation to Scripture, the Puritans saw themselves as active agents in God's overall program for human history. We will later see how typology's relation to millennialism factors into the Puritan interpretation of history and their view of themselves.

For now, what were some of the figures in Puritan typology? In other words, how was typology applied in the Puritan theological system?

Several examples can be readily identified. The nation of Israel was a powerful figure in Puritan typology. Samuel Danforth, in his "Brief Recognition of New England's Errand into the Wilderness," saw that the Puritans who were carving out a civilization in the wilderness of North America were much like the children of Israel wandering in the desert. The children of Israel were on God's errand in the wilderness as were the Puritans. Danforth asked, "To what purpose did the Children of Israel leave their Cities and Houses in Egypt, and go forth in the Wilderness? Was it not to hold a feast to the Lord, and to sacrifice to the God of their fathers?"[12] But during their sojourn, the Israelites forgot their God and turned inward. They became dull to God's law, and God judged them because of their rebellion. Danforth went on to ask, "To what purpose then came we into the Wilderness, and what expectation drew us hither? Was it not the expectation of the pure and faithful Dispensation of the Gospel and the Kingdom of God?"[13] Just as the children of Israel had turned their backs on God in the desert, so were the Puritans dangerously flirting with the same sin. Danforth was identifying ancient Israel with his own people, not just as a powerful sermon illustration, but as a type. As God's new Israel, the Puritans could look to the example of ancient Israel and understand exactly how God would deal with them, for well or ill, depending on their faithfulness to him as his covenant people.

There were other powerful figures featured prominently as types in Puritan writings; for example, in Mather's *Magnalia*, the churches established by the Puritans were the golden candlesticks of Revelation, shining the light of the gospel in the dark recesses of America. The prophet Nehemiah served as a type of John Winthrop. Mather referred to Winthrop in exalted terms, as *Nehemias Americanus* in the fourth chapter of the first volume of *Magnalia*. And the Puritans generally took the New World as a whole to be more than just a piece of land separated by the sea from Europe, but the stage on which God was about to bring to fulfillment all of history. The New World was Canaan, the Old World, Egypt. God had brought his chosen people out from the oppressions of the old country and into the wilderness. They were to prepare the way of the

Lord, much as John the Baptist was to fulfill Isaiah 40:3-5 when he went into the wilderness to prepare Israel for the coming of the Christ. As Bercovitch wrote, "The remnant that fled Babylon in 1630 set sail for the new promised land, especially reserved by God for them. . . . Unmistakably, the New World was part of the history of salvation."[14]

Millennialism. The third aspect of the Puritan theological structure I am identifying is the notion that history is progressing toward a Christian utopia, that God is using nations to bring about his kingdom on earth—and as Ernest Lee Tuveson wrote, "The finger of Providence had pointed to the young republic of the West."[15] The millennium is the biblical thousand-year reign of Christ, described in Revelation 20, to begin after the second advent. Satan will be bound and imprisoned, Christ will personally reign on the earth and his church will reign with him. The millennium precedes the final and absolute defeat of Satan, the creation of the new heaven and the new earth, and the ushering in of the eternal age.

Millennialism is a view of history that sees humankind progressing toward the second coming and the personal reign of the glorified Christ. According to this view, humans actually take part in laying the groundwork for the millennial kingdom, through obedience, spreading the gospel to the uttermost parts of the earth, and establishing the Christian ethical ideal through the expansion of Christian civilization. Further, God's agents in preparing the world for the millennium are the nations, and particularly those nations that represent him faithfully. To the Puritans, and later the American colonists as a whole, America was the millennial nation.

Prior to the Reformation, Western civilization had not understood history to be progressing toward any particular telos through the active agency of human beings. During the Middle Ages and through the Renaissance, Augustine of Hippo (AD 354–430) provided the West with the prevailing view of history in his work *The City of God*. Augustine cast civilization in terms of two groups, or cities: one was the city of man, the other, the city of God. The city of man, for Augustine, consisted of the empires established by human strength and greatness, like the Roman Empire. Human empires, while powerful, were bound up in time and ultimately doomed to fall. But the city of God consisted of those who were faithful to Christ, that is, the church, which for Augustine equated to the kingdom of God on earth. The city of God would be persecuted by the city of man, but ultimately will prevail when Christ returns and judges the living and the dead at the great white throne (Revelation 20:11-15). The millennium described in Revelation, according to Augustine, is not to be taken literally, but allegorically. The thousand years in Revelation 20 denote a long and indefinite period of time—thus Augustine's eschatological position is termed *amillennialism* ("no millennium," no "thousand years"). Since his resurrection, Christ reigns over his people, the church, and Satan's binding takes place from Christ's resurrection until the second advent. At that time, Satan will be released only to meet his final destruction in the lake of fire. The city of man is doomed to follow him there.[16]

The upshot of Augustine's view of history is that, even though Satan is bound during the age of the church, ills resulting from Adam's fall still persist. This condition is not going to change, at least not until Christ's return at the end of the age. If evils can still wreak their desolations upon humans, even while Satan's power is muted, then surely nothing can be done by mere mortals to improve their lot. It is vain for humans to try and effect hope in this transitory and decaying world. The only answer is to wait for a better world in the afterlife. This was the prevailing view of things in western Europe during the roughly thousand-year period from the fall of Rome to the sixteenth century.

The Augustinian view of history was supplanted by a new view, one that came about as a result of the Protestant Reformation in the sixteenth century. A general reconsideration of the meaning and authority of the Bible was central to the project of the Reformation. Included in this reconsideration was a new interpretation of the book of Revelation, and with it, the meaning of the millennium. Perhaps Revelation pointed to an actual thousand-year period in the not-too-distant future, when true Christian civilization would reign triumphantly over the forces of the devil and the Antichrist. Could it be possible that God would actively use the nations to bring about this triumph? If so, then it would seem that humanity could bring about the culmination of history after all. Instead of forlornly waiting around for Jesus to return, humans could effect the glorious reign of Christ by their own efforts of cooperating with divine providence, as God actively and purposefully brought about the culmination of history.

Many Protestants saw the Reformation as the major turning point in God's program for history. The Reformation struck a death blow to the Roman papacy, which English Protestants in particular considered to be the Antichrist. And what a mystery was revealed when America was discovered in 1492, a land hidden by providence until the very eve of the Reformation! The discovery of America and the dawn of the Reformation, occurring at roughly the same time, appeared to many Protestants as the beginning of the end of an old order. Tuveson described it this way: "Mankind might be over the hump at last. Thus the Reformation became the assurance that the long era of superstition, injustice, and poverty was ending and that light was breaking over the world. A great age of achievement had begun."[17]

In the millennial view of history, as opposed to the Augustinian view, progress was the defining factor in the human experience.[18] The events of Revelation were not allegories, but were literal events, taking place at a future date, but nevertheless, in real time. This notion comes through in the apostle John's recounting of Jesus' command to write down everything in his apocalyptic vision—"the things that you have seen, those that are and those that are to take place after this" (Revelation 1:19). If anything, Jesus seems to be referring to literal "things" to be "seen" with the eyes—things in the past, present and future time. It hardly seemed possible, especially to Protestant thinkers that we will consider shortly, that Jesus could be referring to an allegorized set of circumstances.

As the Reformation opened and developed in the sixteenth century, the New England colonies were established in the seventeenth, and the colonial wars in America culminated in the mid-eighteenth, the lines were clearly drawn. The New England Puritans (and most of English Protestantism) considered the French Roman Catholic kingdom to be the physical manifestation of the forces of the Antichrist. Specifically, the

Louisbourg expedition of 1745 provided an occasion for English colonial thinkers to divide the French and English forces into those of darkness and light respectively. For example, Mark Noll pointed to William Stith of Virginia who showed "how biblical precedents"[19] framed the conflicts between Britain and France. But with the rupture between the American colonies and Britain at the close of the French and Indian War in 1763 came a new conception of the division between the forces of light and darkness. From the mid-1760s through the early 1780s, Americans increasingly saw England as tyrannical, pursuing the people of the colonies as Pharaoh pursued the ancient Israelites under Moses. Ultimately, many Americans came to see their Revolution as a logical historical upward trend toward the millennial triumph from the discovery of America to the Reformation to the founding of the United States of America.

POLITICAL ROOTS

The theological roots of the tree of American exceptionalism go deeper and are more intricate than the other roots supporting it. You might say that theology is the taproot of the tree, anchoring it firmly to the ground. But exceptionalism is supported by a system of roots. Let us move on from theology and now consider the political roots of the concept of exceptionalism.

The United States originated in the Revolution as a political union of independent states. This union coalesced into a federal republic under the Constitution, which was signed in 1787 and went into effect in 1789. But the union of the thirteen original states did not emerge out of thin air. The states joined together around the common cause of independence from Britain, and that cause was undergirded by the liberal ideas expressed in the Declaration of Independence. And the ideas expressed in the Declaration had their origins even further back. The Western philosophical tradition has included liberal ideas for a long time, but for our purposes here, let us trace those liberal ideas back to England during its tempestuous seventeenth century.

The English Civil War (1642–1651) and the Glorious Revolution (1688) were two crucibles in English history that ultimately helped shape that nation into the liberal constitutional monarchy that we recognize today. The trend toward the making of England's liberal government is long indeed, and space does not permit an extended analysis of that trend. But in the seventeenth century, things definitely came to a head. The English confronted the issue of the extent of monarchical power. Would the monarchy (read, the executive) hold the reins of power, or would the Parliament (the legislature)? Is power arbitrary, and does it rest in the hands of a divinely appointed monarch? What is the relationship between the people and their government? Does the king rule a people like a father rules his children? Or do the people delegate power to their rulers? Does power rest in an elected body of legislators, and is the monarch answerable to that body? Do the people have the right to change their government, if that government abuses its power over the people? Is government ordained by God, or does it exist by the consent of the people? And what is the proper relationship between the church and the state?

These were some of the questions contended over during the seventeenth century in England. Often those questions were dealt with on the battlefield, as at Marston Moor in 1644, Naseby in 1645 and Preston in 1648. The forces loyal to Charles I (1600–1649), known popularly as the Cavaliers, were defeated by the Puritan New Model Army under Oliver Cromwell (1599–1658). Charles I was put on trial and publicly beheaded on January 30, 1649. No one can tell the story of Charles's execution like Will and Ariel Durant:

> Prince Charles [Charles I's son, later Charles II] dispatched from Holland a sheet bearing only his signature, and promised the judges to abide by any terms they would write over his name if they would spare his father's life. Four nobles offered to die in Charles' stead; they were refused. Fifty-nine judges, including Cromwell, signed the death sentence. On January 30, before a vast and horror-stricken crowd, the King went quietly to his death. His head was severed with one blow of the executioner's axe. "There was such a groan by the thousands then present," wrote an eyewitness, "as I never heard before and desire I may never hear again."[20]

After Charles was executed, the monarchy was replaced by the Protectorate under Cromwell until just after his death. In 1660, the English monarchy was restored with the coronation of Charles II, who ruled until 1685. When Charles's son James II ascended the throne, it was said that his desire was to return England to Roman Catholicism and rule as an absolute monarch. Parliament was in no mood to take chances with James, and the body invited William of Orange and his wife Mary (James's Protestant daughter) to cross the Channel, land in England and replace James. The catch was that, as monarchs, they would have to recognize the supremacy of Parliament. They agreed, and landed in England with fourteen thousand soldiers on November 5, 1688. James, having little support, and thus no real ability to control events, fled for his life to France. The ascension of William and Mary to the throne in 1688 is known as the Glorious Revolution—a bloodless affair, unlike the Civil War.

John Locke (1632–1704) wrote his famous *Two Treatises on Civil Government*, which was published in 1690, largely to bring credibility to the actions of Parliament, particularly in inviting the rule of William and Mary. Locke said that governments ruled by the consent of the people. Rulers possessed political power, but they possessed it in trust from the people, and they maintained their power by protecting the basic rights bestowed on them by nature at birth. Thus, rulers do not have the power to rule arbitrarily. Rulers may only legitimately exercise their power in such as way as to protect the natural rights of the individual. Locke wrote, "[Power] can have no other end or measure, when in the hands of the Magistrate, but to preserve the Members of that Society in their *Lives, Liberties, and Possessions*; and so cannot be an Absolute, Arbitrary power over their Lives and Fortunes, which are as much as possible to be preserved."[21] Locke also penned his famous *Letter Concerning Toleration*, which advocated for religious toleration. According to Locke, the state only possessed power over temporal affairs. It had no jurisdiction over the individual conscience.

Events in England leading up to the Glorious Revolution led to the formation of two strong political parties oriented around the liberal ideas articulated by Locke in his *Two Treatises*, namely, the Tories and the Whigs. The Tories were conservatives who favored aristocratic privilege, a strong bond between ecclesiastical and civil authority, and the passive obedience of subjects to the political/ecclesiastical order. The Whigs were firmly against these positions. Their liberalism won the day in the Glorious Revolution of 1688. Seventeenth-century thinkers such as John Locke, Algernon Sidney, John Milton and James Harrington articulated liberal views such as religious toleration, liberty of the press, parliamentary supremacy and rule by consent. Later thinkers, influenced by these and other earlier figures, sharpened and focused liberal ideas in the face of what they saw as overreach by George II's prime minister, Robert Walpole, in the 1720s. In particular, John Trenchard and Thomas Gordon advocated for religious freedom and individual rights in their 1720–1723 collection of essays titled *Cato's Letters*. They represented well the ideas of Real Whig ideology, a body of thought that stressed the most sweeping liberalism yet seen. Real Whig thought, as expressed by Trenchard and Gordon, was popular not only in England but also in America, especially during the 1760s and 1770s. During these years, Real Whig thought became the driving intellectual force of the Revolution. The Real Whigs took Locke's views on toleration to their logical terminus, advocating for complete religious freedom. Religious freedom became a hallmark of the writings of Trenchard and Gordon, for example. Pauline Maier wrote of Real Whig political philosophy that "the [American] revolutionary movement takes on consistency and form only against the backdrop of English revolutionary tradition."[22] And the writings of Trenchard and Gordon were those that were among the most influential Real Whig writings on this side of the Atlantic.

How does Real Whig ideology fit into American exceptionalism? The answer is simple—it is manifested through what Mark Noll called "Christian republicanism."[23] Christian republicanism is an amalgamation of Real Whig ideology and Protestant theology occurring in American literature and rhetoric in the years leading up to and during the Revolution. The unifying themes between these two strands of thought are freedom of religious dissension, a reaction against ecclesiastical privilege and a millennialism that saw America as God's chosen nation to bring about the final defeat of the forces of the Antichrist.

Christian republicans in America, like Jonathan Mayhew of Boston, sought to biblically justify rebellion against the mother country. Mayhew's sermon "A Discourse Concerning Unlimited Submission," which he gave on January 30, 1750 (the 101st anniversary of the execution of Charles I), defended the justice of the Puritans' overthrow of Charles I. Romans 13:1-5 served as Mayhew's text, and he preached that Charles's overthrow was entirely just. In his letter to the Romans, Paul was not writing about submitting to a government that was evil, but a government that was a "servant for your good" (Romans 13:4). Just as it is entirely right for a child or a servant to disobey a parent or a master who rules them unjustly, a people who resist the rule of a tyrant are innocent of wrongdoing. Mayhew appealed to the principle of self-defense here—a people have the right, even the responsibility, to protect themselves against a tyrant, just as the people did in 1649 when they executed Charles I. Mayhew thundered,

> A PEOPLE, really oppressed to a great degree by their sovereign, cannot well be insensible when they are so oppressed. . . . Nor would they have any reason to mourn, if some HERCULES should appear to dispatch him—For a nation thus abused to arise unanimously, and to resist their prince, even to the dethroning him, is not criminal; but a reasonable use of the means, and the only means which God has put in their power, for mutual and self-defence.[24]

Mayhew serves as an important figure in the years leading up to the Revolution for several reasons. First, Mayhew was a New England preacher heavily influenced by Real Whig political thought, like the idea that rulers rule by the people's consent. Second, he was a Christian who accepted republican ideas despite the fact that, as Mark Noll has pointed out, republicanism is at odds with key aspects of Christian theological doctrine.[25] And third, Mayhew, like many others in his generation, baptized Real Whig ideas in the waters of biblical theology. Mayhew is representative of a Christian republicanism that began occurring in the mid-eighteenth century, and continued into the revolutionary and early national periods. That religious brand of republicanism forms the foundation of a distinctive American civil religion, which Mayhew, along with many other figures, helped to create.

EXEGETICAL ROOTS

Puritan theology, Real Whig ideology and Christian republicanism are key elements in the development of the notion that America is normatively exceptional, set apart by God for a special identity and purpose. What brought these sources together to help shape this notion was the exegetical tradition of late-eighteenth-century America expressed through sermons, including jeremiadic literature. Sermons have been a powerful medium through which Americans, especially Protestant Americans, have understood who they are and what their place in the world should be. And sermons demonstrate how many, if not most, Americans have interpreted the Bible over the centuries, and read themselves and their unique story into it. Witham described this reality when he said, "To the extent that America is an idea, and owes its shape to generations of religious rhetoric, the heritage of the sermon tells the national story like no other chronicle."[26] And because of this fact, the biblical exegesis and preaching of the eighteenth century deserves consideration as a conspicuous source of civil religion in America, and thus exceptionalism.

Thus far, we have seen some hints at how Puritan theology and Real Whig ideology influenced biblical exegesis and preaching. The Puritan jeremiad is a potent example of how New England preachers interpreted the Bible and used it to their purposes. But let us consider some more specific examples of sermons in the colonial and revolutionary periods to see how exceptionalism as a concept began to take shape.

First, how was the idea of covenant expressed in colonial sermons? In 1662, Michael Wigglesworth wrote his famous poem, "God's Controversy with New England." The poem, an early jeremiad, starts off with a reference to Isaiah 5:4—"What could have been done more to my vineyard, that I have not done in it? wherefore, when I looked that it should bring forth grapes, brought it forth wild grapes?" Clearly, Wigglesworth meant

to apply the biblical passage to his own people, even though it was orig-
inally directed at ancient Judah. With this passage, and this exegetical
method in mind, it is appropriate here to quote some of Wigglesworth's
lines to see how the theme of covenant comes through so strongly, and
how the Israelite covenant is shifted over to apply to New England.

> Are these the men that erst at My command
> Forsook their ancient seats and native soil,
> To follow Me into a desert land,
> Contemning all the travel and the toil,
> Whose love was such to purest ordinances
> As made them set at nought their fair inheritances? . . .
> With whom I made a covenant of peace,
> And unto whom I did most firmly plight
> My faithfulness, if whilst I live I cease,
> To be their Guide, their God, their full delight;
> Since them with cords of love to Me I drew,
> Enwrapping in My grace such as should them ensue?
> If these be they, how is it that I find
> Instead of holiness, carnality;
> Instead of heavenly frames, an earthly mind;
> For burning zeal, luke-warm indifferency;
> For flaming love, key-cold dead-heartedness;
> For temperance (in meat, and drink, and clothes), excess? . . .
> Ah dear New England! Dearest land to me!
> Which unto God has hitherto been dear—
> And may'st be still more dear than formerly
> If to His voice thou wilt incline thine ear.
> Consider well and wisely what the rod,
> Wherewith thou art from year to year chastised,
> Instructeth thee: repent and turn to God,
> Who will not have His nurture be despised. . . .
> Cheer on, sweet souls, my heart is with you all,
> And shall be with you, maugre Satan's might.
> And wheresoer this body be a thrall,
> Still in New England shall be my delight.[27]

Notice the covenantal language Wigglesworth used here—God called
the colonists of New England out of their native land and to go to a land
where he would show them. He promised that he would demonstrate
faithfulness and blessing to them if they would follow him and his ways.
But they sinned against their God, and God was punishing them—with
a drought, in this case—for departing from the covenant. But with punishment, God invites the people to repent and return to him. They are
still his chosen people, and they can be restored to God and to a state of
blessedness that far exceeded anything before, if they would but return
to him. These themes we see repeated in the Bible again and again, but
Wigglesworth presented the New England colonists as God's covenantal
people, and New England itself as the apple of God's eye.

Next, consider how typology appeared in the exegesis of colonial
sermons. Recall that typology is a common premodern approach to
work out redemptive history spanning Old and New Testaments together
in and through Christ. Further, premoderns traditionally used typology
to cast post–New Testament events in redemptive terms. Whether any
given premodern exegete followed an Augustinian or millennial view of
history, the belief was always that God, by his providence, was overseeing
all events to culminate in Christ's return. Because of this, premodern
biblical exegetes like those of the revolutionary period frequently saw
biblical types in modern individuals and events.

One example is the 1777 sermon in East Haven, Connecticut, by
Nicholas Street. In this sermon, Street defined the Americans in explicitly biblical terms. Specifically, he envisioned the Israelite exodus
from Egypt as the type for the American struggle for independence from
Britain. Table 1.1 supplies the subjects of this particular sermon and the
typological figures Street assigned them.

In classic jeremiadic style, Street called the people of East Haven to
repent from their complaining about the strife of the struggle, and to
renew themselves to faithfulness to the American cause. He said, "Are you
not ready to murmur against Moses and Aaron that led you out of Egypt,
and to say with the people of Israel, 'It had been better for us to serve the
Egyptians, than that we should die in the wilderness' Exod. 14.12."[28]

Street's primary argument was that God deals with his people in the same way he always has—to test them to see what is in their hearts. Street preached that just as God tried and tested his people Israel in biblical history, he is trying and testing his people in America to see if they will be faithful to him. Street's closing exhortation is, "Let us be humble, kiss the rod and accept the punishment of our sins—repent and turn to God by an universal reformation—that God may be intreated for the land, spare his heritage, and not give it up to a reproach but restore to us our liberties as at the first, and our privileges as at the beginning."[29]

Table 1.1. Comparisons in Nicholas Street's 1777 sermon

Biblical Figure	Typological Fulfillment
Children of Israel (Exodus) Post-exilic Jews (Ezra, Nehemiah)	American colonists
Moses and Aaron	Leaders of the revolution
Egypt Medo-Persia Assyria	Britain
Wilderness	Time of trial and testing
Egyptians Sanballat (Nehemiah) Haman (Esther)	British Tories
Red Sea	Military struggle
Canaan	Victory, freedom and blessing
Pharaoh of Egypt (Exodus) Hazael of Syria (2 Kings)	George III

Lastly, we have considered how many colonial thinkers saw millennialism as a way to situate America's significance in history. Jonathan Edwards (1703–1758) believed that God had hidden American shores from the eyes of civilization until such a time as to prepare it for the culmination of salvation history in Christ's second coming. Edwards wrote, "This new world is probably now discovered, that the new and most glorious state of God's church on earth might commence there."[30] More and more thinkers held the belief that the American colonies represented a turning point in history, and was destined to advance human civilization to the millennial reign of Christ as the eighteenth century progressed. Abraham Keteltas, preaching in 1777 to the Presbyterians in Newburyport, Massachusetts, equated the cause of America with the cause of God. America's cause against Great Britain was the cause of liberty, justice, rule of law and individual rights—not only for those who were living, but also for those generations yet to be born.

America's cause, for Keteltas, was the cause of good against evil. As such, it was God's own cause. And Americans could take comfort in the fact that God will be faithful to champion the American cause because, in doing so, he was safeguarding his own cause. Keteltas did not envision the struggle with Britain as merely a political struggle. He saw it as part of the struggle of good against evil that had been going on since the fall in the Garden of Eden. Not only that, he saw the Revolution as part of the same cosmic struggle that Christ himself engaged in with the devil in his Passion. "Our cause," wrote Keteltas, "is not only good, but it has been prudently conducted: . . . it is the cause of truth against error and falsehood; the cause of righteousness against iniquity. . . . It is the cause of reformation against popery. . . . In short, it is the cause of heaven against hell—of the kind Parent of the universe, against the prince of darkness, and the destroyer of the human race."[31]

Keteltas preached this sermon from Psalm 74:22—"Arise, O God, plead thine own cause" (KJV). His sermon clearly reveals a particular exegetical method guided by millennialism. He envisioned the American colonies as being engaged in the apocalyptic struggle of the forces of Christ against the forces of the devil. Samuel Sherwood is yet another example of a preacher reading Scripture and the events of his time in this way. His 1776 sermon, "The Church's Flight into the Wilderness," is one of the most strikingly millenarian sermons of the time. His text was Revelation 12:14-17,[32] and his exegesis is strongly typological. Sherwood's typology, not surprisingly, is informed by millenarianism. And what is further interesting about Sherwood's exegesis of the text is how he conflated the church with the American colonies. For instance, Sherwood preached that God brought the church into North America, a land of enormous size and bounty, and planted the church here to flourish. God, said Sherwood, "brought her as on eagles' wings from the seat of oppression and persecution . . . nourished and protected her from the face of the serpent."[33] But Sherwood had in mind more than merely religious people of a Protestant persuasion. He had all the people of the colonies in mind when he spoke of "the Church." Sherwood spoke of how the British civil and ecclesiastical powers had inflicted their abuses of power upon the colonies. These abuses of power were to destroy the people's liberty and property, so that they themselves became the property of the state. Sherwood recounted the situation in this way:

> Now, the administration [of the dragon, typified by Britain] seems here described, that has for a number of years, been so grievous and distressing to these colonies in America, claiming an absolute power and authority to make laws. . . . I say, the administration seems described, and appears to have many of the features . . . of the image of the beast. . . . And the language of our pusillanimous foes, and even their adherents amongst us, seems plainly predicted, Rev. xiii.4[:] "Who is like unto the beast? Who is able to make war with him[?]"[34]

The exegesis of colonial religious leaders, as seen in their preaching, clearly displays the theological themes found in Puritanism. And it is fascinating to see how the American premodern preaching reflects an exegetical style that has a long history dating back to the earliest centuries of church history. The sermons of the colonial period, especially those from 1763 through the end of the eighteenth century, contributed powerfully to the idea that Americans were an exceptional people in the eyes of God.

HISTORIOGRAPHICAL ROOTS

Our final root of the tree of American exceptionalism is historiography. Historiography is, broadly speaking, the study of how historians write history. Let's keep in mind the fact of the difference between history and the past. Historians recognize that the past and history are not one and the same. The past is simply the events and persons of the days, months and years previous to the present. History is the product of those intellectual types who take the things left behind in the past and seek to make sense of them for a present-day audience. Because history is the product of human beings living in a time removed—sometimes far removed—from the past, there is a subjective element to history. And in that regard, it is important to remember historian John Fea's admonition that all history is revisionist to some degree. Historians make use of sources and evidence that may not have been available to earlier historians studying the same subject. Fea wrote, "As new evidence emerges and historians discover new ways of bringing the past to their audiences in the present, interpretations of specific events change. This makes history an exciting and intellectually engaging discipline."[35] And if I may add to Fea's observation, it is this fact also that can solidify a particular way of seeing the past in the minds of an entire culture, sometimes to the extent that a historian's perspective on the past becomes a kind of orthodoxy in and of itself.

Historians of the nineteenth century who studied the origins of the United States both experienced and oversaw changes in how history itself was written. American historians writing at the end of the eighteenth century shared common backgrounds and assumptions. Figures like Mercy Otis Warren, Jeremy Belknap and Hugh Williamson were not like the professional historians we have serving in history departments at colleges and universities. These historians of the Revolution were usually wealthy elites who thought and wrote about history from a leisurely standpoint. They saw history as containing strong moral messages. They were strongly nationalistic, even though most of them wrote histories of the Revolution from a local perspective. And they generally treated the leaders of the Revolution as heroes who could do no wrong.

By the early nineteenth century, historians were becoming more and more specialized and academic. They were more interested in objectivity. They placed a higher premium on primary sources. And they saw history as a discipline separate from ethics, philosophy or theology. In other words, history was becoming a modern academic specialty in the nineteenth century. Eileen Ka-May Cheng noted that "if [antebellum] historians were in many ways even more committed than their predecessors to the nationalist function of history, they at the same time, unlike their predecessors, increasingly came to view history as an autonomous discipline."[36] This was a trend occurring in Europe as well as in America. During the antebellum period, some of the most noteworthy historians were from New England, and cast the story of America's development as the story of New England writ large. Figures such as Edward Everett,[37] Richard Hildreth, William H. Prescott and John Gorham Palfrey were part of an elite group of Bostonian historians. George Bancroft (1800–1891) was also a member of this elite group.

Bancroft was one of the most significant American historians in the nineteenth century. He wrote a ten-volume history of America from colonial foundings to the Constitution over the forty-year period between 1834 and 1874. And Bancroft was, simply put, an American exceptionalist historian. Like many Puritans before him, Bancroft saw the Reformation as a central turning point in history because through it individual liberty was introduced into the souls of common people. The American Revolution was a logical progression of the Reformation because it represented how liberty was growing and taking root in not just the religious realm, but in the economic, social and political realms also. Not only was it a logical progression from the Reformation; the Revolution was inevitable for Bancroft, because it was part of a providential plan for all human history.

Bancroft wrote his history in a context in which Americans' confidence in themselves as a people was growing. Jack Greene wrote that Americans already saw themselves as set apart from their European cousins. They lived in a New World after all, a land of enormous promise and potential. This was a clean slate in so many ways for so many people emigrating to the American colonies from overpopulated urban centers, religious persecution, poverty and a host of other ills of a civilization set in its ways. But the notion that America was superior to other nations was new in the nineteenth century. It came about because of American independence, but also because the new nation had survived a second confrontation with Britain in the War of 1812. Although the war was not a decisive victory of America over Britain, it did prove that the republic could meet an existential threat and emerge from it intact. This view of superiority that began to prevail in the early nineteenth century formed the basis of the idea that America would serve as an example to the rest of the world in the near future. As Greene wrote, "British North America, reconstituted as the United States after 1776, would project their hopes for a better world into the future, and it would thereby make a significant contribution to the Enlightenment and its program of social and political reform."[38]

Bancroft, as an exceptionalist historian writing in the tumultuous and formative years bestriding the Civil War, was a contributor to this idea of a superior America serving the world as exemplar. He conceived of nations as having a life span, much as individual persons do. Persons are born and develop through a childhood, an adolescence and an adulthood. Bancroft historian Jonathan Boyd termed this notion "organic nationalism."[39] According to Boyd, for Bancroft, "the United States no less certainly existed in embryonic form throughout the colonial period as the various parts of its body formed, grew in strength and coordination, and ultimately cut the umbilical cord from its European mothers."[40] America's growth and development as an exceptional nation would continue, but not for its own sake. American exceptionalism pointed to what other nations could become. In that sense, there is a distinct internationalism to Bancroft's nationalism.

Bancroft believed that God's providence is the agent bringing all this to fruition. Bancroft, as a member of the Boston elite, was heavily influenced by the Puritanism of his forebears. He was also influenced by German idealism and the Hegelian view of history, through his intellectual upbringing at the University of Göttingen. Bancroft thought that God had indeed chosen America for a special mission in the world, to serve as an example of religious, moral and political liberty. And in doing so, God was manifesting a providential plan for all humanity, thus acting to bring human history to completion. America was the civilization that was ushering in a new chapter of human history. It was the agent of advancement, of progress. In Boyd's words, "Bancroft's chief end in writing the two million words of his history [was] to show one nation fulfilling its divine calling. Hence, he would argue that, although the work centers on and even glorifies America, his historiography serves a universal purpose."[41]

CONCLUSION

To sum up, the ideology of American exceptionalism has a multistructured intellectual root system: theological, political, exegetical and historiographical. By the early nineteenth century, Americans largely took it for granted that their nation represented a break from the past and a decisive turn toward a future defined by progress and advancement. And millions of people emigrated to the United States in the nineteenth century to tie their own personal destinies to that of America, whose destiny seemed poised to advance from triumph to triumph.

A civil religion, with exceptionalism as one of its essential aspects, developed after the Revolution. The Declaration of Independence was one of the foundational documents in a civil religious canon that was taking shape. The Declaration made objective, transcendent, authoritative statements about the nature of humanity, the role of the government in relation to the people it represented, and God's having established a particular order that could not be thwarted or overturned. The Declaration was followed by other documents that formed the civil religious canon: the Constitution, the Bill of Rights, Washington's Farewell Address and others.

As the nation grew in numbers and in territorial size between the Louisiana Purchase of 1803 and the Mexican War ending in 1848, American exceptionalism divided into two articulations. One of these articulations was more strongly religious, and more certain of God's providence concerning the future of the United States and its status alongside other nations. It was also decidedly racist. The other articulation was more agnostic concerning the providence of God, but was nonetheless certain that God had set it apart to be a moral example to the rest of the world. America could show other nations what a nation conceived in liberty might look like, how it might behave and what ideals it might pursue for the benefit, in theory if not in practice, of all humanity.

Americans struggled to figure out their place in the nineteenth century after their break with their mother country, Great Britain. They looked for their place, not only in the world doing "all other Acts and Things which Independent States may of right do," as the Declaration of Independence suggested, but also their place in human history. As they struggled, they did many things that seem strange to us in the twenty-first century. William Walker is an example of such a person. But someone who most Americans have come to admire and acknowledge as the greatest president ever to hold the office—Abraham Lincoln—was motivated by the idea of American exceptionalism, as Walker was. The tree of American exceptionalism, fed by its roots, was taking its shape in the antebellum period during the nineteenth century. It continued to grow and flourish well into the twentieth and into our own century. It has yet to cease growing and developing as a civil religious idea that Americans continually look to for guidance as they try and make sense of their significance in space and time.

For Further Reading

Bercovitch, Sacvan. *The Puritan Origins of the American Self.* 1975. Reprint, New Haven: Yale University Press, 2011.

Gamble, Richard M. *In Search of the City on a Hill: The Making and Unmaking of an American Myth.* London: Continuum, 2012.

Greene, Jack P. *The Intellectual Construction of America: Exceptionalism and Identity from 1492 to 1800.* Chapel Hill: University of North Carolina Press, 1993.

McKenna, George. *The Puritan Origins of American Patriotism.* New Haven: Yale University Press, 2007.

Stout, Harry S. *The New England Soul: Preaching and Religious Culture in Colonial New England.* 1986. Reprint, Oxford: Oxford University Press, 2012.

Tuveson, Ernest Lee. *Redeemer Nation: The Idea of America's Millennial Role.* Chicago: University of Chicago Press, 1968.

Expansion, Slavery and
Two American Exceptionalisms

No country has been so much favored, or should acknowledge with deeper reverence the manifestations of the divine protection. An all-wise Creator directed and guarded us in our infant struggle for freedom and has constantly watched over our surprising progress until we have become one of the great nations of the earth.

PRESIDENT JAMES K. POLK, 1846

ON OCTOBER 18, 1842, rashness got the better of prudence in the mind of Commodore Thomas Ap Catesby Jones, commanding the US Pacific Squadron from his flagship, the USS *United States*. Jones ordered his squadron to drop anchor in the picturesque harbor of Monterey in what was then Alta California, Mexico. He sent word to Governor Manuel Micheltorena that hostilities between the United States and Mexico had commenced and that he was to surrender Monterey at once. The confused governor was unaware of any existing hostilities with the United States. Yet, he found himself staring down the yawning barrels of the guns from three American warships, so he complied with Jones's demand. American marines landed. The Mexican flag was run down. The Stars and Stripes were run up. Jones proclaimed California to be US territory.

Oops—Jones received a message just hours later that no state of war existed between the United States and Mexico after all. He thought war had broken out because he took counsel of rumors while cruising off the coast of Peru. Jones dashed north to seize California because he wanted to prevent the British from claiming it in the event the United States became distracted in a brawl with its Spanish-speaking neighbor to the west and south.

There was good news and bad news for Jones when he received word that no war existed. The good news was that Governor Micheltorena accepted Jones's profuse apologies and hosted everyone at a lavish ball. And Jones ordered the American squadron to boom a salute to the re-stored Mexican flag upon departing. No harm, no foul. Except for one thing: the Mexicans now knew that the Americans were certain to make an attempt on California in case war broke out over the issue of Texas. Jones, in his haste to take the initiative, had tipped his hand. When Texas was annexed three years later, things were coming to a head between Mexico and the United States. Mexico was convinced that war over Texas was exactly what the Americans wanted all along—not only for Texas, but for all the territory from Texas to the Pacific Ocean, territory that belonged to Mexico as far north as the boundary along the forty-second parallel dividing Alta California from Oregon.[1]

President James K. Polk dispatched John Slidell to Mexico City shortly after the US Congress finalized the annexation of Texas in December 1845. Slidell's mission was to settle disputes over Texas's boundary with Mexico—would it be along the Nueces or the Rio Grande Rivers? Mexico did not recognize Texan, and subsequently American, claims to the Rio Grande. To try and satisfy both parties, Polk authorized Slidell to offer to purchase California and assume all Texan claims against Mexico in exchange for a boundary drawn along the Rio Grande. Mexican officials refused to even see Slidell, much less listen to him.

At this rebuff, Polk sent General Zachary Taylor and his forces across the Nueces down to the Rio Grande in an effort to annoy the Mexican army into starting a fight. This move had the desired effect. On April 25, 1846, Mexicans under General Mariano Arista attacked an American unit camped in disputed territory along the Rio Grande and killed sixteen American soldiers. Days later, on May 11, Polk asked Congress for, and received, a declaration of war with Mexico. In his war address, Polk made the amazing statement that "Mexico has passed the boundary of the United States, has invaded our territory and shed American blood upon American soil."[2]

The results of the Mexican-American War of 1846–1848 are starkly evident on a map of North America. All or parts of the present-day states of Texas, New Mexico, Arizona, California, Nevada, Utah, Colorado, Kansas, Oklahoma and Wyoming were ceded by Mexico to the United States as stipulated by the 1848 Treaty of Guadalupe-Hidalgo. The US acquisition of these lands, as well as that of the Oregon Territory (by treaty with Great Britain in 1846) represents the largest amount of new territories acquired under a single presidential administration, that of Polk. The 1.2 million square miles[3] added to the United States from 1846 to 1848 exceeded even the 909,390 square miles[4] added by the Louisiana Purchase in 1803 during the Jefferson Administration. Louisiana was added to the original 890,000-square mile territory of the United States, the land east of the Mississippi River that was conceded to the United States by Great Britain after the Revolution ended in 1783.[5]

The Mexican-American War represented the triumph of manifest destiny, the idea that God in his wisdom had foreordained that the United States must possess the North American continent to the Pacific Ocean. But the problem with the enormous influx of territory, particularly Texas and the Mexican Cession in 1848, was slavery. The question of whether or not the territories seized from Mexico would be open to the expansion of the peculiar institution was on the minds of everyone in the United States as soon as the shooting started in 1846. A freshman representative from Pennsylvania, David Wilmot, proposed that slavery not be extended into territories won from Mexico (excluding Texas). While the House accepted the Wilmot Proviso, the Senate rejected it. John C. Calhoun of South Carolina argued against the Wilmot Proviso by appealing to the Fifth Amendment, which prevented the government from depriving persons of their property (read: slaves). Senator Thomas Hart Benton of Missouri likened Wilmot's and Calhoun's positions to a set of scissors—historians George Tindal and David Shi summarized Benton's metaphor: "Neither blade alone would cut very well, but joined together they could sever the ties of union."[6] And the issue of slavery, aggravated as it was by territorial expansion, ultimately brought on the Civil War. In this way, Ralph Waldo Emerson's prophecy rang true: "The United States will conquer Mexico, but it will be as the man swallows the arsenic, which brings him down in turn. Mexico will poison us."[7] James McPherson's assessment of Emerson's prophecy is simple and exact: "He was right."[8]

In the last chapter, I likened the idea of American exceptionalism to a two-stemmed maple tree. The idea has an intricate root system, comes up out of the ground and then diverges into two stems. In the nineteenth century, our tree's stem splits in two. Because of rapid territorial expansion and the attending issue of the expansion of slavery, many expressed American exceptionalism in the years leading up to the Civil War as either (1) the closed exceptionalism of John L. O'Sullivan's manifest destiny or (2) the open expression of exceptionalism of Abraham Lincoln. Since the Civil War, American exceptionalism as civil religion continued to be articulated in terms of closed and open, exclusive and inclusive, imperialist and exemplarist. In this chapter, I will give a brief background to territorial expansion and slavery, then lay out the aspects of exceptionalism as articulated by O'Sullivan and Lincoln. I will compare and contrast the two, and set the path for the remaining chapters of the book.

TERRITORIAL GROWTH OF THE UNITED STATES

The story of American expansion in the nineteenth century is, if anything else, dramatic. When the United States won the Revolution, Jefferson thought it would take a hundred generations of Americans to fill up the lands east of the Mississippi River. Jefferson was among many who, at the end of the eighteenth century, thought that the North American continent might be peopled by sister republics at peace and harmony with the United States. Still, hardly anyone could have predicted the speed and efficiency by which the United States embraced the continent. But most Americans were elated to see it happen, especially those, like

Jefferson, who profited from land speculation and slavery.

The 1783 Treaty of Paris, which ended the Revolutionary War and brought British recognition of American independence, was particularly generous. The boundaries of the United States stretched as far west as the Mississippi River. But as expansive as the new nation was, the strategically important port of New Orleans was not part of US territory. Furthermore, Jefferson in particular feared that if a rival nation colonized the territory west of the Mississippi, control of the river could be a point of major dispute leading to hostilities. To make matters worse, the Spanish closed the port to American commerce in 1802, leading Jefferson to take measures to rectify the problem once and for all.

The Louisiana Purchase of 1803 became the solution to this troubling situation. France's claims to Louisiana dated back to the seventeenth century. The territory passed into the hands of Spain after the French and Indian War ended in 1763. But in 1800, the Spanish agreed to cede Louisiana back to France (as of 1802, Spain had yet to vacate New Orleans). President Jefferson authorized Robert Livingston to see about purchasing New Orleans from France for up to $10 million. Unbeknownst to the Americans, Napoleon had given up on colonizing the Louisiana Territory, in part because he lost control of Saint-Domingue (Haiti) due to a massive slave revolt, and because he needed money to pursue his imperial agenda in Europe. Thus, he offered to sell the whole of Louisiana to the United States for $15 million. Livingston, who was a bit hard of hearing, could hardly believe his ears when the French offered the entire territory, but the deal was struck in April and ratified by the US Senate in October. For about four cents an acre, the United States acquired the territory, which doubled its size.

The northwestern boundary of the Louisiana Purchase ran along the Continental Divide in the Rockies (Jefferson called them the "Stony Mountains"). The lands west of the Divide to the Pacific Ocean constituted Oregon country, which was claimed by Britain, Spain and Russia at the time of the Purchase. The United States was able to make a claim to Oregon after Lewis and Clark explored and mapped the country along the Columbia River to the Pacific in 1805 and 1806. After 1824, Spain and

Russia no longer claimed Oregon, and Britain and the United States agreed to a ten-year joint claim after 1818 and renewed it indefinitely in 1827. By 1845, the year that Texas was annexed to the United States, American settlers in Oregon vastly outnumbered British settlers. Some in America, most notably John Quincy Adams, wanted to take all of Oregon country up to the northern boundary with Russia at 54°40′, even if it meant war with Britain (hence the popular "Fifty-four forty or fight" meme). But President Polk oversaw the peaceful division of Oregon along the forty-ninth parallel in 1846, which had established the northern border between the United States and British North America (Canada) east of Oregon by treaty in 1818. Polk did not want a war with Britain, but he was less cautious with Mexico.

So, the northwestern extent of US territory reached to the Pacific between 1803 and 1846. During this time, Americans expanded southward as well. To the south of the original thirteen states was Florida, specifically West and East Florida, territories Spain held at the close of the Revolution in 1783. West Florida consisted of a narrow strip of land along the Gulf Coast stretching east from the Mississippi River to Pensacola on what is now the Alabama-Florida state line. East Florida comprised the rest of the Gulf Coast and the peninsula. West Florida had been occupied by Americans during the War of 1812 because the Seminole tribe offered freedom to escaped slaves. Andrew Jackson invaded West Florida and took Pensacola in 1818. In 1819, John Quincy Adams negotiated the purchase of the Floridas from Spain for $5 million, set the southeastern boundary with Spanish Mexico (future Texas) along the Sabine and Red Rivers, and established the northern boundary at the forty-second parallel (the present northern boundaries of California, Nevada and Utah).

Texas came into the picture as early as 1821, when Stephen F. Austin and his followers settled along the Brazos River at a place they named San Felipe. Mexico won its independence from Spain in 1821, and began inviting Americans to settle in Texas to form a buffer between Mexico and the United States. By 1830, there were about twenty thousand Americans settled in Texas, which began to alarm authorities in Mexico City. To aggravate things, slavery was illegal in Mexico, to the great annoyance

of many American settlers. Mexico banned any further American settlement in Texas in 1830, but it was a measure too little, too late. By 1835,
the Texans were in revolt against the Mexican government. General Antonio Lopez de Santa Anna (1794–1876) invaded Texas and killed the
American defenders at the Alamo outside of San Antonio on December
10, 1835. On April 26, 1836, Texan forces under Sam Houston routed Santa
Anna's army at the battle of San Jacinto. This battle was something of a
Texan Yorktown, since Santa Anna was captured and then agreed (under
extreme duress) to take his army out of Texas and acknowledge its independence. The Mexican Congress did not officially recognize Texan independence, but from 1836 to 1845, the Republic of Texas operated inde-
pendently of Mexico.

In 1837, under the leadership of Sam Houston, Texas appealed to the
United States for annexation. Northern Whigs in the United States feared
the spread of slavery into Texas, and opposed annexation; the US Senate
thus rejected the idea. But with the election in 1844 of Democratic slave-
holder James Polk, a supporter of Texan annexation, the prospects for
Texas being admitted to the Union improved substantially. In 1845, the
United States annexed Texas by way of a joint resolution of Congress, and
on December 29, Texas officially joined the Union.

What is missing in this story of territorial expansion is the slavery
issue. The Southern economy depended on slavery. When the United
States acquired new territories, the question of whether or not Congress
would allow the extension of slavery into those new territories was both
perennial and highly divisive. The question would ultimately be settled
on battlefields of decision across the states of the shattered Union during
the years 1861 to 1865.

THE EXPANSION OF SLAVERY

In 1841, slave catchers in Washington, DC, kidnapped a free black man
named Solomon Northup of Hebron, New York. He was taken south to
Virginia and loaded onto a ship bound for New Orleans to be sold into
slavery. Two others with him on board had also been kidnapped. Together they planned a mutiny, but one of the conspirators got smallpox

and died. Northup's captors changed his name to Platt when he got to New Orleans to erase his identity as a free man and make it impossible for anyone from his past to track his whereabouts. To his friends and family, Northup simply disappeared.

While he was a slave, Northup saw and experienced firsthand the exacting hardship endured by slaves working Louisiana cotton and sugar plantations. James and Lois Horton wrote, "Northup and his fellow slaves were paraded around for prospective buyers. He had to demonstrate his muscles and agility and show that he had strong healthy teeth."[9] Northup eventually became a slave driver, and was so agile with the whip that he could snap the tail so close to a man's skin without making contact that he could fool just about anyone under the right circumstances into thinking he was a brutal sadist. As Northup told it, he could bring "the lash within a hair's breath of the back, the ear, the nose, without reaching either of them."[10] Eleven years after having been kidnapped and sold into slavery, and after many sorrows, Northup finally trusted a Canadian carpenter named Samuel Bass to help him secure his freedom. Twelve years after his kidnapping, in January 1853, Northup was freed and returned home. He wrote a memoir titled *Twelve Years a Slave* shortly after his captivity ended. His captors were never punished for what they did.

The institution of slavery was deeply ensconced in the antebellum Union politically, economically and socially. By the 1850s, slavery was outlawed in the North, but it penetrated the Southern states from Delaware to Texas. It was horrendous and brutal—families underwent separation, men and women were brutalized, treated like dogs, made to work for produce enjoyed by others, were denied the most basic of rights and liberties taken for divinely granted by white Americans. Slavery existed here, in America—in beautiful, fruitful and varied places like river valleys, along the coasts, and in the foothills of places like Georgia and North Carolina—for nearly 250 years. Slavery was so brutal that thousands did everything they could to escape it. It forced many people to do unthinkable things to protect themselves and their children from it. A slave named Margaret Garner escaped from Kentucky with her family in 1856 and went into hiding in Cincinnati, Ohio. When slave catchers caught up with them there, she tried to murder her own children to save them from being caught and forced to live a life in bondage. She killed her baby before the slave catchers stopped her from killing every one of her children.[11]

The first African slaves came to America when a Dutch slaver landed with its human cargo in Virginia in 1619. Since the invention of the cotton gin by Eli Whitney in 1793, slavery became the engine of the antebellum Southern economy. In 1860, the institution of slavery existed in fifteen of the thirty-three states of the Union. In Brazoria County, Texas, where I live, nearly seventy-five percent of the population was in bondage in 1860. That statistic pales in comparison with other places in the South like Washington County, Mississippi, where over ninety-two percent of the population were slaves.[12]

Slavery was the most important and divisive political, economic and moral issue in America during the years leading up to the Civil War. Congress tried three political compromises in the forty years prior to the election of Abraham Lincoln in order to peacefully settle the slavery issue to the satisfaction of both North and South. Each attempt failed, and with each failure the question of whether or not the Union could peaceably cohere became more and more uncertain. These compromises were the Missouri Compromise of 1820, the Compromise of 1850 and the Kansas-Nebraska Act of 1854. Each measure came about as a result of the acquisition and organization of new territories. Slavery and territorial growth were thus inextricably linked. Missouri was part of the Louisiana Purchase, as was Kansas and Nebraska. Utah and New Mexico Territories, which Congress opened to slavery in the Compromise of 1850, were part of the Mexican Cession of 1848. The introduction of these new territories, and the future carving out of states from them, affected the delicate balance of power in Congress between slave and free states. There was also the pressing economic issue of the future construction of a transcontinental railroad. Both sides in the debate wanted the planned route of the railroad to proceed through the West in order to forward their own political and economic interests. Ultimately, the failure of these compromises deepened the rivalries between North and South and played a major role in Southern secession and civil war.

Of course, there were profound legal and moral ramifications to the issue of slavery, as Solomon Northup's memoir attests. An obvious example is from 1857, in which the Supreme Court decided on a case involving Dred Scott. Scott was the slave of army surgeon John Emerson, who took Scott with him to the free state of Illinois and the free territory of Wisconsin in the course of his duties. Later, they traveled back to Missouri, Louisiana and Florida, all of which were slave states. Emerson died in 1843, and in 1846, Scott sued for his freedom. Under Missouri case law, if a slave had lived in a free state or territory and then returned to Missouri, that slave was entitled to freedom. The Circuit Court of St. Louis County freed Scott, but Emerson's widow appealed that decision to the Missouri Supreme Court. The state supreme court overturned the lower court's ruling. The case then made its way through the federal court system until it was heard by the US Supreme Court in 1856. By this time, as Walter Ehrlich wrote, the national slavery debate had "transformed the litigation from a routine freedom suit to a *cause célèbre*."[13]

In the first application of judicial review since *Marbury v. Madison* in 1803, the Supreme Court under Chief Justice Roger B. Taney ruled against Scott 7–2 in *Scott v. Sandford*. Taney wrote in the majority opinion that Scott (1) was still a slave, (2) had never been anything but a slave and (3) as a slave was not a citizen of the United States (and thus had no standing in court). The Court considered Scott as nothing more than property

DRED SCOTT.

Figure 2.1. Dred Scott

under the Constitution. Furthermore, Taney wrote, the Missouri Compromise was unconstitutional.

A clearer ruling endorsing slavery could not possibly be imagined.

The Court rendered the whole concept of "free states" and "slave states" legally absurd. The Dred Scott decision opened the door to the legalization of slavery everywhere in the Union. Ehrlich summed up the decision's aftermath: "With the intrusion of the Court into the slavery issue, many felt that any compromise over slavery was now impossible, and the North and the South moved inexorably toward civil war."[14]

Eighteen fifty-seven was a bad year. Things got worse by 1860. The Dred Scott case figured prominently in the 1860 election, when four major candidates ran for president and the winner, Abraham Lincoln, carried no Southern states (as the 1860 cartoon "The Political Quadrille" depicts). With the secession of eleven states, the Confederate attack on Fort Sumter and the commencement of the Civil War, 1860 and '61 witnessed the culmination of animosity between North and South. But it was now only a matter of time before the issue of slavery would finally be settled. In calling free African Americans in 1863 to arms in the war,

Figure 2.2. "The Political Quadrille" (1860). This cartoon parodied the effect of the Dred Scott case on the 1860 election. Dred Scott plays a dance for the presidential candidates, namely, John Breckinridge (with James Buchanan, portrayed as a goat), Abraham Lincoln (with an African American woman, to mock his position on slavery), Stephen Douglas (with an Irishman, because of his alleged pro-Catholicism), and John Bell (with a Native American, because of his sympathies for their interests).

Frederick Douglass said, "The tide is at its flood that leads on to fortune. From East to West, from North to South, the sky is written all over, 'Now or never.'"[15]

What does all this on territorial expansion and slavery have to do with American exceptionalism? Quite a bit. When the United States bought Louisiana from France in 1803 and doubled in size, the nation's identity ceased to be oriented toward the Eastern seaboard. From 1803 on, America turned westward, and this westward expansion fed the already mature notion that America was exceptional, chosen by God, immune to the forces of history, a millennial nation with a God-given mission and a sacred land peopled and led by the greatest of the great. But with territorial expansion came slavery. Slavery presented an enormous moral challenge to America's liberal founding ideals and Protestant consensus, both of which supposedly contributed to the nation's exceptional quality. Territorial expansion gave birth to the closed exceptionalism of manifest destiny. The stain of slavery exposed American hypocrisy, and necessitated one of two outcomes—the death of the exceptional union of free and independent states or, as Lincoln put it in the Gettysburg Address, "a new birth of freedom." Lincoln's vision of an America reborn, cleansed from the abomination of slavery, became the animating quality of open American exceptionalism.

JOHN L. O'SULLIVAN AND THE CLOSED EXCEPTIONALISM OF MANIFEST DESTINY

During the heady days of territorial expansion, particularly from the 1830s to the 1850s, the phrase *manifest destiny* became a popular means of expressing the notion that God had chosen the United States to bring civilization to the continent of North America. Manifest destiny was, as Anders Stephanson described, "more than an expression: it was a whole *matrix*, a manner of interpreting the time and space of 'America.'"[16] In the antebellum period, it was an imperialist matrix articulated and advanced mainly by Democrats. This was fitting, given that Democratic icons like Thomas Jefferson and Andrew Jackson acted for territorial expansion in ways that reflected their individual proclivities and personalities: Jefferson by diplomacy and purchase, Jackson by conquest.

The person most often credited with coining the term *manifest destiny* was John L. O'Sullivan (1813–1895), the editor of the influential *United States Magazine and Democratic Review* until 1846. O'Sullivan graduated with his AB and MA degrees from Columbia University and practiced law in New York City. He also served as the American minister to Portugal in the Pierce administration (1853–1857). He helped launch the *Democratic Review* in 1837, and he also helped start the *New York Morning News* in 1844 with future Democratic presidential nominee Samuel J. Tilden. The *Democratic Review* became an important and widely read periodical, regularly featuring such literary greats as Nathaniel Hawthorne, Edgar Allan Poe and Alexander H. Everett. But the secession crisis and the Civil War undid O'Sullivan. Although leading up to the war he was opposed to slavery, on paper at least, he defended the right of the Southern states to secede from the Union. He fled to England during the war, but later returned to New York City where he died in 1895.[17]

During the summer of 1845, as Congress worked through the process of annexing Texas, O'Sullivan penned an editorial defending Texas's annexation and admission into the Union. He suggested that all acrimony over the issue must cease now, because nothing could stop Texas from being embraced by the rest of the states of the Union. "Patriotism already begins to thrill for her too within the national heart. It is time then that all should cease to treat her as alien."[18] He went on to criticize foreign powers, particularly England, for trying to undermine Texas's annexation, and thus, America's inevitable upward march to first-rate status. Specifically, according to O'Sullivan, other powers sought to "[check] the fulfillment of our manifest destiny to overspread the continent allotted by Providence for the free development of our yearly multiplying millions."[19] Five months later, O'Sullivan wrote, "[The American claim] is by the right of our manifest destiny to overspread and to possess the whole of the continent which Providence has given us for the development of the great experiment of liberty and federative state government entrusted to us."[20] Manifest destiny defined a palpable attitude of expansionism in America during the antebellum period, and again during the 1890s with the acquisition of colonial overseas territories after the Spanish-American War (1898).

What was the basis of this concept of manifest destiny as O'Sullivan articulated it? From reading O'Sullivan, it seems clear that the basis of the concept is twofold: providential certainty and Anglo American supremacy. O'Sullivan read the providence of God like one may read a five-day weather forecast. He interpreted the signs of the times and confidently drew the conclusion that God's business was about establishing the supremacy of the Anglo American race in North America. God chose America to spread democratic principles and bring the whole continent into the American Union. In O'Sullivan's musings about the destiny of America, he gave not the slightest hint of doubt to the idea that America was especially favored and chosen of God, and that it would—it *must*—be triumphant.

Providential certainty and white supremacy were distinct but logically connected ideas for O'Sullivan. When he spoke of God's activities in behalf of the United States, he spoke in terms of inevitability. No one— no rival nation, no people group, no series of setbacks—could prevent the United States from fulfilling its destiny of expanding from coast to coast. O'Sullivan believed that by 1945, one hundred years from the annexation of Texas, the US population would stand at 250 million, and thus, "Texas has been absorbed into the Union in the inevitable fulfillment of the general law which is rolling our population westward."[21]

What did O'Sullivan mean when he spoke of this "general law"? He was convinced that the events of history unfolded by a meticulously ordered plan of providence. This plan was to culminate in the perfection of humanity. The starting point was barbarism; the ending point was democratic civilization. Thus, for O'Sullivan, history was working toward a man-centered purpose, a telos, that would make every event along the way meaningful and significant.

Human history for O'Sullivan was divided into five orders: (1) pure barbarism, something akin to a Hobbesian state of nature; (2) theocracy, in which kings ruled by the fear of divine wrath and power; (3) statism, especially that of ancient Rome, in which the power of the state engulfed all aspects of society; (4) aristocracy and feudalism, particularly as it occurred in Western Europe during the medieval period; (5) democracy, the last order of civilization, which had its first appearance here in the United States.[22] God had ordained that the white race complete and perfect human history by ushering in the democratic order of civilization through the founding of the United States. He wrote, "To this result the discipline of Providence has tended from the earliest history of the Anglo-American race."[23]

O'Sullivan's articulation of providential history is similar to German philosopher G. W. F. Hegel's (1770–1831) philosophy of history. Hegel

Figure 2.3. John Gast's *American Progress* (1872) depicts the darkness of the West receding before the approach of American civilization.

envisioned orders of civilization that progressively advanced under the operation of *Geist* (Spirit) from tyranny to freedom, but he saw Germany as the place in which human perfection was to be attained. The point is that O'Sullivan constructed manifest destiny on a view of history animated by the workings of a meticulous and irresistible providence in behalf of the white race—and that the workings of providence were not only measurable in the past, but they could be precisely predicted for the future.

Since the white race was the pinnacle of humanity, it followed that providence would use it to complete human history and usher in perfect freedom. Ultimately, O'Sullivan believed that African and Native Americans would disappear from the mainland of America completely, because their assimilation into the white political and economic order was not going to happen. In commenting on Tocqueville's views on the racial future of America, he wrote,

> Our author predicts, with apparent conviction, the entire disappearance, at no very remote period, of the few existing remnants of the native tribes. Of the fate of the blacks he is less confident, but . . . includes to the opinion, that while they will triumph in the West Indian Islands, they will ultimately disappear from the continent. This opinion is, in our view, extremely probable. . . . The very decided superiority of an entire free population over a mixed population of freemen and slaves . . . will gradually make itself felt over the whole surface of our territory.[24]

And furthermore, "the attempt to raise [African Americans] to a political equality with the white race has not succeeded in practice in the States where it has been carried into effect in theory. It will probably never be made in the States where the slaves constitute a large proportion of the population."[25]

Thus, the destiny of the United States—understood and articulated by O'Sullivan as exclusively white—was to overspread the continent of North America. As it expanded, it was to plant the liberal ideas of political equality and representative government after uprooting barbarism and tyranny. O'Sulllivan thought that all North America would become part of the United States. Mexico was unable to govern itself liberally, and needed to be taught how to cultivate a republican society. O'Sullivan minced no words: "Beyond a question the entire Mexican vote would be substantially below our national average both in purity and intelligence."[26] Still, O'Sullivan did not advocate a violent takeover of Mexico. He believed that the Mexican people required strong central government to rule them at first, but as they matured as a people, they would become enlightened enough to follow the example placed before them by the American people. If the United States compelled Mexico by force to enter

the Union, that would betray its destiny. Still, by force of a pure democratic example, Mexico would not be able to resist destiny's call. At that
time, "we make no doubt, that the whole of this vast continent is destined
one day to subscribe to the Constitution of the United States."[27]

O'Sullivan's manifest destiny frequently entailed the appropriation of
Christian theological themes and applied them to America and to
American political ideals. Because of this, manifest destiny became a civil
religion complete with a system of theological doctrines giving it a coherent and transcendent framework. But the use of Christian theology
in the framework of manifest destiny, in effect, was really a hijacking.
Proponents of manifest destiny like O'Sullivan appropriated only those
aspects of Christianity that could be used to advance a nationalistic
agenda. The result was an arbitrary civil religious system, a cherry-picked
construction that ultimately militated against both Christianity and the
Declaration of Independence.

O'Sullivan's writings demonstrate numerous examples of how
Christian theology was incorporated into manifest destiny. The doctrine
of providence is the most obvious one. Christianity does not affirm any
inevitable order of advancement from human barbarism to perfection.
Nor does Christianity affirm that any single nation-state will usher in
some sort of utopia. And most Christians do not believe they can speak
with certainty on providence in history, unless there is specific infor-
mation given in special revelation, that is, Scripture. Christianity affirms
that the divine attribute of sovereignty is applied through providence,
and that history will be brought to a culmination at the return of Christ.
Christ is at the center of the doctrine of providence, as he is at the center
of all Christian doctrine.

Another Christian theme annexed to (pun definitely intended) manifest destiny is the dominion mandate. The dominion mandate is found
in Genesis 1:28: "Be fruitful and multiply and fill the earth and subdue it,
and have dominion over the fish of the sea and over the birds of the
heavens and over every living thing that moves on the earth." As war
between the United States and Mexico ramped up, Congressman
Timothy Pillsbury of Texas argued in 1846 that Mexicans were not able

to fulfill the dominion mandate, and since they could not, their lands were forfeited to those who could. Pillsbury said, "A country kept vacant by the policy of a nation which claims the right of ownership over it is common property, and reverts to the situation in which all land was before it became property."[28] John Quincy Adams, sixth president of the United States, had a similar racist understanding of the dominion mandate. Adams based his argument for American possession of all of Oregon to 54°40′ on the notion that God had commanded humans to develop the land and make it fruitful, not merely use it for trapping and trading with Native Americans (who, in his mind, were even less worthy of possessing it). Adams said, "We claim that country [Oregon] . . . to make the wilderness bloom as the rose, to establish laws, to increase, multiply, and subdue the earth, which we are commanded to do by the first behest of God Almighty."[29]

The biblical dominion mandate has none of the racial overtones of manifest destiny, which makes its appropriation by figures such as Pillsbury and Adams all the more distressing. Likewise, the dominion mandate is at the heart of what it means to be made in God's image—as Scripture teaches, all men, women and children bear the image of God no matter the color of their skin or their ethnicity. Still, proponents of manifest destiny in the antebellum period commonly called on the dominion mandate to justify the taking of lands worked and used by Native Americans and Mexicans.

Lastly, proponents of manifest destiny, O'Sullivan in particular, equated democracy with Christianity. As we have seen, there was not much new in terms of seeing America and democratic principles in millennial terms. But O'Sullivan took things to another level by suggesting that democratic principles were the animating force of Christianity, and that salvation itself was to be found not in the person and work of Christ, but in democracy. Thus, the teachings of Christ were rooted in democracy, and democracy was the light of men.

> The annunciations of [Christianity's] lofty Teacher embodied truths after which the nations in their dim twilight had long struggled in vain. . . .

These potent doctrines were the inherent dignity, the natural equality, the spiritual rights, the glorious hopes, of man. . . . They speak to him in a voice of infinite power; . . . they awaken hope; they administer consolation; they cherish the sense of personal worth; they strengthen faith in truth; they reveal the highest excellence; they demand unceasing progress; they worship the soul as of the higher importance than all outward worlds.[30]

What is particularly egregious about manifest destiny is its native hypocrisy. On the one hand, the idea extolled the virtues of democratic principles: equality, individual rights, rule of law, personal freedoms and virtuous society. On the other hand, it absolutely denied those principles to nonwhites. Thus, it is one of the most explicit expressions in US history of closed American exceptionalism. As an exclusionary system with an imperialistic agenda, as well as an idea that inappropriately annexed Christian theological themes to itself, manifest destiny was a betrayal of the affirmations made in the Declaration of Independence and a counterfeit of the gospel of Christ.

But manifest destiny was not the only exceptionalist game in town during the antebellum period. Let us turn now to another expression of exceptionalism, one that is in many ways distinct from that of O'Sullivan and the purveyors of manifest destiny. This expression arose not out of the territorial expansion of the United States, but from the great crises of the mid-nineteenth century that came with that expansion: disunion, slavery and civil war.

ABRAHAM LINCOLN'S OPEN AMERICAN EXCEPTIONALISM

Abraham Lincoln (1809–1865) is perhaps our most celebrated president. His rise to prominence was both unlikely and yet eminently suited for the classic narrative of the American dream. He had minimal formal schooling, had a small taste of military experience (compared to his Civil War counterpart, Jefferson Davis), and grew up in an obscure and distant corner of the country (compared to his 1860 Republican rival, William Seward). Still, his rise to national prominence was meteoric. In 1858, he ran against Stephen A. Douglas for the US Senate seat from Illinois. Even though he was defeated, he became known all over the state as a master debater, and demonstrated himself to be a balanced thinker on the slavery issue. He was morally opposed to slavery and wanted to see it ultimately abolished. Yet, he knew that the institution was not going away anytime soon, so he took the position that it should be not extended into the territories beyond where it already existed. This was his public position on slavery until January 1, 1863, when he formally issued the Emancipation Proclamation.

Lincoln's rhetorical skills and logical thinking garnered national attention in the newly formed Republican party. He was nominated as a compromise candidate for president on the Republican ticket at the Chicago convention in 1860, winning out over William H. Seward. Seward had served as governor of New York and a US senator, and he seemed to most at the time to be the likely person to win the nomination. But since the Republican party held the convention in Lincoln's home state, and because many feared that Seward would be too polarizing on the issue of slavery, Lincoln became more attractive as a moderate who could be acceptable to both North and South. Lincoln was nominated on the third ballot, and went on to win the 1860 election, despite the fact that three other candidates were running and Lincoln did not carry a single Southern state. In fact, Lincoln's election was the last straw for many Southerners, and was one of the most important reasons given by the Southern states for secession.

Lincoln is famous for a great many things—that might even qualify as the understatement of the year. More books have been written on Abraham Lincoln than on any other American. McPherson estimated in 2009 that sixteen thousand books have been written on Lincoln, and more than two hundred bronze and marble statues across the country depict and honor him.[31] One significant contribution Lincoln made to American culture was his particular expression of civil religion. Bellah said that Lincoln was America's greatest civil theologian. William Wolf called Lincoln one of "America's latter day prophets."[32] Lincoln's conception of America was wrought out of his Puritan upbringing, experiences growing up on the frontier, his hard work and perseverance in the face of much failure and tragedy, his reading of history and the Declaration of Independence, and finally the unique trial of leading the nation through a bitter and bloody civil war. His position on American exceptionalism starkly contrasted with O'Sullivan's manifest destiny, in that Lincoln's view was inclusive while manifest destiny was exclusive. Thus, Lincoln gave us the first developed form of open American exceptionalism.

While O'Sullivan based manifest destiny on providential certitude and Anglo American superiority, Lincoln's exceptionalism—particularly when applied to the question of slavery—was based on a clear understanding and articulation of right and wrong. It is true that Lincoln often looked the other way when it came to the exploitation of workers in the industrial North. But he called on the moral authority of right and wrong—justice—again and again in his speeches and writings on slavery. Specifically, he based his articulations on opposition to slavery, equality, the rule of law, the dignity of work, the indissolubility of the Union and God's providence on an objective, transcendent standard of justice. For example, in his sixth debate with Stephen Douglas, Lincoln attacked slavery on moral grounds, saying, "The Republican party think [slavery] wrong—we think it is a moral, a social, and a political wrong. . . . Because we think it wrong, we propose a course of policy that shall deal with it as a wrong. We deal with it as with any other wrong . . . and so deal with it that in the run of time there may be some promise of an end to it."[33]

The Declaration of Independence was the most important political document in Lincoln's political philosophy and civil religion. As Bellah observed, the Declaration stands as part of a civil religious canon. This was certainly true for Lincoln, since he appealed to it as an unassailable authority frequently in his oratory. The Declaration contained truths that applied to everyone, regardless of race, circumstance, ethnic origin and so on. It transcended even the Constitution, not only because it predated it, but also because the Constitution was simply a working document that prescribed how the federal government was to function. Allen Guelzo wrote, "Immigrants who read the Constitution, Lincoln argued, saw only the rules and regulations of a foreign country; but when they read the Declaration, they found principles and ideas that reached over the head of language or section or previous nationality and bound Americans together . . . seeking life, liberty, and the pursuit of happiness."[34]

How Lincoln understood the equality clause in the Declaration exemplifies his estimation of its moral, political and civil religious authority. Lincoln believed that the "all men are created equal" clause in the Declaration applied to all people, not just to whites. Stephen Douglas criticized this assertion, because Jefferson owned slaves and could not possibly have had African Americans in mind when he wrote the clause. But Lincoln answered Douglas's critique by reminding him that Jefferson, even as a slave owner, was opposed to the institution of slavery per se. Lincoln said that Jefferson feared the judgment of God upon the nation because it tolerated slavery. Furthermore, Lincoln argued that Douglas's idea of the inapplicability of the equality clause to slaves was an innovation. Not until the Democratic party sought to ensconce and extend slavery did this false notion take root. Lincoln said, "I believe the entire records of the world, from the date of the Declaration of Independence up to within three years ago [1855], may be searched in vain for one single affirmation, from one single man, that the negro was not included in the Declaration of Independence."[35]

Justice dominated Lincoln's thought process as he considered the American system of laws protecting slavery. Lincoln criticized the Supreme Court's Dred Scott decision on the basis of a transcendent and objective understanding of justice. In so doing, Lincoln was being consistent with Locke's views of justice as he defined them in the *Second Treatise of Civil Government*.[36] The civil laws were always to be followed, except at such times when those laws violated justice. When laws that are unjust are handed down by the civil authority, they are to be overturned by the people. Civil laws do not, in themselves, define what is right and wrong; they are to be made to conform to a higher standard of right and wrong. When they defy moral objectivity, they should be changed. Lincoln argued this point in 1838: "I do mean to say, that, although bad laws, if they exist, should be repealed as soon as possible, still while they continue in force, for the sake of example, they should be religiously observed. . . . [But] let proper legal provisions be made for them with the least possible delay."[37]

When it came to laws supporting slavery, such as the Dred Scott decision and the Fugitive Slave Act of 1850, Lincoln was prepared to submit to those laws for the moment but also wanted to eagerly seek legal corrections as soon as possible. In particularly applying this principle to slavery, Lincoln was closer to Locke than even Jefferson, the sage of Monticello who penned the Declaration of Independence and saw Locke as one of the greatest men in history. Because Lincoln consistently argued that slavery violated the rights of African Americans to liberty and property, the right of consent of the governed, and the right to overturn unjust government, he took Locke's political philosophy to its logical conclusion, going beyond Jefferson. It was Lincoln's clear vision of justice that directed his understanding of the equality clause in the Declaration.

The ways of providence featured prominently in Lincoln's thought, particularly in his view of past events and as he sought to find meaning in the conflagration of the Civil War. In a way, the fact that Lincoln had a strong regard for providence is similar to O'Sullivan, who also had a high view of providence. But what separates Lincoln from O'Sullivan on the issue of providence is that whereas O'Sullivan thought he possessed epistemic certainty, Lincoln had no such presumptions. Lincoln knew that he had no idea what God was up to in his dealings with America. In 1862, while brooding on the subject of why God was allowing the bloodshed to continue, Lincoln wrote down some thoughts on God's providence. He grappled with the fact that God could, at any time, bring the war to an end. He could at any time give Union arms victory or defeat, and yet the war went on. Lincoln wrote, "God cannot be *for* and *against* the same thing at the same time. In the present civil war it is quite possible that God's purpose is something different from the purpose of either party."[38] Ultimately, all Lincoln could say for certain was that God would do what pleased him, and whatever that proved to be was the best outcome.

But Lincoln even saw the doctrine of providence through the lens of justice. He once stunned some clergymen in 1862 who expressed their belief that God was on the side of the Union. This is certainly a natural assertion to make when engaged in a war. And it was certainly the belief of people like O'Sullivan, who believed that God was always on America's side. But Lincoln was not prepared to make such a bold assertion. Consistent with Joshua 5:13-14, Lincoln's inclination was to reject the notion that God favored the North in the war. He said, "I know that the Lord is *always* on the side of the *right*. But it is my constant anxiety and prayer that I and the *nation* should be on the Lord's side."[39] And he famously surmised in his Second Inaugural Address that perhaps God was bringing his chastisement upon America for allowing slavery, a great moral evil. Still, he recognized that "the Almighty has his own purposes" and "if God wills that it continue . . . so it still must be said 'the judgments of the Lord are true and righteous altogether.'"[40] Lincoln considered the principles of righteousness and submission to the inscrutable will of God to be preeminent in applying the Christian doctrine of providence to particular circumstances. He shied away from making dogmatic claims on matters he knew were too wonderful for mortals to know.

CLOSED AND OPEN AMERICAN EXCEPTIONALISMS IN O'SULLIVAN AND LINCOLN

Let us now consider some similarities and differences in the way O'Sullivan and Lincoln approached America's identity and importance.

First, there appear to be at least two similarities in the thought of these two men. Both O'Sullivan and Lincoln considered American-style democracy to be the pinnacle of human existence, and both held paternalistic attitudes toward nonwhites. We have already seen in O'Sullivan's philosophy of history the inevitable human progress culminating in democracy, and in particular, the democracy established by Americans. O'Sullivan located the heart of democracy in what he called the "voluntary principle," under which all human activities could be trusted to flourish without the intervention of the government. This voluntary principle, according to O'Sullivan, "is borrowed from the example of the perfect self-government of the physical universe, being written in letters of light on every page of the great bible of Nature."[41] Lincoln, in his December 1862 Annual Message to Congress, cast the American Union as "the last, best hope of earth."[42] The Union was worth the fathomless cost in human lives, Lincoln told the 166th Ohio Regiment in 1864, because in securing "this free government . . . you may all have equal privileges in the race of life, with all its desirable human aspirations."[43]

We have also seen how O'Sullivan based the civil religion of manifest destiny in part on racism. But Lincoln could not escape the traps of racist thinking himself, even though justice was the foundation of his own civil religion. Lincoln's understanding of equality, while far advanced of O'Sullivan's, was still quite limited, at least in his first 1858 debate with Douglas. In this debate, Lincoln saw African Americans as equal in terms of being entitled to enjoy the fruits of their own labors, but he was not willing to acknowledge them as his intellectual, or even his moral, equals.[44] And Jean Baker noted that Lincoln, as evidenced in his support of colonizing freed slaves in Africa and the Caribbean (which he supported at least as late as 1862), believed "that the nation's exceptionalism would be undermined in a biracial society."[45]

But there are many more differences in the civil religious exceptionalism expressed by O'Sullivan and Lincoln. The fundamental and defining difference between the two, as stated previously, is the difference between exclusivism and inclusivism. From this irreconcilable distinction, we see the two expressions of exceptionalism depart over conceptions of justice, equality, human rights, slavery, the workings of divine providence and a host of other pertinent issues. For example, O'Sullivan and Lincoln both extolled the virtues and potentialities of democratic principles in a government that exists under them. But Lincoln could claim to be more consistent than O'Sullivan in both his rhetoric and his actions to advance those democratic principles. O'Sullivan, in striking contrast, constantly spoke out of both sides of his mouth—he hyperbolically gushed about the virtues of democracy while noxiously denying the dignity, equality and rights of nonwhites.

Human nature is another important point of departure for O'Sullivan and Lincoln. O'Sullivan believed that, in American democracy, the people were always right. The people could be left entirely alone to behave justly, and God could be unconditionally depended on to work through the activities of the people to bring prosperity to the nation. He said, "We may then safely trust the people, for they will always, in their final decisions, be right in every sense, as they will act in harmony with truth and virtue. . . . Then the voice of the people . . . will be one with the voice of God."[46]

While Lincoln also believed that God's providence worked through the people, his explanation of how this occurred was more realistic and nuanced than O'Sullivan's—because his view of human nature was rooted in an objective conception of justice. Lincoln knew that the vision cast in the Declaration of Independence was an ideal one, but that the true American path was the one that constantly pursued that ideal. Lincoln knew that the presence of slavery in America exposed a great hypocrisy, and also knew that emancipation was an enormously difficult proposition. Still, to Lincoln, it was unthinkable that Americans would not ultimately deal with this particular hypocrisy and abolish slavery, even if that meant an indefinite prolonging of the war, as he said in his Second Inaugural Address. Sidney Mead wrote that, for Lincoln, the voice of the people was the voice of God only insofar as the people were acting in accordance with God's moral laws. In other words, when the people are inclined toward justice—the doing of right and the shunning of wrong—then and only then would providential agency work through the people. Because the people are not always going to pursue the right, and at times the right is not easy to discern, the providence of God is often not apparent. This was why religious freedom was an important part of Lincoln's conception of America. As Mead said, Lincoln believed religious freedom created "a situation where every religious opinion and practice, having the right to free expression, would continually contend with all others in order that error might be exposed to view and the truth be recognized."[47] Religious freedom does not appear at all as a factor in manifest destiny as expressed in O'Sullivan's writings.

CONCLUSION

In the nineteenth century, America's territorial growth and the deepening crisis of slavery that came with it introduced a divergence in the concept of exceptionalism. The American conviction that they were an exceptional people was not new. But in the national adolescence, when the nation was growing and coming to grips with its place in the world, competing exclusivist and inclusivist conceptions of American exceptionalism developed. To be sure, the inclusivist conception of exceptionalism that Lincoln championed was not always consistently applied. Still, in some measure, the contest of the Civil War between the Southern Confederacy and the Union was a contest between these competing views of exceptionalism.

In the next five chapters, we will consider some theological assertions entailed in closed American exceptionalism. As we have already seen in manifest destiny, closed American exceptionalism appropriates —even hijacks—Christian theology, having the effect of equating Christianity with patriotic devotion. We Americans should seek balance on the issue of our place in the world, and this balance is possible in an open concept of exceptionalism, similar to the national vision our sixteenth president articulated.

For Further Reading

Baptist, Edward E. *The Half Has Never Been Told: Slavery and the Making of American Capitalism*. New York: Basic, 2014.

Clary, David A. *Eagles and Empire: The United States, Mexico, and the Struggle for a Continent*. New York: Bantam, 2009.

De Beaumont, Gustave. *Marie; or, Slavery in the United States*. Translated by Barbara Chapman. Baltimore: Johns Hopkins University Press, 1999.

Howe, Daniel Walker. *What Hath God Wrought: The Transformation of America, 1815–1848*. Oxford History of the United States, edited by David M. Kennedy. New York: Oxford University Press, 2007.

Morgan, Ted. *A Shovel of Stars: The Making of the American West—1800 to the Present*. New York: Touchstone, 1996.

———. *Wilderness at Dawn: The Settling of the North American Continent*. New York: Touchstone, 1994.

Stephanson, Anders. *Manifest Destiny: American Expansion and the Empire of Right*. 1995. Reprint, New York: Hill and Wang, 1996.

3

The Chosen Nation

We Americans are the peculiar, chosen people—the Israel of our time; we bear the ark of the liberties of the world. . . . God has predestinated, mankind expects, great things from our race. . . . Long enough have we been skeptics with regard to ourselves, and doubted whether, indeed, the political Messiah had come. But he has come in us, if we would but give utterance to his promptings.

HERMAN MELVILLE, 1850

The white man excused his presence here
by saying that he had been guided by the will of his God;
and in so saying absolved himself of all responsibility for
his appearance in a land occupied by other men.

LUTHER STANDING BEAR, 1933

Uncle Sam's hands are dripping with blood,
dripping with the blood of the black man in this country.
He's the earth's number-one hypocrite. He has the audacity
—yes, he has—imagine him posing as the leader of the
free world. The free world!

MALCOLM X, 1964

✦✧✦

QUEEN MARY OF ENGLAND (1516–1558; r. 1553–1558), the only surviving child from the union of Henry VIII and Catherine of Aragon,
inherited the throne after the death of her half-brother, Edward VI, in
1553. From childhood to adulthood, she suffered the misfortune of being
the only daughter of the king's rejected wife. When Catherine did not
provide Henry with a surviving male heir, he divorced her and married
Anne Boleyn. Mary was declared illegitimate and separated from her
mother, whom she dearly loved, at the age of fifteen. When Henry died
in 1547, his ten-year-old son Edward succeeded him as king. Edward
reigned only until he was fifteen, when in July 1553 he died after an illness
in which he is reported to have "coughed and spat blood, his legs swelled
painfully, eruptions broke out over his body, his hair fell out, then his
nails."[1] Edward had tried to keep Mary from succeeding him because she
was Roman Catholic. He wanted to ensure that his cousin, Lady Jane
Grey, ascended the throne. When Edward died, Jane was acclaimed as
queen. But after only ten days, Mary raised an army, deposed Jane and
rode into London triumphantly in August 1553.

Despite her royal lineage, Mary had lived a troubled life. And despite
the fact that the throne was finally hers, her troubles had only just begun.
In her zeal for the Catholic faith, she married Philip II of Spain (1527–
1598) and incurred the wrath of many of her people, both Catholic and
Protestant, who feared that England would become subservient to Spain.
Philip II was the son of the great Habsburg emperor Charles V. Philip
ruled Spain when that kingdom was at the pinnacle of its world power.
Spain's possessions included a vast empire in the Americas, the Phil-
ippine Islands (which were named for Philip) as well as numerous territories in Europe. While married to Mary, he claimed the title of king
of England. And it was Philip that later launched the ill-fated Spanish
Armada against Elizabeth I's English fleet to secure the English Channel
for a planned invasion of England in 1588. Mary barely survived a coup
attempt in 1554 (Wyatt's Rebellion), but once she did, she became deeply
suspicious of plots against her as well as Protestant threats against her
beloved Catholic church.

In 1555, Mary initiated a brutal policy of persecution against Protestants. Many Protestants had already fled to the continent, hoping to wait Mary out and try to place Elizabeth, her half-sister, on the throne when the time was right. But between 1555 and 1558, more Protestants fled England to escape the awful torment of being burned at the stake. "Bloody Mary" oversaw the burning of about three hundred persons during her reign. Victims were bound to the stake surrounded by a great pile of dried brush swathed in pitch and tar. To show a bit of mercy, the executioners sometimes strangled the condemned before lighting the pyre. Others were secured to the stake with bags of gunpowder hung around their necks that were supposed to explode, and thus dispatch them quickly. Some victims to whom the executioners showed no mercy took up to an hour to die. Archbishop of Canterbury Thomas Cranmer, who annulled Henry's marriage to Catherine of Aragon and wrote the *Book of Common Prayer* to replace the Mass, was among those to perish in flame on the pyre.

Several Protestants fleeing England sojourned in German and Swiss cities during the persecution. While in Europe, they absorbed Reformation theology and the writings of William Tyndale,[2] the English reformer who translated the Bible into English. Tyndale embraced the national covenant theology expressed in the Old Testament, and believed that God continued to work in human history through national covenants. English Protestants adopted Tyndale's view of national election during the Marian persecution and believed that England existed in covenant with God as his chosen people. And they believed that it was their duty to restore England to right relationship with God in order to stave off his wrath that was sure to consume the nation because of Catholic Mary's reign. These Protestant exiles, who returned to England after Mary died in 1558, formed the vanguard of the Puritan movement. Richard Hughes wrote that "Tyndale's vision of covenant . . . was the soil in which the notion of chosenness would slowly germinate until, finally it would spring full-blown in the United States."[3] So it was the Puritan tradition, informed by Tyndale, arising from the Marian persecution that advanced the vision of the chosen nation first in England and later in New England.

The story shows how deeply rooted the idea of national/ethnic election, or chosenness, is in England (in general) and America (in particular). As we will see, American proponents of national/ethnic election have frequently violated the Christian gospel, along with the Christian conception of justice as a universal moral standard. In this chapter we will explore the theology and history of national/ethnic election as an aspect of closed American exceptionalism, consider the ramifications and search for a more just and appropriate method of expressing patriotic devotion in open American exceptionalism.

NATIONAL/ETHNIC ELECTION AS A CIVIL THEOLOGY

The Scriptures are the most important source of the civil theology of national/ethnic election (hereafter referred to as *election* or *chosenness*). The model for chosenness is the national covenant existing between God and ancient Israel as articulated in the Old Testament. Specifically, the Abrahamic and the Mosaic covenants from the books of Genesis through Deuteronomy were the models for the idea of covenant expressed by the Puritans of New England and carried over into the United States.

The Abrahamic covenant is at the heart of the founding of the nation of Israel as God's chosen people. It is found in Genesis 12:1-3: "Now the LORD said to Abram, 'Go from your country and your kindred and your father's house to the land that I will show you. And I will make of you a great nation, and I will bless you and make your name great, so that you will be a blessing. I will bless those who bless you, and him who dishonors you I will curse, and in you all the families of the earth shall be blessed.'" At this commandment, Abram took his family, left his ancestral homeland in Sumer, and went to Canaan. In Genesis 17, God changed his servant's name from Abram to Abraham. At this point, God told Abraham in Genesis 17:7, "And I will establish my covenant between me and you and your offspring after you throughout their generations for an everlasting covenant." In other words, for the first time, God established a covenant with Abraham that would have no end. But this covenant had a key stipulation—Abraham was to walk with God in righteousness. God founded his covenant with Abraham on this condition in Genesis 17:1-2:

"I am God Almighty; walk before me, and be blameless, that I may make my covenant between me and you, and may multiply you greatly." Thus, central to the idea of a national covenant is the condition that the nation be blameless, in order that it may continue in covenant relationship to God as his chosen people.

The Mosaic covenant is defined and described through the narratival structure of the books of Exodus through Deuteronomy. But in Deuteronomy, we see how the Abrahamic covenant extended the Mosaic covenant. For example, in Deuteronomy 5:2-3, referring to God's handing down of the Ten Commandments from Sinai (also known as Horeb), Moses said, "The LORD our God made a covenant with us in Horeb. Not with our fathers did the LORD make this covenant, but with us, who are all of us here alive today." In Deuteronomy 7:6, 8, Moses reminded the people that they were chosen of God, "to be a people for his treasured possession . . . because the LORD loves you and is keeping the oath that he swore to your fathers." In this passage, the Abrahamic covenant was enlarged to encompass the entire nation of Israel, and the theme of national election was explicitly defined. But ancient Israel also understood the Mosaic covenant in terms of specific conditions, which were outlined in Deuteronomy 5–30. In these chapters, Moses presented the nation's requirements of living under the covenant, and he gave a litany of both blessings and curses that were to follow their faithfulness or unfaithfulness in Deuteronomy 27–30. Moses said in Deuteronomy 27:9-10, "Keep silence and hear, O Israel: this day you have become the people of the LORD your God. You shall therefore obey the voice of the LORD your God, keeping his commandments and his statutes, which I command you today." If the people walked in faithfulness to the covenant by obeying the law, they would prosper, flourish and multiply in the land God had given them. If they broke faithfulness with the covenant, they would be punished. Moses said in Deuteronomy 28:58-59, "If you are not careful to do all the words of this law that are written in this book, that you may fear this glorious and awesome name, the LORD your God, then the LORD will bring on you and your offspring extraordinary afflictions, afflictions severe and lasting, and sicknesses grievous and lasting." Thus, the nation had to keep the moral stipulations of the covenant in order to demonstrate their uniqueness as God's elect.

Given this Old Testament model of covenantal chosenness, what are some of the necessary aspects of national/ethnic election as expressed in American civil religion? Anthony Smith wrote about what he called "the cult of authenticity," and identified this notion with the biblical theme of holiness, or being set apart and morally pure as ancient Israel was to be under the covenant.[4] Authenticity, as Smith described it, is understood as that which is pure, undiluted from the outside and an expression of the true and the real. Authenticity also refers to that which is simple and pristine, and in its simplicity stands as a given.[5]

In defining authenticity, and in identifying it as a necessary aspect of the civil-theological doctrine of election, Smith put his finger on one of its more poignant and descriptive aspects. That is, if a particular nation is divinely chosen, then by definition all others are only known as they stand relationally and ontologically *outside* of the chosen nation. Thus, all other groups that are not found within the chosen nation are categorically separated. Smith said it this way: "The authentic is the irreplaceable and fundamental, that which we cannot do without or think away. It is this necessity that separates 'us' from 'them,' our nation from all others, and makes it and its culture unique and irreplaceable."[6] This idea, that all people groups not found within the chosen nation are known perpetually as an Other, is in large measure at the heart of racist attitudes and policies held by the "elect." We will explore the consequences of this idea further later in the chapter.

National election is one of the legacies of the New England Puritans that continues to manifest itself in contemporary times. One of the ways election has always been manifested in American culture is through the concept of covenant—that if America will but walk in God's ways, then he will bless the nation, but if it rejects God, then the nation will suffer divine punishment. The Christian America thesis—the proposition that America was founded as a chosen nation, that it has been uniquely blessed and strengthened by God to fulfill a special mission in the world—is alive and well in the twenty-first century. Proponents of the

Christian America thesis continually call on America to "turn back to God" or else face the removal of "God's hand of blessing" that the nation has come to take for granted.

But the idea that America is a chosen nation in covenant with God is not a recent idea. As John Fea has recently demonstrated, the Christian America thesis has taken many forms, and has existed in America for the entirety of the nation's lifetime.[7] Over the past thirty or so years, since the formation of the Moral Majority and the publication of Peter Marshall and David Manuel's *The Light and the Glory* in 1977, the Christian America thesis has grown considerably in popularity and does not seem to be going away anytime soon. And we can thank the New England Puritans, in large measure, for bequeathing the legacy of national election to generations of Americans. George McKenna identified five enduring aspects of that legacy related to chosenness: (1) America as the new Israel, (2) America on a divine mission, (3) covenant theology, (4) America at war with the Antichrist, and (5) what he called "anxious introspection."[8] This introspection is the special American desire to be on the side of the right, and not to be satisfied with injustice, hypocrisy or lawlessness— even though as a nation they often act unjustly, hypocritically and lawlessly. Nicholas Guyatt called the punishment of God for breaking the covenant "judicial providentialism" and noted that it was a hallmark of the Northern abolitionist movement.[9] But the fear of God's punishment for national transgression is found throughout American history, even though sometimes that fear is more explicit in certain generations and circumstances than others.

AMERICAN NATIONAL/ETHNIC ELECTION IN HISTORY

The notion that America is a new Israel, God's chosen people, has been around for a long time, but during the period from the success of the American Revolution (1783) to the end of the Civil War (1865), chosennation rhetoric was at its height. The primary source of the idea of national election is, of course, the Bible. The Bible had always been important in America. Once the former colonists won the Revolution, affirmed religious freedom in the First Amendment and concluded the

War of 1812, the Bible took on a new significance in American life. The First Great Awakening saw the rapid spread of the gospel through itinerant preaching in the first half of the 1700s. At the beginning of the 1800s, a second awakening began, which had the effect of "democratizing" and voluntarizing Christianity in America.[10] In the Second Great Awakening, many Christians wanted to get copies of the Bible into everyone's hands. The American Bible Society, one of numerous voluntary organizations that came out of the Second Awakening, was formed in 1816 for that purpose. Eran Shalev wrote that the Bible's "narratives and language dominated the intellectual and spiritual lives of untold millions of Americans."[11] And during this period from the 1780s to the 1860s, the Old Testament in particular provided the vital paradigm for the United States as it commenced its career as an independent power on the Western hemisphere.

The Old Testament book of Exodus provided some of the most salient images for Americans of the early national period. The narrative of Yahweh taking his people out of Egypt, bearing them out of slavery, as it were, "on eagles' wings" (Exodus 19:4), destroying their enemies before their eyes and leading them to a good, beautiful and fertile land "flowing with milk and honey" (Exodus 3:17), seemed to supernaturally correspond to their own experience. Benjamin Franklin proposed that the Great Seal of the United States depict the Red Sea crossing to commemorate American independence. John Adams wrote to his wife, Abigail, that Franklin's seal showed "Moses lifting up his Wand, and dividing the Red Sea, and Pharaoh, in his Chariot, overwhelmed with the Waters."[12] Adams said that Thomas Jefferson's own proposed design portrayed the Israelites "in the Wilderness, led by a Cloud by day, and a Pillar of Fire by night."[13] In his second inaugural address, Jefferson called upon the help of "that Being in whose hands we are, who led our fathers, as Israel of old, from their native land and planted them in a country flowing with all the necessary and comforts of life."[14] And as we have seen previously, the figures in the Exodus narrative, such as the Red Sea, Pharaoh's army and Moses, served as types of persons and events from the war with Britain.

How did the idea of national/ethnic election take hold in the American colonies? And once the Americans secured their independence, how did they express the idea of American chosenness in the early national period? Let's consider these issues by thinking first about the enormous significance of the first European contact with America.

European discovery of America. Europeans from Spain, Portugal, France, Russia, the Netherlands, England and even Sweden came to North America to explore and establish colonies of settlement and extraction after Christopher Columbus's famous voyage in 1492. We in America are accustomed to saying that Columbus "discovered" America. To be sure, this is an overstatement—the native peoples who lived in the Americas for millennia knew it was here. But to the Europeans, who prior to 1492 had no idea that two major continents existed west of the world they knew—Europe, Africa and Asia—the Americas *were* a new-found world. And because of this fact, both Europeans' and Native Americans' fundamental, paradigmatic categories framing their understanding of reality were permanently dislocated. And from the beginning, Europeans laid down patterns that defined almost every encounter henceforth.

It is difficult for us to appreciate the magnitude of this reality. We in the twenty-first century look back on the European "discovery" of America, and to most of us, the story is pretty well rehearsed. We know (or we think we know) how it all progressed. It is easy for us to fall into the trap of present-mindedness when we consider the first contact of Europeans to what they called "the New World." We have to do our best to put ourselves into the shoes of the people of the past in order to appreciate the impact upon their scientific, epistemological, ethical and metaphysical commitments. As Fea recently put it, we have to try and show empathy when thinking of those events, because empathy allows us to "see the world as they did, to understand them on their own terms and not ours."[15]

When Europeans first encountered the Americas, what they found was categorically different than anything they had known previously. While Africa and Asia were still largely unknown to them, they were at least aware of their existence, and Western civilizations had come into contact with African and Asian civilizations many times before. But here was a land completely unknown to them, one that seemed as pristine and innocent as Eden, and new peoples whose ways and customs were a thoroughgoing enigma to Europeans. To try and reach an understanding of what Europeans and Native Americans experienced in their contact with one another, imagine in our own day astronauts landing on an alien planet that is beautifully lush and rich in resources, and inhabited by civilizations whose appearance, worldview and ways of life are vastly different than anything we ever encountered in our own world. Such a circumstance would alter the conditions of life for both civilizations forever. And the patterns established in the first contacts would define future contacts and relationships forever as well.

This was the situation when Europeans first came to America. In order for Europeans to harmoniously relate to native peoples, and in order to treat their new discoveries in a way that was not totally ethnocentrically exploitative, Europeans would have required entirely new intellectual and practical categories. But this requirement proved too tall an order for them, just as it likely would for most people. This is not to excuse them, but it is to acknowledge the historical situation as it was. The result was that Europeans placed America and Native Americans into their long-established categories, because those categories were all they knew. The land was occupied by people who seemed to Europeans to lack the basic marks of a civilization, which for them had to resemble their own to be legitimate. As Jack Greene wrote of the European perspective, "Hairy people who lived like wild beasts in the woods without clothes, housing, agriculture, religion, law, any apparent social and political or-ganization, or reason to restrain their darker passions, savages had long been an established social category in European thought."[16] Thus, Euro-peans thought indigenous people were inferior to themselves, as the In-ferior Other, as subhumans to be acted upon much as animals are acted upon by their human masters. And since they regarded native peoples in this way, they regarded the vast and bountiful lands on which they lived as practically vacant and ripe for the taking.

The newness of America presented Europeans with what seemed to them an opportunity to remake society almost from scratch. The overpopulation, disease, poverty and ceaseless fighting over the limited resources and lands of Europe could be left behind and forgotten in the limitless Americas. Even though the great powers were carving out empires in America, there was so much land that for a long time there was comparatively little contact between rival powers. So when the Puritans came to North America to establish a "city upon a hill" in 1630, they hoped to fulfill a dream of building an ideal society that was God ordained. And since the discovery of America coincided in time with the Reformation, it seemed to them that their venture was part of God's master plan for history. Greene wrote,

> Virtually every one of the new English colonies established in America after Virginia represented an effort to create in some part of the infinitely pliable world of America . . . some specific Old World vision for the recovery of an ideal past. . . . Far and away the most ambitious was the surprisingly successful attempt by English puritans to establish a redemptive community of God's chosen people in [New England].[17]

National/ethnic election in America. The Puritans who colonized New England in the seventeenth century brought from England a keen sense of national election based upon covenant theology as expressed in the Old Testament. By the first half of the eighteenth century, American colonists in British North America were beginning to find themselves. They had experienced the colonial wars with the French, closer economic ties within the colonies and the religious and social impact of the First Great Awakening. Alan Heimert summed up the Awakening's contribution to the growing sense of unity among the thirteen colonies, saying, "Not liberty, nor even equality, was, as it turned out, the essence of the Awakening, but fraternity. In the course of the eighteenth century many Calvinists were to be shocked as they saw the single end toward which all the streams of Providence and grace tended. But the spirit aroused in 1740 proved to be that of American nationalism."[18]

As American identity developed from the surge of religious revivals in the 1740s, to the British victory in the French and Indian War in 1763, to the outbreak of Revolution in 1775, to the securing of American independence in 1783, the Old Testament was particularly applicable in American self-identification. In the fifty years between 1740 and 1790, Americans had witnessed the decentralization and individualization of religion, wars that fundamentally altered the social, economic and political fabric of North America, and the founding of a new political entity in the form of thirteen United States. Taken by themselves, each of these events was momentous enough. Taken together, they represented a movement that took on biblical significance to many in America. It is no wonder that the Old Testament was so influential during this time. Shalev wrote, "Americans of the early republic thus clearly preferred the deeply nationalist and territorial Old Testament for elaborating their political theologies."[19] The theme of chosenness seemed eminently appropriate to Americans at the commencement of their national career, because they interpreted their success in the Revolution as evidence of God's particular favor. Speaking of the seriousness with which Americans of the early national period took God's providence, Fea wrote, "If the United States was ever a 'Christian nation,' it was so during the period between the ratification of the Constitution (1789) and the start of the Civil War (1861)."[20]

The Whigs and the Democrats were the two main political parties from the 1830s to the 1850s. Members of these parties expressed national chosenness consistent with their particular political and economic agendas. The Whigs were the party of consolidating the national infrastructure through internal improvements, such as roads, canals and later railroads, that would link Americans together. Fea observed that the Whigs believed it was God's will for them to craft a nation, and "some even believed that American economic and moral progress would usher in the second coming of Christ."[21] The Democrats favored expansion through purchase and conquest when necessary, such as the case with Mexico. They also favored the expansion of slavery into the new western territories taken from Mexico after 1848. The Democratic party was the party of manifest destiny, especially during the 1840s and '50s.

The issues of slavery, disunion and civil war seriously challenged the notion that America was chosen by God and existed in covenant relationship with him. Whereas Americans of the revolutionary period and shortly after emphasized the similarities between ancient Israel and the United States, many antislavery activists underscored the differences between the two. Ancient Israel allowed for slavery, but the chattel slavery that existed in the United States was of a cruel and barbaric sort not seen in ancient Israel. Furthermore, if, as James Byrd wrote, "moral nations prospered while immoral nations suffered"[22] under a covenantal arrangement, then America was acting unfaithfully to God for allowing slavery.

Slavery, disunion and the Civil War led to what Mark Noll described as a profound "theological crisis." Both North and South believed in divine chosenness under a covenantal arrangement between God and the people. But during the war between North and South, "God appeared to be acting so strikingly at odds with himself."[23] The North believed that the Union was the chosen nation because God had brought it to success during the Revolution and because the Union championed the abolition of chattel slavery. Southerners believed that the Confederacy was God's chosen nation because they acknowledged God in their Constitution, and because they believed that slaves were being evangelized through their system of slavery. Thus, as Fea wrote, "the people of the Confederate States of America believed that they were citizens of a Christian nation *precisely because* they upheld the institution of slavery."[24] The theological crisis exposed by the war was simple—both sides were confident that they were the divinely favored nation, and that God was sure to grant their respective sides victory, but both sides could not be right. Lincoln himself underscored this logical problem inherent in the providential certainty both sides expressed in his second inaugural address. Referring to both sides' belief that they were God's chosen people, Noll wrote, "The chorus, though singing different notes, sang them all in the same way."[25]

By the end of the Civil War, the rhetoric of national chosenness waned. But this did not mean that the belief in national chosenness declined.

Once the crisis of the Civil War passed, the frontier pacified and closed, and America became more proactive in international affairs in the late nineteenth and early twentieth centuries, Americans still saw themselves as chosen, but chosen for a particular mission. Mission had been a key aspect of election, especially as expressed in manifest destiny before the Civil War. But chosenness manifested itself as mission after the Civil War, especially during the twentieth century. We will turn to the theme of mission in the next chapter—for now let us explore some ethical and theological challenges to the theme of chosenness.

RACISM AND NATIONAL CHOSENNESS

The American nation established itself as an independent power in the Revolution, confirmed itself as such in the War of 1812, and began its career of territorial expansion beginning with the Louisiana Purchase in 1803. At every stage of development and expansion, white Americans came into contact with people of other races. Colonial Americans had dealings with Native Americans from the outset of colonization, and Americans had also been in contact with Africans since the first slaver arrived on Virginia's shores in 1619. And in the early nineteenth century, whites came into contact with Mexicans in Texas, and ultimately met them in battle during the Mexican War. White attitudes toward each of these three groups, Native Americans, African Americans and Mexicans, varied from generation to generation. At the same time, whites' consistent view of these groups was that they were outside the "authentic" nation, and were thus part of a group collectively regarded as the Inferior Other. The fact that whites as a whole saw these races as Inferior Other meant that they considered them bereft of human dignity, and thereby open to being acted upon at will. Whites as a whole also believed that their freedom to act upon these groups was God-ordained. Racism proved to be the logical corollary to national election.

How were native people, African Americans and Mexicans viewed and characterized by whites during the period when the idea of chosenness was at its height in America? Again, views varied, but the consistent theme was that they were outside of the divinely favored people;

thus, they were the Inferior Other to be acted upon at will by the Chosen.

Native Americans. Whites were at times fascinated, mystified and terrified of native peoples from their earliest encounters with them. At times they saw them in terms of a vast mission field, ripe for evangelism, as Massachusetts Puritan John Eliot did in the mid-1600s. Other times, they saw them as being educable and teachable along the lines of white culture. And at still other times, many whites saw them as irredeemable—at best, as uneducable, as Benjamin Franklin believed, or at worst, as impish and among the damned, as Cotton Mather asserted.[26] Nicole Guétin said that most Americans through the nineteenth century believed that ultimately Native Americans would die out as the white population overspread the continent. We have already seen that John L. O'Sullivan concurred with Alexis de Tocqueville in predicting Native American extinction. Guétin wrote, "As a rule, Americans recognized some virtues in the Indian race, but could not prevent themselves from thinking that the Indians were destined to be erased from the American continent, either by a decision from the Almighty, or according to the inexorable process of natural laws."[27]

White attitudes toward Native Americans hardened between the eighteenth and nineteenth centuries after independence, population growth and territorial expansion. Enlightened leaders such as Washington and Jefferson in the eighteenth century believed that Native Americans were fellow human beings who would ultimately be brought into the community of Americans through education and assimilation. And Elias Boudinot (1740–1821), first president of the American Bible Society, believed that Native Americans were actually part of the lost tribes of Israel. As such, Boudinot argued for their rights. After all, according to Boudinot, if Native Americans were members of the lost tribes, that fact alone would do much to justify the idea that America was to have a role to play in the millennium.

But by the second and third generation of Americans, leaders such as Andrew Jackson believed that assimilation of indigenous people was neither possible nor desirable, and they needed to be removed to remote portions of American territory. There were also economic reasons for this removal, since gold had been found on Cherokee lands in northern Georgia, and for the whites, that meant the Native Americans had to go. Reginald Horsman wrote of the removal of Native Americans from the southern Appalachians: "Indian removal as developed between 1815 and 1830 was a rejection of all Indians as Indians, not simply a rejection of unassimilated Indians who would not accept the American lifestyle."[28] In the effort to remove Native Americans to the interior of the continent, and in particular from the most desirable lands, we see whites applying the notion of the Inferior Other to Native Americans. In sum, Native Americans were in the way. They did not belong. They were not "authentic." Even the Cherokee—who lived in Georgia, South Carolina, North Carolina and Tennessee, a tribe that had a written constitution—were not to be acknowledged by the American government. They were destined to be either completely assimilated or eradicated. Either way, Native Americans were not to be allowed to maintain their identity or integrity as a people group distinct from, but equal to, whites.

Figure 3.1. President Andrew Jackson

African Americans. Whites consistently saw African Americans as inferior, and their status as slaves only reinforced the idea. Many whites believed that, as slaves, African Americans were good only for physical labor. Horsman asserted that many whites believed that African Americans were not inferior to whites because they were slaves. Rather, they were slaves because they were inferior to whites. In other words, the only conceivable station that blacks could have, if they were to survive as a race, was to be enslaved. And, particularly to eighteenth-century Englishmen, the black skin of an African was a mark of his debased nature: "Blacks were heathen, savage, and 'beastly.'"[29] Thus, whites were justified in enslaving them. And to many nineteenth-century Southerners, slavery was a blessing to African Americans because they were being evangelized.

There were notable exceptions, of course. Not all white people saw African Americans in this way. This is true of how whites viewed Native Americans and Mexicans also. Charles Anderson and Albert Gallatin are two examples of white men who deplored the notion that Anglo Americans were the chosen nation of God and were theologically justified in doing as they liked with people of other races.[30] But whites *as a race* generally looked on blacks *as a race* in terms of the Inferior Other—as outside God's chosen and favored people. The evolution of the conception of black people as inferior to white people is, as David Brion Davis suggested, deeply rooted and complex. No chronological explanation in history can coherently explain why dark-skinned Africans became regarded as fit only for slavery. Still, Davis located the origins of Western racism against black people in these categories: "Color symbolism; the significance of Islamic and then Christian geographic expansion and conflict; changing interpretations of the biblical 'Curse of Ham' (really Canaan), connections between Spanish fears of having their blood 'contaminated' by intermixture with Jewish converts and then by blacks, and . . . 'scientific' racism in the eighteenth and nineteenth centuries."[31] By the nineteenth century, in both North and South, the idea that African Americans were an inferior race was firmly ensconced in the American mind. Even Abraham Lincoln, the one man credited more than any other for the abolition of slavery, struggled to bring himself to acknowledge African Americans' moral and intellectual equality with whites.

Horsman cited Thomas R. Dew's 1832 pamphlet titled *Review of the Debate in the Virginia Legislature of 1831 and 1832* as an example of one of the most developed arguments in favor of black inferiority. Dew wrote the pamphlet while Virginia was contemplating abolishing slavery, and he argued that giving African Americans their freedom would be disastrous, for they would simply not know how to use their freedom in a responsible, nondestructive way. In other words, African Americans were not capable of living outside of slavery. Referring to African Americans, Dew wrote, "He forever wears the indelible symbol of his inferior condition; the *Ethiopian cannot change his skin, nor the leopard his spots.*"[32] Dew's position was representative of an overall attitude of whites toward African Americans in the slaveholding South especially—that African Americans, not only would not, but could not conceivably become part of the chosen nation. They were, like Native Americans, part of the Inferior Other.

Mexicans. Contact between Mexicans and Anglo Americans came comparatively late in American history. But by the middle of the nineteenth century, whites had formed the opinion of Mexicans that they, like Native and African Americans, were an inferior race of people. One of the ironies about the 1840s debates between Whigs and Democrats concerning the issue of whether or not to go to war with Mexico was that people from both parties agreed that Mexicans could not be assimilated into the Anglo community. Generally speaking, Whigs opposed the war while Democrats favored it. But many Whigs opposed the war because they did not want to see the Union embrace members of an inferior race within its boundaries. The Whig-leaning newspaper *Richmond Palladium* of Indiana opposed the war and criticized President Polk because it was fought "to get hundreds of thousands of a mongrel and debased population upon which to found a representation in Congress."[33]

Another irony about whites' racism directed toward Mexicans lies in the essence of manifest destiny. According to this doctrine, it was God's will that the Anglo-dominated Union polity was to expand from Atlantic to Pacific, and that northern Mexico (up to the 1819 border) was destined to become part of the United States. But many of those same Anglo Americans who trumpeted manifest destiny did not want the people who lived on the land they coveted. Thus the Treaty of Guadalupe-Hidalgo, as negotiated by Nicholas Trist, was finally satisfactory to

President Polk and most Americans because it transferred that Mexican territory to the United States that had the fewest Mexicans. Horsman even suggested that the primary reason why the United States did not take all of Mexico was not because of opposition to the expansion of slavery, but because the country did not want to absorb so many Mexicans into the United States.[34]

During the period when the idea of chosenness was most popular, racism against nonwhites was, if not at its peak, flourishing and unchallenged by most whites. What is certain is that violence against nonwhites, in the name of racial superiority, was at its height in years leading up to the Civil War—with the forced removal of Native Americans, the Mexican War waged in large measure because of manifest destiny, and the institutionalized slavery of African Americans. If ever there was a time in American history when the cult of authenticity was demonstrated in the contrast between the Chosen and the Inferior Other, it was during this period from the Revolution to the Civil War.

African Americans and chosenness. Despite the fact that African Americans were not assimilated into US polity, they were heavily evangelized by Protestant denominations. The Methodists were the most engaged of any denomination in slave evangelization during the nineteenth century, and Baptists had even more slave members than Methodists. Slaves also belonged to the Presbyterian, Quaker, Episcopalian, Church of Christ and Lutheran denominations, as well as the African Methodist Episcopal Church, founded in 1787 by former slave Richard Allen (1760–1831). John Blassingame wrote, "Including black Sunday School scholars and catechumens, there were probably 1,000,000 slaves under the regular tutelage of Southern churches in 1860."[35]

Because slave culture was closely tied to Christianity, African Americans developed a chosen nation concept of their own. Like their white American counterparts, the Bible was the primary source for their notion of chosenness, and particularly the book of Exodus. Recall that Franklin and Jefferson both proposed Great Seal designs that borrowed from the Exodus narrative. The Exodus narrative was particularly salient for slaves also, but for them, the British did not represent the oppressive Egyptians—

white Americans did. And while whites talked of slavery in a figurative sense, black slaves were living it in reality. The Israelites' state of bondage was a graphic and tangible figure for American slaves, and the hope of deliverance was a powerful sustaining idea for generations. Davis observed that "much of the Hebrew Bible turns on the fact that God responded not to the grandeur of kings exuding wealth and power but to the pleas and cries of lowly Hebrew slaves. Their deliverance from bondage in Egypt was clearly intended to teach the world some kind of lesson."[36] That lesson was not lost on African Americans in bondage, as is seen in the expressions of the slave culture.

One of the ways slaves expressed themselves as chosen, and whites as Other, was in music. James Cone wrote extensively about the importance of the Exodus narrative to the American slave experience, and the significance of the spiritual in communicating hope in God's presence with them as well as their eventual deliverance from bondage. Cone wrote,

> Blacks reasoned that if God could lock the lion's jaw for Daniel and could cool the fire for the Hebrew children, then he could certainly deliver black people from slavery.
>
> My Lord delivered Daniel
> Why can't He deliver me?[37]

Slaves often employed ambiguous language in their spirituals about freedom from bondage so that overseers would not punish them for being subversive. Since they were often exhorted to be obedient and submissive to their masters, songs about freedom from slavery would indeed be subversive and put them at great risk. So, many spirituals used theological language as code to encourage the slaves that their time in bondage was temporary, and that brighter days lay ahead. Many slaves looked forward to heaven, to be sure, but they also were assured that God would not allow them to live in bondage forever. So they sang songs like this one:

> I got shoes, you got shoes,
> All God's children got shoes.
> When I get to heaven, gonna put on my shoes,
> Gonna dance all over God's heaven.[38]

African Americans have also grappled with whether or not it was appropriate for them to even contemplate assimilation into an American society that considered them as Inferior Others for hundreds of years under slavery, and subsequently under Jim Crow segregation. During the civil rights movement of the 1950s and '60s, the rhetorical and practical styles of Martin Luther King Jr. and Malcolm X are illustrative of this tension within the African American community. King famously advocated a nonviolent response to white racism in hopes that whites and blacks could live in harmony with one another in American society. He based his vision for the civil rights movement on natural law expressed in the Christian philosophical tradition. This is evident in his "Letter from a Birmingham City Jail," in which he wrote to white clergy, "One may well ask, 'How can you advocate breaking some laws and obeying others?' The answer is found in the fact that there are two types of laws: there are *just* and *unjust* laws. I would agree with St. Augustine that 'An unjust law is no law at all.'"[39]

But Malcolm X advocated for black separatism. And furthermore, while Malcolm did not argue that African Americans ought to initiate violence against white society, he did not back away from advocating in favor of violence in self-defense. For him, America would be nothing without the contributions of African Americans, for it had been they who invested the most in America, receiving the least return. Therefore, he said,

> Right now, in this country, if you and I, 22 million African-Americans— that's what we are—Africans who are in America. You're nothing but Africans. Nothing but Africans. In fact, you'd get farther calling yourself African instead of Negro. Africans don't catch hell. . . . They don't have to pass civil-rights bills for Africans. An African can go anywhere he wants right now.[40]

Black separatism, as expressed by Malcolm, called upon the themes of black chosenness developed in slavery, the conviction that God had chosen African Americans, and that no matter what the white man did to them, nothing could change the fact of their chosenness. As Cone said,

"Whites could drive them, and beat them, and even kill them; but they believed nevertheless that God had chosen black slaves as his own and that this election bestowed upon them a freedom to *be*, which could not be measured by what oppressors could do to the human body."[41]

Still, one critical element exists in both King's and Malcolm's speeches and writings. Even though they took different views on how the civil

Figure 3.2. Malcolm X

rights movement should proceed, they based their differing approaches on an objective and universal conception of justice. King spoke of the difference between just and unjust laws. In his "Letter," he defined a just law as one that comported with God's moral law. An unjust law "is a human law that is not rooted in eternal and natural law. . . . Any law that degrades human personality is unjust."[42]

Thus, Jim Crow laws that subjected the entire African American population to discrimination, barred them from equal opportunities to pursue happiness and stunted their growth as free individuals in a free society—these laws were unjust, and therefore needed to be broken. Malcolm, although he advocated for black separatism, still held to this same conception of justice. In his "Ballot or the Bullet" speech, he spoke of the difference between civil rights and human rights. Civil rights are those that are acknowledged and granted by the US government, the same government that he said rejected and demeaned African Americans for centuries. But human rights are inherent, universal and undeniable. Malcolm said, "Civil rights means you're asking Uncle Sam to treat you right. Human rights are something you are born with. Human rights are your God-given rights."[43]

The Christian conception of justice as objective, universal and theistically framed is essential to an ethical critique of national/ethnic election, and of closed American exceptionalism as a whole. When Americans have held to an exclusivist model to identify themselves, such as chosenness, this has necessarily led to racism. Anyone outside of the Chosen is thus lumped together in the Inferior Other. At that point, the Inferior Other becomes objectivized, and the Chosen can justify acting upon them in any way they deem appropriate. This acting upon can arise from altruistic intentions—such as efforts to evangelize the Inferior Other to bring them the gospel. But more often, this acting upon the Inferior Other is degrading, discriminatory and violent, as Native Americans, African Americans and Mexicans can attest from their historical, collective experience. And ultimately, such an exclusivist expression of patriotism leads to the breaking apart of the national community. David Koyzis wrote, "When states break up, it is often because the people of the successor states did not believe they were receiving justice under the old system."[44] A nation, no matter how devoted a portion of its members are, if equal justice is not secured for all, by all, cannot maintain itself and will ultimately implode.

THEOLOGICAL PROBLEMS WITH NATIONAL/ETHNIC ELECTION

The concept of national/ethnic election is inherently civil-theological. Therefore, it is appropriate to critique the concept on biblically informed, theological grounds. Much could be said, but national/ethnic election— as an aspect of American exceptionalism—is theologically wrongheaded because the concept militates against the Christian gospel as explained in the Bible.

Election is presented in Scripture in two different contexts—one context is governed by the national model as expressed through the Abrahamic and Mosaic covenants in the Old Testament. Ancient Israel was chosen by God to be a holy nation, so that he would reveal himself to all nations through it. This is at the heart of God's calling of Abraham in Genesis 12. In the New Testament, through the person and work of Christ, election took on a more explicit salvific meaning. The Old Testament model of national election was fulfilled in Christ, because he came and took the sins of the world upon himself on the cross. In the New Testament, election was wrapped up in the completed work of Christ on the cross, such that anyone who put their trust in Christ would be saved. Those who were saved were described by Paul in Romans 8:33: "Who shall bring any charge against God's elect? It is God who justifies." And who are the elect, according to Paul? He wrote in Romans 8:29-30 that the elect are those "he also predestined to be conformed to the image of his Son. . . . And those whom he predestined he also called, and those whom he called he also justified, and those whom he justified he also glorified."

National election in the Old Testament was not explicitly an election to salvation. Just because a person was a Jew, it did not follow that the person was saved. John the Baptist scolded the Pharisees and Sadducees in Matthew 3:8-9: "Bear fruit in keeping with repentance. And do not presume to say to yourselves, 'We have Abraham as our father,' for I tell you, God is able from these stones to raise up children for Abraham." But in nationalistic concepts of election, according to Smith, the goal is not salvation in the sense of the Christian gospel. Rather, by being identified with a particular national group, the people "act as a model or *exemplum* of what it means to be holy, and hence like God. . . . The ultimate purpose of the covenant is, therefore, global salvation."[45] But as Luke stated in Acts 4:12, salvation is an empty concept without the gospel. Absent Christ, from what is a nation saved? "And there is salvation in no one else, for there is no other name under heaven given among men by which we must be saved," that is, reconciled to God on the basis of Christ's death and resurrection.

One final problem with national/ethnic election is that Scripture has already identified the chosen nation. The Old Testament, of course, identified ancient Israel as God's chosen nation. But in the New Testament, the chosen nation was identified in the form of the church. First Peter 2:9 states, "But you are a chosen race, a royal priesthood, a holy nation, a people for his own possession, that you may proclaim the excellencies of him who called you out of darkness into his marvelous light." To be in the church means that one has been shown the grace of God through Christ's atoning work. And, if one is in the church by faith in Christ, one is saved on the basis of grace through faith and is therefore chosen of God. And the invitation to be saved, and thus to be included among God's chosen, the church, is given universally. The final invitation of Scripture is given in Revelation 22:17: "The Spirit and the Bride say, 'Come.' And let the one who hears say, 'Come.' And let the one who is thirsty come; let the one who desires take the water of life without price." Thus, while the gospel's conception of election is exclusive, it is not prohibitive. But the nationalistic form of election in closed American exceptionalism shuts out anyone who is classified, explicitly or implicitly, as Inferior Other.

It is imperative to distinguish between the Christian gospel and the concept of national chosenness in closed American exceptionalism. The gospel and closed American exceptionalism are mutually exclusive. To accept the gospel is necessarily to reject closed American exceptionalism, not only because they are two different things, but because their objects of loyalty are two distinct entities in opposition to one another. The nation as divinely chosen itself becomes an object of veneration. But the nation-state, contrary to the rhetoric of O'Sullivan, is fallible, and often violates justice. The gospel communicates God's justice revealed in Christ to human beings. As Paul wrote in Romans 3:26, Christ came to serve as a sacrificial victim on the cross for everyone who believed on him, "so that [God] might be just and the justifier of the one who has faith in Jesus." The exceptionalist expression of national/ethnic election is not equal to that found in the Bible. The biblical expressions of election must not be required to pay for the sins of the nation. Rather, the Christian gospel should be allowed to speak on its own terms as it is articulated in Scripture, and thus be accepted or rejected without reference to America.

CONCLUSION

Exceptionalism, as it relates to the concept of chosenness, has little of value to offer the citizen. But does that mean the citizen must reject any and all forms of exceptionalism? The answer is no. Here, Koyzis's distinction between nationalism and patriotism is helpful. Nationalism is tribalistic, triumphalist, idolatrous, exclusivist and violates justice. But patriotism is an expression of devotion to country that is defined by justice. In other words, patriotism is love expressed to the national community, but it is love properly measured and applied. Patriotism acknowledges a proper place for devotion, loyalty, gratitude and sacrifice for one's country. But patriotic expressions do not exclude others by necessity. They only do so if those exclusions are just—necessary for the protection of the whole. Koyzis wrote, "We are here referring to that community of citizens created by political power but deepened in the development of a shared commitment to, and love of that community. . . . Such loyalty is not idolatrous worship of a nation; rather, it is a limited affection for a community of fellow citizens."[46]

Patriotism, according to this articulation, is understood by using the conception of justice handed down to us in the Christian philosophical tradition, especially as King described it in his "Letter." And while much of Malcolm's rhetoric is jolting, his conception of justice, expressed in his distinction between civil and human rights, is consistent with the Christian view of justice. When patriotism is rooted in justice, then it does not blind itself to the flaws and failings of the nation. Rather, patriots seek to rectify those flaws, and learn from the failures so as not to repeat them. The result of this attitude is that patriots create potential for the flourishing of the whole community.

While closed exceptionalism is nationalistic, open exceptionalism is patriotic. It does not deny religious people their prophetic voice. It does not accept the insistence that the nation can do no wrong. It does not shut out groups on arbitrary, man-made grounds. It is not contrary to the Christian gospel. Under the conception of open exceptionalism, a person like Walter Rauschenbusch can express himself as a patriot, even though he argued against involvement in World War I. He can be regarded as a patriot, even though his views were outside of the mainstream. He said, "It takes a higher brand of patriotism to stand against the war clamor than to bellow with the crowd."[47] Sometimes patriotism means calling the nation out on moral grounds, because the nation is not always right. Closed exceptionalism is a philosophy denying such a thing is possible. Open exceptionalism is one that anticipates it, but that yet seeks opportunity to set the nation on a more sure moral footing.

Furthermore, open exceptionalism as a civil religious paradigm does not deistically rule out God's immanence and the doctrine of providence. Indeed, Christians hold to providence because without it the flow of history is left devoid of meaning. The use of providence in attempting to interpret history can lead to problematic conclusions, to be sure. Providence can be abused in many ways, both knowingly and unknowingly. Providence, as a theological paradigm, does not suffice as a rendering of history. But belief in providence is not necessarily a problem. It becomes a problem when providence is constructed around particular events, and people claim comprehensive or epistemically certain knowledge of it. This was the problem for many on both sides during the Civil War. As Noll wrote, "The difficulty was not trust in providence as such but trust in providence so narrowly defined by the republican, covenantal, commonsensical Enlightenment, and—above all—nationalistic categories that Protestant evangelicals had so boldly appropriated with such galvanizing effects."[48] But when the interpreter of past or present events acknowledges providence in a humble and critical way, allowing for it but claiming no certain knowledge of its application, the interpreter can then align himself with Christian doctrine and appropriately express patriotism. A patriot, one who sees American exceptionalism in open terms, may acknowledge providence as Lincoln did—with the ever-present admission that when speaking of God's purposes in human events, one can always be wrong.

In the next chapter, we shall consider the civil-theological theme of mission. Chosenness entails mission. It is the practical application of an ontological affirmation. The United States has historically seen itself on a righteous mission in the world, and many of its actions in the past have been informed by a strong sense of mission. As with chosenness, there is a closed and open exceptionalist expression of mission. We turn then to consider mission as a civil-theological paradigm through which Americans have historically self-identified.

FOR FURTHER READING

Davis, David Brion. *Inhuman Bondage: The Rise and Fall of Slavery in the New World*. Oxford: Oxford University Press, 2006.

Fea, John. *Was America Founded as a Christian Nation? A Historical Introduction*. Louisville: Westminster John Knox, 2011.

Horsman, Reginald. *Race and Manifest Destiny: The Origins of American Racial Anglo-Saxonism*. Cambridge: Harvard University Press, 1981.

Koyzis, David T. *Political Visions and Illusions: A Survey and Christian Critique of Contemporary Ideologies*. Downers Grove, IL: IVP Academic, 2003.

Shalev, Eran. *American Zion: The Old Testament as a Political Text from the Revolution to the Civil War*. New Haven: Yale University Press, 2013.

Smith, Anthony. *Chosen Peoples: Sacred Sources of National Identity*. Oxford: Oxford University Press, 2003.

4

The Commissioned Nation

The issues that face us are momentous, involving the fulfillment or destruction not only of this Republic but of civilization itself. They are issues which will not await our deliberations. With conscience and resolution this Government and the people it represents must now take new and fateful decisions.

REPORT TO THE NATIONAL SECURITY COUNCIL—NSC-68, 1950

This Nation was conceived with a sense of mission and dedicated to the extension of freedom throughout the world.

SECRETARY OF STATE JOHN FOSTER DULLES, 1956

One day, it will save the world.

MARQUIS DE LAFAYETTE, 1825

IN AUGUST 1957, a twenty-four-year-old aspiring comedienne named Carol Burnett appeared on the *Ed Sullivan Show* to perform a parody song titled "I Made a Fool of Myself over John Foster Dulles." Burnett sang as a crazed fan amorously obsessed with President Dwight D. Eisenhower's secretary of state. Burnett performed her song with what became her trademark rubber facial expressions, unforgettable singing voice and hilarious acting. But what made the song truly funny was its irony—

Dulles was famously staid and serious, popularly known at the time as the "Most Boring Man in America." Winston Churchill reportedly described him as a "dour Puritan, a great white bespectacled face with a smudge of a mouth."[1] He was not the first person one might have thought of as a charismatic celebrity fawned over by adoring fans, like, say, Elvis Presley or Johnny Cash. Burnett sang her song, brought the house down and launched her career.

Burnett performed the song on network television venues numerous times over the next several days. And despite his reputation for being fervidly grave, Dulles revealed that he indeed had a clever and dry sense of humor. Dulles appeared on *Meet the Press* about a week after Burnett's first performance and was asked about what he thought of it. Burnett happened to be watching the interview, and she described Dulles's response to her act:

> And so it was, you know, all the serious talk about what the Secretaries of State talk about. And then at the very last part of the show, the moderator said, well, all right, we're going to leave now, but, Mr. Dulles, just tell us what is this about you and that young girl that sings that love song about you. And I looked—oh, I got real close to the television set. And he got a twinkle in his eye and he said, "I make it a matter never to talk about loves in public."[2]

As secretary of state, John Foster Dulles (1888–1959) believed intensely that God tasked America to perform a mission of righteousness and justice in a world threatened by what he called the "godless communism" of the Soviet Union. Dulles was certainly not the first nor the last person to conceive of America as the exceptional and indispensable nation with a God-given commission in the world. In holding his conviction about America's global responsibilities, he showed himself consistent with a long American intellectual and religious tradition. And Dulles's particular conception of America's mission in the world—how he defined it, and how he justified it—was both a product of his times and a paradigm to which later American policy makers adhered.

We considered the civil religious concept of national election in the last chapter as an aspect of closed exceptionalism. National election entails national mission. That is, to affirm that God chose a particular nation carries both a passive and an active meaning. The nation is chosen by God, so its identity is defined by a special relationship to God. This notion, while passive, is powerful, as we have seen. But as a chosen nation, it not only bears a unique identity. It has a job to do. It is divinely chosen to *be* something in order to *do* something. The civil religious concept of national mission, fraught with activism, is the subject of this chapter.

Generally speaking, the divine commission is that Americans extend free institutions to the world. Various figures have articulated the mission in different ways across the generations. The earliest settlers in the seventeenth and eighteenth centuries expressed the mission in millennial terms. Proponents of manifest destiny expressed it in imperialist terms. And Lincoln expressed it in

Figure 4.1. Secretary of State John Foster Dulles

exemplarist terms. Manifest destiny had a revival of sorts in the 1890s, and the mission was extended to the new territories America acquired in its war with Spain. And after World War I, the mission was cast in terms of spreading and defending democracy worldwide. The national election that Americans have historically articulated is, in Anthony Smith's words, "*missionary* election . . . heavily influenced by the *covenantal* type of ethnic election, mainly as a result . . . of the spread and impact of the Bible."[3] Richard Gamble, writing of a continuous rhetorical tradition in presidential speeches since Woodrow Wilson, said, "To one degree or another and with varying motives and consequences, each of these men continued to speak of the United States as if it were the *Salvator Mundi*, following a pattern of thought that has endured for more than four centuries."[4]

We will consider Dulles as a representative example of an American policy maker who so forcefully articulated the notion of national mission that he almost embodied it. Dulles served in the highest levels of the American government during the first full decade of the Cold War, when he helped set important precedents in foreign policy that conformed to exceptionalist notions of national mission. The idea that America has been set aside by God to fulfill a special destiny dates back to the formation of the first American colonies in the seventeenth century. But believers in America's national mission enlarged the notion to a global scale during the twentieth century, particularly after World War II (1939–1945). John Foster Dulles was at the tip of the spear in this effort during his tenure as America's chief diplomat. He was America's foremost Cold Warrior in the 1950s. As such, he not only confirmed the idea of America's moral and spiritual indispensability on the world stage in specific details of foreign policy during his tenure as secretary of state; he also articulated American indispensability in a way that most Americans have taken for granted ever since. Stephen Kinzer wrote that, for Dulles, the idea of American exceptionalism was "not a platitude, but the organizing principle of daily life and global politics."[5] His was among the purest expressions of the closed exceptionalist notion of national divine commission since the end of World War II.

SITUATING DULLES IN AMERICAN HISTORY

Dulles entered and exited this world in America's capital city, Washington, DC. He was born in 1888 and died in 1959. These years span the rapid rise of the United States, first to continental power, then to world power and finally to superpower status. With this rise in power and influence, the United States also met its most extreme existential challenges: the threats imposed by the dictatorships of the Axis powers in World War II and the nuclear age animated by the ideological conflict with the Soviet Union in the Cold War. When Dulles died on May 24,

1959, the United States and the Soviet Union were approaching the height of Cold War tensions, culminating in the Berlin Crisis of 1961 and the Cuban Missile Crisis of 1962. Within ten years of Dulles's death, the United States was mired in an unwinnable war in Vietnam. Twenty years on, the American embassy in Tehran was seized by Iranian Islamic revolutionaries in retaliation for America's support of the Shah. Both of these humbling events were the direct legacies of Dulles's vision of the American world mission and policies that he pursued as secretary of state in Vietnam and Iran in the 1950s. But thirty years after his death, the Berlin Wall came down and the Eastern European countries that had been dominated by the Soviet-led Warsaw Pact bolted from Moscow's control. Soon after in 1991, the Soviet Union itself collapsed. Dulles's exceptionalist vision for American foreign policy appeared to be vindicated by many Americans. And after the terrorist acts perpetrated by al-Qaeda on 9/11 initiated the global war on terror just over forty years after his death, Dulles's idea of a cosmic war between forces of good and evil—and America's role in it—seemed to take on a new form in the rhetoric of George W. Bush and the neoconservative element in the Republican party.

When Dulles was two years old, the government took the 1890 census, and it stated that the American frontier was officially closed. The continental United States was rounded out, territorial expansion was completed and the Indian wars were over. A young historian named Frederick Jackson Turner, a professor of history at the University of Wisconsin, gave a paper at the 1893 meeting of the American Historical Association in Chicago in which he attempted to make sense of the frontier's meaning pertinent to America's place in the world. The paper was titled "The Significance of the Frontier in American History," and in it, Turner argued that "the existence of an area of free land, its continuous recession, and the advance of American settlement westward explain American development."[6] In other words, it was the reality of the continuous expansion of the population into an untamed, uncharted and uncultivated western frontier—the continuous movement, occupation and settling of the frontier—that defined the American identity. The democratic prin-

ciples that Americans brought with them into the frontier were the defining features of their expansive mission. The act of westward movement,
animated by democratic principles, represented "a new field of opportunity, the gate of escape from the bondage of the past,"[7] for Turner.
Turner's "frontier thesis" broke new ground in American historiography
by casting US history in exceptionalist terms and laying the basis, not for
Americans to desist in their project of expansion, but to continue it.

In 1898, the United States declared war on Spain, and by the end of
that year, it had absorbed territories that Spain had possessed since as
early as the fifteenth century: Cuba, the Philippines and Puerto Rico. The
Philippines became the site of America's first sustained project in car-
rying out its mission of bringing democratic civilization to a foreign
people. Theodore Roosevelt, the one man who was more responsible
than anyone in spurring America to war with Spain, lectured Americans
about their duty as a great civilizing national force to fulfill its destiny in
the Philippines, in order to bless the Filipinos and to be blessed themselves. While governor of New York, he said in 1899,

> We have taken it upon ourselves . . . a great task, benefitting a great nation,
> and we have a right to ask of . . . every true American, that he shall with
> heart and hand uphold the leaders of the nation as from a brief and glorious
> war they strive to a lasting peace that shall redound not only to the interests
> of the conquered people, not only to the honor of the American public, but
> to the permanent advancement of civilization and of all mankind.[8]

Dulles was eleven when then-Governor Roosevelt made that speech.

With the onset of World War I in 1914, the United States initially
remained neutral. But the Germans inflicted losses on American mer-
chant shipping, and also enraged the nation by sinking the *Lusitania*
in 1915, killing over a thousand civilians, 114 of them Americans. By
January 1917, the Germans committed themselves to attack every
American ship headed toward Great Britain, even though the United
States took an officially neutral position. On April 2, 1917, President
Woodrow Wilson asked Congress to declare war on Germany, and thus
began American involvement in the war against the Central Powers.

American troops broke the stalemate between the Allies and the Germans in France and Belgium in the summer and fall of 1918, and by November 11, an armistice between the belligerents ended the war. Dulles was thirty at war's end.

Wilson saw America fulfilling a cosmic mission to bring Christian civilization, enlivened by democracy, to a world gone mad. In a 1920 message to Congress, Wilson said, "This is the time of all others when Democracy should prove its purity and its spiritual power to prevail. It is surely the manifest destiny of the United States to lead in the attempt to make this spirit prevail."[9] Wilson had been a professional historian and political scientist before entering politics, authoring several books including a five-volume history of the United States. He was a Presbyterian and a proponent of both Turner's frontier thesis and Protestant eschatology. He believed that God had chosen America to complete John Winthrop's 1630 mission—to establish a model Christian state that would be an example to the rest of the world. As Milan Babík wrote, during the peace talks at Versailles in 1919, "the old Puritan dream of returning to the old world from the transatlantic refuge in order to spread the American millennium worldwide seemed to him on the verge of fulfillment."[10] Through his vision of the League of Nations, Wilson saw America as God's appointed nation to bring peace to world civilization, and himself as God's appointed servant. Babík wrote that Wilson considered the League to be "a giant presbytery of nations" and "in this presbytery, Wilson regarded himself as the presiding minister, a new Moses selected by divine providence to explain the modern Tablets of the League Covenant to national leaders."[11]

Imperial Germany posed a great threat to the world in World War I. After all, Germany invaded Belgium, Luxembourg, France and Russia and was at war with a host of other nations whose territory it never violated, like the United States and Great Britain. But the threat posed to the United States and the world by Nazi Germany in World War II was a far more profound threat to civilization as a whole. Most Americans saw the struggle against Nazi Germany and expansionist Japan as the most authentic war for democracy, self-determination and human flourishing they had ever waged. President Franklin D. Roosevelt cast the struggle in those very terms almost a year before the United States declared war. In his January 6, 1941, message to Congress, Roosevelt called for the securing of a new world order once the Axis dictatorships were defeated. This world order would be marked by specific freedoms that would be comprehensively upheld and defended:

> In the future days, which we seek to make secure, we look forward to a world founded upon four essential human freedoms. The first is freedom of speech and expression everywhere in the world. The second is freedom of every person to worship God in his own way everywhere in the world. The third is freedom from want, which, translated into world terms, means economic understandings which will secure to every nation a healthy peacetime life for its inhabitants everywhere in the world. The fourth is freedom from fear—which, translated into world terms, means a worldwide reduction of armaments to such a point and in such a thorough fashion that no nation will be in a position to commit an act of physical aggression against any neighbor—anywhere in the world.[12]

Roosevelt had a keen Christian awareness that many observed was eminently simple. He was an Episcopalian for whom Jesus' moral teachings served as foundational religious principles. Of the many foundations on which democracy is built, Roosevelt believed that religious freedom was of prime importance especially in a society marked by pluralism. Andrew Preston wrote that "in wearing his theology lightly but holding his faith closely, Roosevelt was closely in turn with the religious sentiments of most Americans, who valued religion as much for its social utility and spiritual comforts as for any deeper philosophical meaning."[13] When the war ended in 1945, the United States was the most powerful nation on earth. Alone of all the belligerent nations, hardly any of its territory and none of its infrastructure had been touched during the war. In 1945, America was at its height in global economic, diplomatic, military and political stature.

But also by the end of World War II, the West perceived a new threat arising to take the place of Nazi Germany and Imperial Japan—the Soviet Union. The Soviets had been partners with the Western allies against Hitler. But fears of a new world war between the West and the

Soviets became real as soon as 1948, when the Soviets crushed a revolt in Czechoslovakia and attempted to seal Berlin off from the Western powers that oversaw specific sectors in the city. In 1949, the Soviet Union detonated its first atomic bomb, ending America's monopoly on nuclear weapons. With this explosive development (pun intended), Americans possessed a fresh sense of mission.

Americans were particularly nervous about the Soviets because in many ways they represented the worst of both the Nazis and the Japanese. They were worried that the Soviets were expansionist and totalitarian, like the Nazis. And even more ominously, they were worried that they were secretive and prone to making a surprise attack, like the Japanese. Memories of two world wars were fresh on Americans' minds in the late 1940s and '50s. Thus, as Kinzer wrote, many Americans believed "that therefore [the Soviets] must be resisted by every means, no matter how distasteful."[14] Because the Soviet threat seemed so profound, the national mission was of a scope and scale never before seen. In his 1949 inaugural address, President Harry Truman said,

> The United States and other like-minded nations find themselves directly opposed by a regime with contrary aims and a totally different concept of life. That regime adheres to a false philosophy which purports to offer freedom, security, and greater opportunity to mankind. Misled by that philosophy, many peoples have sacrificed their liberties only to learn to their sorrow that deceit and mockery, poverty and tyranny are their reward.[15]

Harry Truman's presidency ended on January 20, 1953. Dwight D. Eisenhower, formerly the general who served as supreme commander of all Allied forces in the European theater during World War II and supreme commander of the newly formed North Atlantic Treaty Organization (NATO), succeeded him. Shortly after Ike's inauguration as thirty-fourth president, he nominated, and the Senate confirmed, Dulles as secretary of state. He turned sixty-five that February.

John Foster Dulles, Christian Diplomat

Dulles was born into a family possessing a unique diplomatic and religious pedigree. He was named after his maternal grandfather, John W.

Foster, who served as Benjamin Harrison's secretary of state. His maternal uncle, Robert Lansing, served Woodrow Wilson as secretary of state during America's involvement in World War I. Young "Foster" was close with both his grandfather and his uncle, and he accompanied both of them on separate overseas missions. He went with his grandfather to the Second Hague Peace Conference in 1907 and with his uncle to the Paris Peace Conference in 1919. On this 1919 trip Dulles had an up-close perspective on the complex negotiations surrounding the creation of the League of Nations. His experiences of seeing the genesis of the League, its struggles to survive without American participation, and ultimately its disintegration influenced him deeply in his later years as he contemplated the creation and mission of the United Nations in the 1940s and 1950s.

While the Fosters were lawyers and diplomats, the Dulles men were ministers. Dulles's paternal grandfather, John Welsh Dulles, went to serve as a missionary to India when he was twenty-six. His uncle, the Reverend Joseph Dulles, oversaw the library at Princeton Theological Seminary. Dulles's father, the Reverend Allen Macy Dulles, was the pastor of First Presbyterian Church in Watertown, New York, until 1904. In that year, young Foster went away to Princeton University while his father went to Auburn Theological Seminary in Auburn, New York, to take up the post of professor of theism and apologetics. Dulles grew up listening to his father's sermons and sitting around the front porch with his family in Watertown, singing deeply theological and didactic hymns. According to his friend Henry Van Dusen, when Dulles was dying of colon cancer in the spring of 1959, he wanted to be comforted by the hymns he had sung as a boy. Van Dusen wrote,

> He longed to hear again the hymns that had nourished his spirit in youth and across the years—not sentimental modern hymns but the grand old affirmations of faith: "The Spacious Firmament on High"; "When Morning Gilds the Skies"; "God of Our Life, Through All the Circling Years"; "Work, for the Night Is Coming"; "All Praise to Thee, My God, This Night."[16]

While Dulles was a devout Christian, he was not a fundamentalist, or even a theological conservative. As Preston observed, had he been a fundamentalist on the order of someone like William Jennings Bryan (Wilson's first secretary of state), he would never have held the positions of influence in the Federal Council of Churches or in the US government in his later career. In describing his theological identity, Preston wrote, "He was not just a Christian; nor was he simply a mainline Protestant. . . . More precisely, and much more importantly, he was an ecumenical Christian."[17] And as an ecumenical Christian, with no particular theological axes to grind, he spoke a great deal on the indispensability of Christian churches of all denominations in striving for international cooperation and world peace. But still, his Christian faith—particularly the missionary aspect of Christianity—was deeply ingrained in him, and his worldview directed his attitudes and actions as secretary of state.

In the 1930s and early '40s, Dulles established himself as a firm internationalist who believed that the threat of war would recede to the extent that national sovereignty was weakened. He was appointed as head of the Commission on a Just and Durable Peace (under the auspices of the Federal Council of Churches, or FCC) in late 1940 to consider the question of constructing a global postwar order that would not repeat the mistakes of that of the 1920s and '30s. Under his leadership, the Commission advocated for a new international body that would be stronger and more effective at preventing war than the League of Nations. One of the keys to the success of such a world body, Dulles believed, was American leadership and the example and efforts of American churches.

But the end of World War II brought the threat of Soviet communism into sharp relief for Dulles. According to Preston, Dulles believed "Soviet communism had always been an evil at least as great as Nazism, and much greater than fascism."[18] To add to his suspicion of communism in general, Dulles did not trust Joseph Stalin, the Soviet premier, who was going back on the promises he made at the 1944 Yalta Conference regarding the allowance of free elections in Soviet-liberated Eastern Europe. While he was in San Francisco for the renovation of the United Nations from a military alliance to an international cooperative body in late 1945, Dulles backed away from some of his internationalism because of fears that the Soviets would take advantage of the United Nations to advance an expansionist agenda. "By the time he became Secretary of State," Inboden wrote, "he saw the United States as God's chosen instrument to accomplish divine purposes in the world"[19] rather than international bodies. But Dulles did not repudiate his internationalism in favor of pure nationalism. Rather, he simply saw that the United States' mission was to defeat the forces of irreligious communism in order to protect his ultimate goal of internationalism. It was as if he had to delay his original vision of a world federation for the moment while the United States, as the theistic leader of the free world, dealt with the threat that Soviet communism leveled at human civilization. Preston put it this way: "From 1946 until his death in 1959, Dulles modified his ecumenical internationalism to do battle with communism in order to rescue ecumenical internationalism."[20]

DULLES AND AMERICA'S DIVINE COMMISSION

As Secretary of State, Dulles broke from John Quincy Adams's vision of American foreign policy that he expressed in a July 4, 1821, speech as secretary of state under James Monroe—"She goes not abroad, in search of monsters to destroy. She is the well-wisher to the freedom and independence of all."[21] Under the leadership of President Eisenhower, and in partnership with his brother, Director of Central Intelligence Allen Dulles, Foster Dulles helped wage secret war in Central America, Latin America and Asia. Clandestinely overturning leaders he suspected of leaning toward communism was much less expensive in lives and treasure than all-out military confrontation. Dulles believed that only America had the spiritual, moral and material capability to save human civilization from the dark forces of communism. According to Kinzer, Dulles "personified this worldview" and "crystallized the Cold War paradigm."[22]

The closed exceptionalist notion of divine commission was a prominent feature of both American Cold War foreign policy and Dulles's personal belief matrix. Three philosophical commitments undergirded Dulles's vision of America's mission to confront the forces of darkness in the world—Manichaeism, religious faith and activism. These three commitments combined in Dulles's outlook and directed his actions as America's chief diplomat during most of the decade of the 1950s.

Manichaeism. Manichaeism is an ancient religious and ethical system that came to prominence in the third century through Mani, a Persian philosopher who died around AD 276. In Manichaeistic metaphysics, good and evil are separate entities in opposition to one another. Both good and evil are equally powerful and are also classified in terms of light and darkness, as well as truth and error. Mani taught that humans have the capacity for good or evil, and that the cosmic conflict between them is carried out, at least in part, through the activities of human beings. In the ancient world, Manichaeans commonly articulated the philosophy using a mixture of Zoroastrianism, Gnosticism and Christianity. In the medieval period, Manichaeism was the doctrine of the heretical group known as the Albigensians. The Albigensians were based in southern France in the thirteenth century, and were wiped out by Louis VIII and Louis IX (St. Louis) by the year 1270. St. Augustine was famously once an adherent of Manichaeism before his conversion to Christianity. It also had an influence on the thinking of eighteenth-century Enlightenment philosophers David Hume and Voltaire. Thus as a worldview Manichaeism has been prominent in Western intellectual and religious history since the ancient period.

Dulles was not a strict Manichaean. But his view of the world after the war ended in 1945 was defined in large measure by the notion of a transcendent battle between light and darkness, truth and falsehood, good and evil. Furthermore, Dulles baptized his Manichaeism in theistic waters. America represented the forces of good because it respected moral laws, the dignity of the individual, individual freedom based on natural rights, the existence of God and the importance of churches in the worldwide struggle. Communism represented the forces of evil because its followers recognized none of these things. It was a system distinguished by atheism, statism and slavery. As such, communism was a great falsehood that must be confronted and destroyed by the Good, the Godly and the True.

In his book *War or Peace*, Dulles laid out some of the distinctives of the Soviet communist system in an effort to help his readers come to "know who generates the enmity that poisons the atmosphere in which we live"—that is, "the relatively small, fanatical Soviet Communist Party."[23] Dulles did not consider the Russian people as a whole America's enemy, but he did consider the Communist Party, dominated by Stalin and the Politburo in the Kremlin, to be the enemy. The Party leaders command obedience of the Soviet people, according to Dulles, and any person or nation that opposes them is treated as an enemy to be destroyed.

At bottom, Soviet-style communism was atheistic. This was the basic problem for Dulles. The fact that the Party leaders in the Kremlin began from an atheistic premise to wield absolute power disturbed Dulles. He believed that violence was the active expression of Communism. Furthermore, since Soviet-style communism was atheistic, any acknowledgment of moral law was impossible. In the Soviet Union, law was thus not based on an objective conception of justice, but was arbitrary, capricious and wielded against those who oppose the state. Dulles wrote that, for the Soviets, "laws are the means, the decrees, by which the dictatorship of the proletariat enforces its will."[24]

Dulles taught that the Soviet system, which is atheistic and rooted in the absolute power of its leaders, defines loyalty and patriotism as strict conformity. Within the Soviet Union, citizens are expected to agree with the policies of its leaders in every respect, or else face instant retribution. Troublesome nonconformers, Dulles said, "are like grit in the wheels of the machine and have to be cleaned out. That explains why the population of Russian concentration camps keeps constantly at around 15,000,000."[25] And conformity to the Soviet system does not only apply to Soviet citizens. It applies to every person everywhere in the world. Any nation that opposes the will of the Soviet leadership is a threat to the Soviet system as a whole, and must be compelled to conform absolutely or be eliminated.

Ultimately, Dulles taught, those who are opposed to Soviet communism are capitalists, and since capitalists can only oppose communism by war, the Soviet Union must build up its capability to defend itself. But according to Dulles, for Soviet communists, the best defense is a good offense. The ultimate goal of the Soviets was to create a global single state dominated by Moscow, and to achieve this goal, it must "first tak[e] over the weaker countries" in order to encircle the stronger ones. Once the weaker countries have been brought into the Soviet orbit, "then all people, everywhere in the world will be compelled to think alike and act in harmony in order to assure the world peace to which the Soviet Communists profess to be dedicated."[26] Still, the expansionist agenda was not to be accomplished through national war, but through class war. Thus, it was not the Red Army that was going to be on the march. The Red Army ensured defense and intimidated the world. The task of expansion belonged to the Communist Party. Expansion of communism, according to Dulles, was "to be carried out by its methods of class war, civil war, penetration, terrorism, and propaganda," and the Party's method was "successful in China, and it is now being followed in Indo-China."[27]

The primary difference between the threat of Soviet communism and that of Hitler's Germany or Imperial Japan was that the latter two programs of expansion were sponsored by individual states and their dictators. But the Soviet brand of expansion was part of a movement, a worldview, a dark transcendent force of which power and impetus was far beyond a mere person or specific state. So for Dulles, the problem would not be going away with the death of Stalin, because Soviet communism did not depend on Stalin to direct its trajectory. "We are up against something that is formidable," Dulles wrote. "It is, for the time being, immutable, though its tactics are flexible and unpredictable."[28]

Because of these realities, Dulles believed that the American people must be cautious. Defeating this foe was not going to be like defeating any other that the Americans had ever before faced. Americans were, by instinct, reactive. Their reaction to something as evil and tyrannical was to confront it directly, to face it in a decisive struggle. In April 1917 and in December 1941, American presidents asked Congress to declare war against nation-states that had thrust war upon them. But in the Cold War, things were going to be different. "We are not witnessing a conventional type of effort by one state to take something away from another state," Dulles said. "It is not operating against us as a nation but against our institutions. What is happening is novel, the like of which men have not seen since, one thousand years ago, the new and dynamic Moslem faith struck out against the established institutions of Christendom."[29] Since the confrontation with the Soviet Union was a unique manifestation of a cosmic war of light versus darkness, truth versus error, good versus evil, and spiritualism versus materialism, Dulles was convinced that the conflict must rely first on moral and spiritual weapons rather than on material forces.

Faith and spirituality. Dulles believed that Christians had an indispensable role to play in the conflict with the irreligious Soviet communist system. It is interesting that the period in which Dulles served as secretary of state witnessed one of the great revivals of spirituality in the United States. Church attendance increased dramatically during the 1950s, as did church building projects. The evangelistic crusades held by Billy Graham were popular all over the country, beginning with his 1949 Los Angeles crusade. Surveys taken during the period show that increasing numbers of Americans believed in God and believed that the Bible was God's Word.

Dwight D. Eisenhower became, in Conrad Cherry's words, "both a leading spokesman and a stellar symbol of the revival."[30] Shortly after hearing a sermon in February 1954 at the New York Presbyterian Church by the Reverend George M. Docherty that commemorated Abraham Lincoln's birthday, Eisenhower sought to infuse an explicitly theistic affirmation into a pillar of American civil religion. Docherty's point was that America was a nation "under God," and that Lincoln knew that the Civil War called on Americans' spiritual strength more than it did their strength in weapons and manpower. Eisenhower praised Docherty for his inspiring sermon, and on June 14, 1954—Flag Day—he signed a bill adding the phrase *under God* to the Pledge of Allegiance. Eisenhower said, "We are affirming the transcendence of religious faith in America's heritage and future; in this way we shall constantly strengthen those spiritual weapons which forever will be our country's most powerful resource, in peace or in war."[31]

As Eisenhower's secretary of state, Dulles could not have agreed more with the president's remarks. In 1952, Dulles gave a speech called "A Policy of Instant Retaliation," in which he advocated for American readiness to respond to a Red Army first strike with enormous power. But in order for Americans to have the ability to respond in this way, the nation had to gird itself up morally and spiritually. Material weapons, according to Dulles, were most effectively wielded and used as complements to the most potent weapons of all, that is, the weapons of ideas. He said, "Nonmaterial forces are more powerful than those that are merely material. . . . We should use *ideas* as weapons; and these ideas should conform us to *moral* principles."[32] In a similar speech titled "The Strategy of Massive Retaliation" he gave in 1954, Dulles said, "The fundamental, on our side, is the richness—the spiritual, intellectual, and material—that freedom can produce and the irresistible attraction it sets up."[33] In other words, freedom as a complete worldview, comprising the religious, epistemological, moral and material aspects of human civilization, is an all-sufficient basis to confront Soviet communism, which is bereft of any moral fabric to sustain a conflict of such grand scope. Freedom, for Dulles, would serve as an irresistible force not only for its utility as a starting point, but also as a model for the world to see and compare to the Soviet system. Because of this, ultimate victory was assured.

In his rhetoric, Dulles made much of the fact that America was founded as a noble experiment in democracy and freedom. For Dulles, this was more than a political or social experiment. American democracy was established by religious people, and that religious heritage is what sustained the experiment and made it successful. The Founders, Dulles said, "were seeking to translate, into living reality, their spiritual convictions."[34] Dulles likened the Founders to those faithful believers celebrated in the biblical book of Hebrews as the "great . . . cloud of witnesses" (Hebrews 12:1). Those "witnesses" served every generation by giving them moral examples to follow in times of great trial, such as the one they were facing in their own times. Dulles said, "Surely we too can feel 'that we are compassed about by a great cloud of witnesses' who are observing our conduct and who by their spirit seek to inspire us to carry forward the great national and international tasks to which they dedicated their lives and to which they committed our nation by their strivings and by their faith."[35] Still, for Dulles, simply having religious faith was not sufficient. There was no such thing as passive faith. Genuine faith is always active. The active faith of Americans was the indispensable element for the successful fulfillment of the American mission.

Zealous activism in the national mission. Dulles believed that America was confronting a unique, Manichaean struggle that threatened not only the American way of life, but human civilization as a whole, and also that Americans' religious faith and heritage was their strongest weapon; thus it followed that God had destined America to fulfill a divine calling to secure human freedom everywhere in the world. This mission was of cosmic significance, of global relevance and based on an invincible ethical and spiritual principle of righteousness, justice and freedom. The United States was the indispensable nation; without the United States, the human race would descend into slavery and moral darkness. In the Soviet system, Dulles said,

> the rulers hold a materialistic creed which denies the existence of the moral law. It denies that men are spiritual beings. . . . As a result the Soviet institutions treat human beings as primarily important from the standpoint of how much they can be made to produce for the glorification of the state. Labor is essentially slave labor, working to build up the military and material might of the state so that those who rule can assert even greater and more frightening power.[36]

For hope in the struggle against such a foe, Dulles looked to Jesus' Great Commission, which he gave to his disciples just before his ascension into heaven. In Matthew 28:19-20, Jesus told them, "Go therefore and make disciples of all nations, baptizing them in the name of the Father and of the Son and of the Holy Spirit, teaching them to observe all that I have commanded you. And behold, I am with you always, to the end of the age." Dulles's confidence in America's Christian foundations persuaded him that Americans would not hoard God's blessings of liberty for themselves. They would do all in their power to share them.

Indeed, because their nation was founded on Christian principles, they were commanded to extend those blessings to all the world. Dulles said,

> Jesus told the disciples to go out into all the world and preach the gospel to all the nations. Any nation which bases its institutions on Christian principles cannot but be a dynamic nation. . . . [The Founders] created a here a society of material, intellectual, and spiritual richness the like of which the world had never known. . . . [The American people] availed of every opportunity to spread their gospel of freedom, their good news, throughout the world.[37]

Thus, Dulles attempted to demonstrate a link between Jesus' Great Commission and an exceptional American democracy in order to justify a divine national commission for Americans in the Cold War.

The Soviets believed they had a duty to export their system to the world also. But Dulles taught that their imperative, while urgent and acute, had no moral basis. That is why it was ultimately impossible for the Soviets to succeed. But their failure would not come about if the United States did not have what Dulles repeatedly called a "dynamic faith." To settle for anything less than a dynamic, active, missionary faith would be to settle for a defensive posture against an aggressive, yet subtle, Soviet policy of expansion. America was commissioned not to merely contain the Soviets, but to push them back and to liberate the peoples they had enslaved.

Dulles could see no possible way that the United States and the Soviet Union could peacefully coexist given the philosophical dynamics at odds with one another in the cosmic struggle of ideas. He said in his "Containment or Liberation" speech in 1953 that "the threat of Soviet Communism . . . is not only the gravest threat that ever faced the United States but the gravest threat that has ever faced what we call Western civilization, or, indeed, any civilization which is dominated by a spiritual faith." Because of this, the United States should not seek simply to contain the Soviets, but commit to a foreign policy of rolling back the Soviets. "We must always have in mind the liberation of these captive peoples," Dulles said.[38] Dulles was confident in America's final victory, even though the struggle might be long and hard. As long as Americans maintained a firm confidence in God, a resolute faithfulness to their spiritual heritage and a commitment to securing justice and righteousness in all parts of the world, they would prevail. Indeed, America had to prevail, for if it lost faith in its divine mission, all of human civilization would be lost. In one of his last speeches before his death, titled "Peace Through Law," Dulles said, "There is no nobler mission that our nation could perform. Upon its success may depend the very survival of the human race. We can, therefore, dedicate ourselves to this mission with supreme confidence that we shall thus fulfill our national destiny."[39]

DULLES'S LEGACY

Dulles's vision of a God-given national mission for America was not original to him, nor did it die with him in the spring of 1959. It animated American foreign policy, in various degrees of similarity, for the rest of the Cold War. And it also found expression after the 9/11 attacks and resulting wars in Afghanistan and Iraq. The American experience in Vietnam in the 1960s and '70s invited serious questions concerning the legitimacy of the concept of mission, especially as Dulles had defined it in the 1950s. President Jimmy Carter, for example, sought to make humility a hallmark of his foreign policy, and the global pursuit of human rights the American mission in the world. Raymond Haberski wrote that "Carter sought to reaffirm the promise of America while paying heed to the perils that had recently befallen the nation."[40] But President Ronald Reagan managed to recover much of Dulles's Manichaean vision and faith in the ultimate triumph of America's mission of triumphing over communism. He famously called the Soviet Union "the focus of evil in the modern world" in his March 8, 1983, speech to the National Association of Evangelicals. And in pure Dullesian form, he went on to stress that spiritual weapons were more potent than material ones. He said, "While America's military strength is important, let me add here that I've always maintained that the struggle now going on for the world will never be decided by bombs or rockets, by armies or military might. The real crisis we face today is a spiritual one; at root, it is a test of moral will and faith."[41]

But even Reagan softened his Manichaean rhetoric, if not his faith in ultimate American success in its mission. When Mikhail Gorbachev succeeded Konstantin Chernenko in 1985, Reagan found someone with whom he could work constructively on reducing nuclear armaments and reducing the tensions that had existed between the United States and the USSR for decades. Reagan's actions are in stark contrast with those of Dulles after the death of Stalin. He saw any Soviet overture toward negotiation as a ruse designed to catch America in weakness and exploit any possible advantage exposed by that weakness.

With the collapse of communism in Eastern Europe in 1989, and the implosion of the Soviet Union in 1991, the Cold War came to an end, thankfully with more of a whimper than a bang. The great Manichaean struggle between good and evil, truth and falsehood—the United States and the Soviet Union—was finished. With no common enemy to confront on the global stage, Americans looked within for a national mission. Thus, the culture wars of the 1990s pitting social conservatives against social liberals over issues such as universal health care, gays in the military and the rise of single motherhood, to name a few, filled the civil religious void left in the wake of the Cold War.

But this situation proved to be only temporary. The terror attacks of September 11, 2001, restored certainty in American exceptionalism and renewed America's national mission, which fixated on eliminating terrorism everywhere in the world. Nationally syndicated columnist Charles Krauthammer rejoiced at the end of the 1990s, a period he believed was unserious and overly introspective. After being "locked in titanic, existential struggle with fascism, Nazism and then communism . . . we needed a rest. In the '90s, we took it." But America found its fighting spirit on 9/11. Krauthammer wrote, "What bin Laden did not understand . . . is that, while on vacation, America remained on call. His mistake was to place the call."[42] President George W. Bush articulated this mission forcefully, particularly in days leading up to and following the invasion of Iraq. On November 6, 2003, eight months after the invasion commenced, Bush said, "The advance of freedom is the calling of our time; it is the calling of our country. . . . We believe that liberty is the design of nature; we believe that liberty is the direction of history. . . . And we believe that freedom—the freedom we prize—is not for us alone, it is the right and capacity of all mankind."[43]

But circumstances in Afghanistan and Iraq severely challenged America's renewed certainty about its place in the world and transcendent mission. Most Americans came to regard the invasion of Iraq as a colossal mistake. As I write this in July 2014, the Islamic State of Iraq and Syria (ISIS) is consolidating its power in Iraq, erasing many of the gains made through the utmost efforts of the US military, made especially between 2007 and 2011. At this point, it is unknown how the rise of ISIS will affect US policy in the Middle East. If there is one lesson America has learned from its experiences in the global war on terror from 2001 to 2014, it is that there are limits to what the United States can do through the use of its power. Andrew Bacevich wrote, "The United States is ill-prepared to wage a global war of no exits and no deadlines. . . . American power has limits and is inadequate to the ambitions to which hubris and sanctimony have given rise."[44]

THEOLOGICAL AND ETHICAL ASSESSMENT
OF NATIONAL MISSION

As an aspect of closed exceptionalism, the concept of national mission is theologically problematic. Since World War II, it has been based on a particular expression of Manichaeism, namely, that good and evil are independent and equally powerful forces at war with one another, and the war is being waged by humans on battlefield Earth. The Christian tradition has historically considered Manichaeism to be heretical, primarily because it denies the atonement for sin made by the God-man, Jesus Christ, through his death, burial and resurrection, and that salvation is provided through Christ, rather than by any effort made by humans. Proponents of national mission also often hijack Jesus' Great Commission for its own nationalistic purposes, as we saw in Dulles's rhetoric. The reason for this is because many national mission proponents, such as Dulles, consider America as a Christian nation. If this be the case, the logic leads inexorably to an American national mission, since Christianity is, in essence, a missional faith. But national mission is also marked by the providential certainty we observed in national election. Whenever there is theological certainty in the absence of specific divine revelation, problems abound.

Ethically speaking, national mission is fueled by hubris, a God complex whereby a nation believes itself omnipotent in the face of any and all challenges to its interests and agendas. Further, national mission has the tendency to direct efforts away from correcting injustices at home, and it also tends to stifle dissent. Dissent has historically been a significant aspect of what it means to be an American, and is thus a significant aspect of open American exceptionalism.

In March 1964, Arkansas Senator J. William Fulbright spoke to the US Senate concerning "Old Myths and New Realities." In this speech, he challenged his colleagues to reject the simplistic, providentially certain worldview entailed in the concept of national mission. Fulbright stressed that there could be more than one way to see the world than in strict terms of good versus evil. There could be more than one way to see freedom in more than moral terms. And there could be more than one way to see communism than as a unified, Kremlin-directed world mission of conquest. "We must . . . come to terms . . . with the realities of a world in which neither good nor evil is absolute and in which those who move events and make history are those who have understood not how much but how little is within our power to change."[45] One might quibble with what appears to be moral relativism in Fulbright's statement, but his larger point is to guard against overweening pride that comes from a superior view of the national self and too much faith in power. Interestingly enough, Fulbright made these remarks less than five months before the Gulf of Tonkin Resolution and the beginning of major US operations in Vietnam.

Fulbright's warnings, however, gained traction even at this early stage of large-scale American involvement in Vietnam. In 1965, a Senate subcommittee issued a report that posed further warnings of placing too much trust in American power to accomplish a national mission. Talk of global mission necessarily leads to expectations that are beyond the reach of even the United States, potentially leading to profound disappointment, the report said. Further, the United States could become guilty of great injustices, either by omission or commission, in the name of national mission. The report concluded by saying, "Our ability to think up desirable goals is almost limitless; our capabilities are limited. . . . We can do a lot, but our power is limited and the first claimant on it is the American people."[46]

This stress on the proper application of power was the subject of a jeremiad Martin Luther King Jr. gave to the 1967 meeting of the Clergy and Laity Concerned at the Riverside Church in New York City. It was the first time that King spoke against the war in Vietnam—a war in which America became involved largely because of Dulles's rejection of the 1954 Geneva Conference agreement that was to recognize South Vietnamese self-determination. In this speech, King spoke of the injustices of the war in Vietnam, not only to the Vietnamese people, but to the American soldiers who were drafted to fight there. He spoke of the tragic irony that America, the symbol of freedom and defiance to tyranny, should be engaged in such a hardheaded militaristic and destructive war against a country that presented not the slightest threat to it or its way of life at all. But what is perhaps the most striking about King's speech is that, in it, he shows himself to be truer to Dulles's method of confronting communism than Dulles was in the way he actually pursued American policy in Vietnam during the 1950s. King advocated for an end to the war, and for America to live up to its democratic and just ideals—to "begin the shift from a 'thing-oriented' society to a 'person-oriented' society. When machines and computers, profit motives and property rights are considered more important than people, the giant triplets of racism, materialism, and militarism are incapable of being conquered." King was echoing Dulles's points about how the moral and spiritual principles that defined America were far stronger than its material assets. And in regard to the nation's mission to defeat communism in the Cold War, King said,

> This kind of positive revolution of values is our best defense against communism. . . . Communism will never be defeated by the use of atomic

bombs or nuclear weapons. . . . We must not engage in a negative anti-communism, but rather in a positive thrust for democracy, realizing that our greatest defense against communism is to take offensive action in behalf of justice.[47]

This comports well with Dulles's stated conviction, that Americans must fight communism using the weapons of moral ideas, ideas rooted in the Christian tradition of justice. Unfortunately, Dulles's Manichaeism seemed to overcome his Christian faith in Vietnam.

Justice gets lost in the closed-exceptionalist notion of national mission, just as it gets lost in the conception of national election. But justice for all is one of the prerequisites of the American democratic tradition. Another prerequisite in that tradition is that of dissent. When a common enemy threatens, and the warfare with that common enemy is cast in Manichaean terms with providential certainty, dissent becomes not only unpatriotic; it becomes treasonous. But as Henry Steele Commager observed in 1947, dissent is necessary to Americanism. In an article titled "Who Is Loyal to America?" Commager criticized the growing climate of suspicion in the years immediately after World War II. He specifically criticized Harry Truman's Loyalty Order, an executive order defining the meaning of loyalty to the US government, which Truman handed down on March 21, 1947.

Commager said that another word for loyalty, as far as Truman's Loyalty Order was concerned, was conformity—"the uncritical and unquestioning acceptance of America as it is . . . regard[ing] America as a finished product, perfect and complete."[48] But conformity, as Commager asserted, is completely un-American. Conformity, as we saw in Dulles's rhetoric, was a hallmark of Soviet communism. Dissent in the Soviet Union, according to Dulles, resulted in deportation to concentration camps. Anyone found in opposition to the Soviet leaders' agenda was to be compelled to conform or to be destroyed. Ironically, conformity was being prescribed in the United States, too, the very country that was supposed to embody righteousness, justice and freedom and was tasked by God to liberate the oppressed all over the world. Commager defined true loyalty in terms of dissent:

[Loyalty] is a willingness to subordinate every private advantage for the larger good. . . . It is allegiance to the traditions that have guided our greatest statesmen and inspired our most eloquent poets—the traditions of freedom, equality, democracy, tolerance, the tradition of the higher law, of experimentation, cooperation, and pluralism. It is a realization that America was born of revolt, flourished on dissent, became great through experimentation.[49]

Open exceptionalism seeks out justice and welcomes dissent. In fact, open exceptionalism acknowledges that justice and dissent are necessary to the American identity. The United States was born in the Revolution— and reborn in the Civil War—through dissent and an objective conception of right and wrong. If America has a mission to pursue in the world, it is the same mission given to all people. President Carter recognized it, although he, like any fallible human being, struggled to find a way to apply it in the midst of authentic struggles against real enemies set against America and American institutions, both at home and abroad. This moral mission revealed in Scripture to all people is found in Micah 6:8—"He has told you, O man, what is good; and what does the LORD require of you but to do justice, and to love kindness, and to walk humbly with your God?" Of this mission, Americans can have certainty.

It is not necessary to abandon the idea of a national mission. Separated from any association with Christ's Great Commission (which is given to Christ's followers, not to any nation-state) and all providential certainty absent divine revelation, a concept of national mission that is animated by justice, self-examination and stewardship of resources is potentially a source of true human flourishing.

George W. Bush is one president who is rightly criticized for being guilty of employing too much Manichaeism, too much certainty and too much bellicosity in the context of the war on terror. But Bush, like Carter, had a keen sensitivity to America's responsibility to act justly in the world, to be true to its oft-stated ideals. Four months after ordering the invasion of Iraq, Bush traveled to Goree Island, Senegal, and spoke of the evils of the slave trade and of America's own particular guilt in advancing that trade in its history. He admitted that even Americans must strive and struggle to achieve the ideals they profess in their foundational documents. President Bush oversaw the dispersal of more American aid to Africa than any of his predecessors, and has been universally praised for his efforts—which is one of the greatest ironies of his presidency. The president known for his blustery rhetoric—"wanted dead or alive" and "bring it on"—and for his certainty that Americans would be greeted as liberators in whatever country they invaded, reached out to peoples on the poorest continent in the world in the name of justice and mercy. And he cast his efforts of aiding African countries in terms of a national mission. He said in 2008 that in Africa "America is on a mission of mercy. We're treating African leaders as equal partners. . . . This mission serves our security interests—people who live in chaos and despair are more likely to fall under the sway of violent ideologies. This mission serves our moral interests—we're all children of God, and having the power to save lives comes with the obligation to use it."[50] This mission is consistent with open American exceptionalism.

FOR FURTHER READING

Babík, Milan. *Statecraft and Salvation: Wilsonian Liberal Internationalism as Secularized Eschatology*. Waco: Baylor University Press, 2013.

Bacevich, Andrew J. *The Limits of Power: The End of American Exceptionalism*. New York: Metropolitan, 2008.

Gamble, Richard M. *The War for Righteousness: Progressive Christianity, the Great War, and the Rise of the Messianic Nation*. Wilmington, DE: ISI, 2003.

Inboden, William. *Religion and American Foreign Policy, 1945–1960: The Soul of Containment*. 2008. Reprint, Cambridge: Cambridge University Press, 2010.

Kinzer, Stephen. *The Brothers: John Foster Dulles, Allen Dulles, and Their Secret World War*. New York: Henry Holt, 2013.

Preston, Andrew. *Sword of the Spirit, Shield of Faith*. New York: Anchor, 2012.

5

The Innocent Nation

This is the "empire" of which the prophetic voice declared "Westward the Star of Empire takes its Way"—the star of the empire of liberty and law, of commerce and communication, of social order and the Gospel of our Lord—the star of the empire of the civilization of the world. Westward that star of empire takes its course.

SENATOR ALBERT J. BEVERIDGE,
"THE STAR OF EMPIRE," 1900

Since the end of hostilities, the United States has invested its substance and its energy in a great constructive effort to restore peace, stability, and freedom to the world. We have sought no territory; we have imposed our will on none. We have asked no privileges we would not extend to others.

PRESIDENT HARRY S. TRUMAN,
INAUGURAL ADDRESS, 1949

In this springtime of hope, some lights seem eternal; America's is.

PRESIDENT RONALD REAGAN,
REPUBLICAN CONVENTION ADDRESS, 1984

✦◇✦

On June 5, 2004, America lost one of its most beloved citizens after his ten-plus-year battle with Alzheimer's disease—former
President Ronald Reagan. His presence on the national political stage,
especially from 1980 to 1989, was a fixture that gave many Americans a
sense of hope and purpose in a rapidly changing world. He contracted
Alzheimer's in the early 1990s, and his farewell letter to the nation of
November 4, 1994, was moving for its wistfulness, but also for its op-
timism, which was so characteristic of Reagan's personality. "I now begin
the journey that will lead me into the sunset of my life," Reagan wrote. "I
know that for America there will always be a bright dawn ahead. Thank
you, my friends. May God
always bless you."[1]

Four days after his death,
Reagan's casket was placed
in the US Capitol to lie in
state for the public to pay
its last respects. Long lines
of people flowed through
the rotunda of the Capitol
to say goodbye for nearly
thirty-six hours. I drove up
to Washington with a
friend from Charlottesville,
Virginia, where I was living
at the time, to join the
many people who were
flowing through the Capitol
to view the president's
casket and reflect on the
meaning of his contribu-

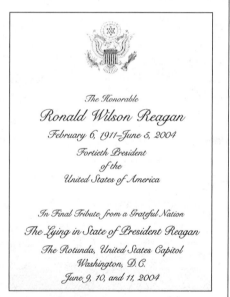

The Honorable

Ronald Wilson Reagan

February 6, 1911–June 5, 2004

Fortieth President
of the
United States of America

In Final Tribute from a Grateful Nation
The Lying in State of President Reagan

The Rotunda, United States Capitol
Washington, D. C.
June 9, 10, and 11, 2004

Figure 5.1. The announcement of the lying
in state of Ronald Reagan. An official presented
each person passing through the rotunda to
view Reagan's casket with this printed
announcement as they proceeded
out of the Capitol.

tions to the nation. We arrived and took our places in line just after
midnight, June 10, just east of the Washington Monument. The line
switched back and forth, and moved slowly but surely all the way to the

Capitol, which was brilliantly lit in the chilly darkness.

The people quietly shuffled along; a palpable sense of grief was in the air. You could also tell that everyone in the line possessed an awareness of the historical significance of the moment. When my friend and I finally passed by the casket six hours after taking our place in line, memories of Reagan flooded through my mind, and I said a prayer for Mrs. Reagan. We emerged out of the Rotunda just after 6:00 a.m., having said our goodbyes to one of the most visionary presidents in our history.

One of the reasons Reagan was admired by so many was he was always hopeful and he had a contagious enthusiasm. He sincerely loved the American people and had definite and determined convictions about what he believed was their special destiny. Reagan said himself as his presidency was drawing to a close that one of his proudest achievements was helping Americans to believe in themselves again—"the resurgence of national pride that I called the new patriotism."[2] One of the ways Reagan sowed the seeds of this "new patriotism" was to characterize the United States as a regenerate, innocent nation that was specially blessed by divine providence. Reagan consistently appealed to this notion of innocence in his public rhetoric, and he expressed it in explicit and implicit ways, it seems, nearly every time he appeared behind a microphone. Perhaps no other president has employed the rhetoric of American innocence so readily and sincerely as Reagan did.

But was Reagan's rhetoric of national innocence helpful or harmful? An important feature of closed American exceptionalism is the notion that America can do no wrong. Delusions of innocence have the potential to bring harm to the republic by inviting corruption to power and trauma to the social fabric. These delusions also fly in the face of Christian orthodoxy and common sense, both of which affirm the fact of human sinfulness. But open American exceptionalism allows for national self-examination and critique, which can have the healing effect that comes from the wisdom of admitting flaws and working to correct them. Innocence is often a prominent exceptionalist theme, but it is fraught with irony and potentially destructive to the American republic that it uncritically extols.

BASIS FOR AMERICAN CLAIMS TO INNOCENCE

Reagan, of course, did not invent the idea that Americans were an innocent people, free from decadence and social ills, and perennially on the rise. Since its discovery by Europeans in the sixteenth century, many have seen America as a land of new beginnings, a place with an Edenic aura. Thomas More (1478–1535) wrote his famous book *Utopia* (Greek for "no place") in 1516, and clearly had the *novus mundum* of Amerigo Vespucci in mind when writing his fanciful account of a place lacking the degeneracy of European political and social life of his time. More's character, Raphael Hythlodaye (translated from Greek as "skilled in nonsense"[3]), visited Utopia and described the (mostly) charmed lives of its inhabitants. In *Utopia,* More had Hythlodaye travel with Vespucci on three of his four journeys, and he placed Utopia in the Atlantic, adjacent to what is now Brazil.[4] Jack Greene wrote that More's work had significance for how Europeans saw both themselves and America. "By associating Utopia with the New World, More . . . effectively directed attention not just to Europe's own internal social, moral, and political problems but also to the as yet unknown potential of the immense New World."[5] And who could forget John Winthrop's description of early New England as a "Citty upon a Hill"—an image he borrowed from Matthew's Gospel and one John F. Kennedy used in his inaugural address and Reagan in his farewell address.[6] Winthrop did not exclude the possibility that the colonists would transgress from following the Lord, but if they were faithful, "soe shall wee keepe the unitie of the spirit in the bond of peace . . . [and] will command a blessing upon us in all our ways, soe that wee shall see much more of his wisdom, power, goodness and truthe than formerly wee have beene acquainted with."[7]

Thus the sheer novelty of America to the early colonists, its seemingly endless potential for human advancement, was one basis for what Richard Hughes called "the myth of the innocent nation."[8] Another basis was the vision of the virtuous republic cast by the American revolutionaries of the eighteenth century. The republican theory of the founding generation entailed the necessity of virtue, manifested in liberal ideas: checks and balances on power, government by consent, an independent judiciary, and religious freedom, to name a few. Puritanism contributed to republican theory, with its traditional emphases on morality, hard work and covenantal community. Ari Hoogenboom observed that "because republicanism rejected monarchy and relied on representative government, its classic ideology stressed the need for virtuous political leaders and citizens willing to sacrifice for the commonweal."[9] Thus, the ideal of a virtuous republic was part of the founding fabric of the United States. Virtue itself was American; vice was anti-American.

Also, Christian republicanism, that fusion of Puritan theology and the political philosophy of Real Whig ideology, presented a particular vision of American innocence by the late eighteenth century. By the time of the Revolution, Christian republicanism held that the United States represented a fresh start for humanity. For example, the reverse side of the Great Seal of the United States declares a *novum ordo seclorum*, or, a new order for the ages. Thomas Paine wrote in *Common Sense*, "We have it in our power to begin the world over again," and "the birthday of a new world is at hand."[10] And America as a "new Israel" was a prominent theme in much revolutionary preaching. Reinhold Niebuhr wrote, "Whether our nation interprets its spiritual heritage through Massachusetts or Virginia, we came into existence with the sense of being a 'separated' nation, which God was using to make a new beginning for mankind."[11] So the notion that America is a nation immune to the forces of history, a nation continually rising and never in danger of falling (like other nations)—this notion has been a powerful one from America's inception.

Further, during the twentieth century, Americans came to see themselves contrasted with the enemies they confronted in World Wars I and II and the Cold War. Americans went to war against Germany in World War I, a country that had invaded Belgium, Luxembourg, France and Russia in 1914. They went to war against Japan in 1941, a country that had attacked the United States without provocation, and went on to aggressively expand into China, Southeast Asia and the Pacific. They also went to war against fascist Germany and Italy, which were national expressions of the epitome of evil for most Americans. And in the decades following World War II, America faced off against the Soviet Union in the Cold War. Reagan was widely criticized in the media for calling out the Soviets as "the focus of evil in the modern world" on March 8, 1983.[12] He used these words in part to forestall the media's exertions to undermine his efforts to increase America's military budget. He wrote in his diary the day before, "The d—n media has propagandized our people against our defense plans more than the Russians have."[13] These critical events of the twentieth century convinced many Americans of their moral superiority in the world. As Hughes wrote, "It is far easier to think of one's self as righteous and pure if one confronts an enemy who can be characterized as utterly evil."[14]

How has the theme of innocence been articulated in American history? It is beyond the scope of the chapter to assess the development of this idea over the centuries, but a few examples will suffice to answer the question. John L. O'Sullivan is one figure that stands out from the pre–Civil War period. In his 1839 essay, "The Great Nation of Futurity," he compared the United States with the countries of Europe, asserting that Americans were rewriting history and making all of civilization in their image. The future belonged to the Americans, not to the Europeans. America had no blood on her hands, and was only interested in the freedom of oppressed peoples. "Our annals describe no scenes of horrid carnage, where men were led on by hundreds of thousands to slay one another, dupes and victims to emperors, kings, nobles, demons in the human form called heroes," wrote O'Sullivan. Furthermore, "We are entering on [the future's] untrodden space, with the truths of God in our minds, beneficent objects in our hearts, and with a clear conscience unsullied by the past."[15] O'Sullivan thus saw the source of America's innocence as a mark of the nation's being in a state of historical transcendence. Since America had no past of which to be ashamed, America stood guiltless, uniquely blessed by God, and the nation of humanity's future. And after referring to America as "the new heaven and the new earth" O'Sullivan asked, "Is not our private life as morally beautiful and good—is not our public life as politically right, as indicative of the brightest prospects of humanity, and therefore as inspiring of the highest conceptions?"[16]

Albert J. Beveridge (1862–1927) was a US senator from Indiana during the first decade of the twentieth century. As a vociferous imperialist, Beveridge supported the annexation of the Philippines in order that Americans might prepare Filipinos to take their place among the civilized nations of the world. His brand of manifest destiny expanded far beyond the North American continent. Since his political career coincided with America's victory over Spain in the Spanish-American War of 1898, Beveridge believed it was God's will that America should one day become the world's preeminent power. And who better to take that exalted place among the nations of the world but America? America's moral purity would be the inspiration of all people everywhere to take up the cause of peace. Beveridge said, "When nations shall war no more without the consent of the American republic: what American heart thrills not with pride at that prospect? . . . When governments stay the slaughter of human beings, because the American Republic demands it: what American heart thrills not with pride at that prospect?"[17] Beveridge foresaw the day, a day in the not-too-distant future, when America would serve the world "as the most powerful of powers and most righteous of judges."[18] To Beveridge, like O'Sullivan before him, nothing was impossible for the young republic with new-found world power.

Figure 5.2. President Lyndon B. Johnson

More recently, as Americans were starting to doubt the doctrine of American innocence during the 1960s, President Lyndon Johnson attempted to remind people that Americans were indeed guiltless of wrongdoing in their application of power in Southeast Asia.

He was responding to Senator J. William Fulbright's *The Arrogance of Power*, in which he said, "Power tends to confuse itself with virtue and a great nation is peculiarly susceptible to the idea that its power is a sign of God's favor."[19] Johnson gave his speech, titled "The Obligation of Power," at Princeton University in November 1966. He asserted that "we have used our power not willingly and recklessly ever but always reluctantly and with restraint." And echoing O'Sullivan's comparison of America with other nations and his theme of American historical transcendence, Johnson said, "Unlike nations in the past with vast power at their disposal, the United States of America has never sought to crush the autonomy of her neighbors."[20] These claims lost their credibility as America's involvement in Vietnam deepened after 1966. By the end of the 1970s, the time was right for someone to mount the national platform and call America back to its vision of innocence.

RONALD REAGAN'S VISION OF AMERICAN INNOCENCE

In 1980, Reagan won the Republican party's nomination for president and then defeated Jimmy Carter. Since the 1964 presidential election Americans had become accustomed to hearing Reagan speak to them on the issues of the their day, both foreign and domestic. He campaigned for Barry Goldwater in 1964 against Lyndon Johnson, served as governor of California from 1967 to 1975, and was a political radio commentator during the late 1970s. He also ran against President Gerald Ford for the 1976 Republican nomination, but lost. Finally, Reagan won the presidency in 1980 on a platform of economic recovery, strengthening America's military and respect abroad, and restoring American's confidence in themselves. Carter had famously identified in a July 1979 speech a spirit of malaise in the American people, "a crisis of confidence . . . a crisis that strikes at the very heart and soul and spirit of our national will. We can see this crisis in the growing doubt about the meaning of our own lives and in the loss of a unity of purpose for our nation."[21] Throughout his presidential campaigns and presidency, Reagan would have none of that kind of talk. The tone of his speeches was continuously positive, emphasizing the fundamental integrity of the American national fabric. Before, during and after his presidency, Reagan described American history, government, society, people and the military in terms of purity and uprightness. Reagan was perhaps the most civil religious president since Abraham Lincoln. Richard Pierard and Robert Linder wrote that civil religion under Reagan was arguably becoming more prevalent in American society than traditional religion. "Never had [civil religion] occupied such an exalted place in national experience," they wrote.[22]

Examples of Reagan's rhetoric on American innocence are readily available in his speeches and writings. Innocence as a theme served as an intellectual framework for Reagan's vision of America. It is a key presupposition in Reagan's speeches and writings. Reagan implicitly and explicitly drew on the theme of innocence in his rhetoric, and in this section, we will consider how he employed innocence in the years while he was a national figure.

Figure 5.3. President Ronald Reagan

First, Reagan appealed to American history in order to illustrate the nation's purity. In 1974, Reagan gave a speech to the Conservative Political Action Committee in which he responded to the charge among liberal commentators that the conservative agenda was regressive, that conservatives were interested in "taking the country back to McKinley." Reagan's reaction to this was to quip, "I never found that was so bad—under McKinley we freed Cuba."[23] Reagan's celebrating the Spanish-American War as nothing less than a war of liberation is typical of how he viewed American history. Americans of the past were heroic people, doing deeds that were unequivocally righteous, and championing those who were being oppressed by the wicked. Few, if any, moral ambiguities were possible, in Reagan's mind, when it came to American actions. This failure to account for moral ambiguity is the hallmark of Reagan's appeal to innocence in the national life.

Second, while Reagan believed that the American government was deeply flawed, he extolled the ideals and documents on which it was founded. In that same 1974 speech, he called the Constitution "the most unique document ever drawn in the long history of man's relation to man." The unique thing about the American Constitution, that which set it apart from all other constitutions in the world, was that it acknowledged the priority of rights over government. He said, "Other constitutions say, 'Government grants you these rights,' and ours says, 'You are born with these rights, they are yours by the grace of God, and no government on earth can take them from you.'"[24] In his 1992 address to the Republican National Convention, he said that America's uniqueness was found in the fact that it put its people before its government. Freedom was what made America great and what made America pure. Unlike the empires of the past, which were defined by their will to power, "we have been set apart by our faith in the ideals of democracy, of free men and free markets, and of the extraordinary possibilities that lie within seemingly ordinary men and women."[25]

Third, Reagan believed in the innate goodness of American foreign policy in general, and the American military in particular. In his 1982 State of the Union address, he described American foreign policy as being one of "strength, fairness, and balance." The military had been weak under Carter's leadership, but since assuming office, Reagan had made strengthening the military one of his chief priorities. In strengthening the military, American foreign policy as a force for good would be advanced rather than stymied by America's foes. "By restoring America's military credibility . . . and by regaining the respect of America's allies and adversaries alike, we have strengthened our country's position as force for peace and progress in the world."[26] After ordering attacks on Libya on April 14, 1986, in response to Muammar Qaddafi's role in terrorism against American servicemen in Germany, Reagan reminded the nation of its patience and long-suffering in the world. "We Americans

are slow to anger," he said. "We always seek peaceful avenues before re-
sorting to the use of force."[27] In this way, Reagan characterized the use
of American force in biblical, necessary and absolute terms.

More than anything, Reagan believed in the goodness and decency of
the American people and society. This is evident in his speeches, his
diary entries and his letters. His positive attitude about America's potential and its future was based in his confidence in the inevitability of
Americans to get it right when faced with profound challenges. He could
not imagine the possibility that Americans might not get it right, might
fail to prevail over any obstacle confronting them. When he accepted his
party's nomination for president in 1980, he said that Americans were
"concerned, yes, but they are not frightened. They are disturbed, but not
dismayed. They are the kind of men and women Tom Paine had in mind
when he wrote during the darkest days of the American Revolution, 'We
have it in our power to begin the world over again.'"[28] Reagan saw all
humanity represented in America, and because every nation had been
assimilated into the American nation, America's greatness was defined
by a pure commitment to justice everywhere in the world. He told the
students at Moscow State University in 1988, "You have to realize that
we are a people that are made up of every strain, nationality, and race of
the world. And the result is that when people in our country think
someone is being mistreated or treated unjustly in another country,
these are people who still feel that kinship to that country because it is
their heritage."[29]

As Reagan appealed to the essential goodness of Americans, he articulated a conception of God that was singularly American. Reagan's
God was not specifically the God of the Bible, but the supreme being of
American civil religion. When Reagan gave his 1974 speech to the Conservative Political Action Committee, he expressed his belief that "there
was some divine plan that placed this great continent between two
oceans to be sought out by those who were possessed of an abiding love
of freedom."[30] He used the same imagery when he gave his 1980 nomination speech on the floor of the Republican National Convention and
when he spoke at the centennial celebration of the Statue of Liberty in

New York City in 1986. For Reagan, God had a particular love for America, setting aside a continent separated by oceans and hidden from civilization until the fullness of time came when God made it a beacon "to be found by a special kind of people from every corner of the world."[31] America was God's instrument to shelter the oppressed, defend the defenseless and secure the peace of the world. For Reagan, America was nothing without God, but God almost seemed powerless without America. He often used Lincoln's expression, that America was "the last, best hope of mankind."[32] He was fond of quoting Pope Pius XII, who according to Reagan said, "Into the hands of Am.[erica] God has placed the destiny of an afflicted mankind."[33] Christianity teaches that God took on flesh in the incarnation of Christ to make atonement for sin and redeem humanity, but Reagan's God looked to America to save the world.

When Reagan offered eulogies for fallen servicemen and women, his conception of an American God was most evident. For Reagan, nothing was more precious in the sight of America's God than the death of his saints, namely, those who wore an American uniform. When he paid tribute to the 248 soldiers of the 101st Airborne Division who were tragically killed in a plane crash on December 12, 1985, he prayed, "Receive, O Lord, into your heavenly kingdom the men and women of the 101st Airborne, the men and women of the great and fabled Screaming Eagles. They must be singing now, in their joy, flying higher than mere man can fly and as flights of angels take them to their rest."[34] Eternal salvation, for Reagan, was a certainty for all who died championing America's causes.

Reagan, it seems, was unable to sort through the ramifications of any substantial moral ambiguity in America. Reagan's inability to reconcile legitimate wrongdoing with his pure vision of the nation he loved is evident in his response to the problem of racism in America. When reflecting on a speech he gave to African American leaders at the White House in 1983 commemorating Martin Luther King Jr.'s birthday, he lamented the fact that he was unable to connect with black people in America. He wrote that African Americans "often mistook my belief in keeping the government out of the average American's life as a cover for doing nothing about racial injustice."[35] But perhaps one of the reasons for this is that

African Americans perceived a lack of realism in Reagan's mind about racism. To Reagan, racism was a collection of episodes of injustice taken as parts of a whole. So, it was natural—and quite believable—for him to insist, "I abhor racism."[36] But he could not see that, during his presidency and continuing into our own day, racism exists as a structural reality in America, such a central and native component in American history and society that defies any one-dimensional explanation.

His reflections on this particular day in his presidency reveal much about this failure to account for this example of unalloyed guilt in American civilization. He said, "Skinheads and white supremacist groups have no place in this country. They are not what we are about, and I wish they would just vaporize."[37] These sentiments, while unassailable, reflect Reagan's failure to acknowledge moral ambiguity in America. Skinheads and white supremacist groups were (and are) not the only racists in America, and racism per se was (and is) not personified in skinheads and white supremacist groups. Racism was (and continues to be) a far more complex and ingrained feature of American civilization. Furthermore, Reagan's desired solution to racism—that racists would "just vaporize"— is not a solution at all. Rather, his statement reflects a desire to simply get rid of the problem of racism, a wistful hope that it would just go away, rather than a commitment to apply power justly and patiently to help dismantle and uproot its structure.

Another example of Reagan's response to wrong is his view of the Iran–Contra affair, namely, the deal American officials in the Reagan administration struck with Iranians to trade arms for American hostages held in the Middle East. Reagan was deeply vexed by this hostage crisis because he sincerely cared about what was happening to the individuals suffering in captivity and because he despised their captors. He compared the situation to the kidnapping of a child—"If your child was kidnapped and someone who wasn't the kidnapper came to you and offered to help you find your child, I think most parents would take that help even if it cost you some money."[38] When Reagan addressed the nation after the Tower Commission Report was published in March 1987, he took full responsibility for actions that he took and those his administration took on his behalf. However, Reagan's struggle to reconcile reality with sentiment is again evident in his speech. First, in this speech, while accepting responsibility, he still denied real wrongdoing. He said, "A few months ago I told the American people I did not trade arms for hostages. My heart and my best intentions still tell me that's true, but the facts and the evidence tell me it is not."[39] Second, he shifted blame to the Iranians, surmising in his reflections on the speech that they had trapped the Americans, luring them into a major failure. On the Iran–Contra affair, he wrote, "I have to say that in looking back I wonder if this whole thing wasn't a setup, a sting operation by the Iranians. Maybe we were conned into believing these were moderate Iranians seeking to reach out to the West, while in reality they were working directly for the Ayatollah just to get some arms. Who knows?"[40] And third, when faced with this particular example of a moral ambiguity in America, Reagan utilized the folksy, aw-shucks style for which he was famous in order to justify himself and dismiss the guilt. One example of this has to do with how he characterized the lack of record keeping during key meetings on the arms-for-hostages plan involving himself and other high officials. He said, "One thing still upsetting me, however, is that no one kept proper records of meetings or decisions. This led to my failure to recollect whether I approved an arms shipment before or after the fact. I did approve it; I just can't say specifically when. Well, rest assured, there's plenty of record keeping now going on at 1600 Pennsylvania Avenue."[41] And that was as much as he was willing to say about the issue of record keeping in that speech.

Reagan's inability to account for moral ambiguity during his presidency is a particular expression of the broader problem with conceiving of America as an innocent and regenerate nation. There is a distinct irony to American history and civilization, as Niebuhr famously wrote, and this irony is the main obstacle standing in the way of the primrose path to American innocence.

OPEN AMERICAN EXCEPTIONALISM AND DELUSIONS OF INNOCENCE

In closed American exceptionalism, America is always right. Anyone or anything that stands against America is, by necessity, wrong. American society is the picture of health. The American Constitution is flawless, inspired of God and perpetually enduring. The American military is long-suffering, a force for justice and irresistible to every conceivable foe. American institutions are pure. The American people are possessed of an unconquerable spirit and limitless potential. America's God lavishes blessings and protection on the nation he specially loves and secures. And the American nation, as the answer to humanity's ills, stands apart from history, immune to the degradation and corruption to which all other nations and empires of the past have succumbed. *America* is a religious faith, one that David Gelernter said "is one of the most beautiful religious concepts mankind has ever known."[42]

But closed American exceptionalism entails a delusional form of patriotism because it denies the reality that America, while striving for high ideals, is often guilty of betraying those ideals. Americans have often failed to live up to their own profession of being a nation "under God" or a nation committed to "liberty and justice for all." There are glaring ironies within the American character that, if ignored, will potentially wreak havoc on American society.

In his book *The Irony of American History*, Niebuhr wrote that one example of a great irony was that America possessed atomic weapons with the potential to bring about unspeakable destruction. America had this dread arsenal in order to defend liberty, the proposition that all are created equal and the innate dignity of all human life. He wrote, "The perennial moral predicaments of human history have caught up with a culture which knew nothing of sin or guilt, and with a nation which seemed to be the most perfect fruit of that culture."[43]

Niebuhr wrote his book in the early 1950s, and it is historically situated in the beginning of the Cold War—the Korean War, the nuclear arms race, the Communist takeover of China and the descent of the Iron Curtain across Europe. But the ironic situation Niebuhr observed is not the only one in American history and culture. Americans characteristically display a sort of schizophrenia when it comes to its stated ideals of liberty, equality and justice. Niebuhr used the term *schizo-*

phrenic to describe Americans' attitude and application of power. At times, Niebuhr wrote, the culture sees its use of power as innocent; at other times, it applies power and attains just ends by accident; and at other times, its ends are justified by the means its power employs.[44] Martin Luther King Jr. also used the term *schizophrenic* to characterize America when it came to facing up to racial and economic inequalities. To the 1961 graduating class of Lincoln University, King said, "Ever since the Founding Fathers of our nation dreamed this noble dream, America has been something of a schizophrenic personality, tragically divided against herself. On the one hand we have proudly professed the principles of democracy, and on the other hand we have sadly practiced the very antithesis of those principles."[45]

Power is a corrupting force. America has held immense power at nearly every point in its history. In the decades before the Civil War, America possessed great power over the people who were held in bondage. America possessed power over people whose lands it seized in the aftermath of the Indian wars and the Mexican War. America's status as a world power and then as a superpower during the twentieth century meant that America faced greater and greater risks of susceptibility to moral irony as it applied its power. The many struggles that Americans have had with moral ironies in their history demonstrate that any belief in an inherent innocence in the American nation is, in fact, a delusion, a fanciful denial of the truth. True patriotism, authentic love of country, does not entail such dishonesty. The denials of closed exceptionalism would seem to be a demonstration of patriotic devotion. But those denials are integral to the tragedy of the many betrayals of the high ideals Americans have rightly expressed and pursued.

Is there a way forward? Open exceptionalism offers us a way to recover the concept of American uniqueness, leading to patriotic devotion that does not deny reality. Fulbright wrote, "To criticize one's country is to do it a service and pay it a compliment."[46] To criticize one's country means that one is thinking deeply about the country's actions toward its own citizens and toward citizens of other countries. One's act of refusing to uncritically accept everything that one's country represents in its values and practices is an act of self-examination. Self-examination bears fruit in wisdom, which points the way toward correcting flaws and altering courses that lead to destruction.

In 1896, W. E. B. Du Bois presented his PhD dissertation to the faculty at Harvard University. His dissertation was titled "The Suppression of the African Slave Trade to the United States of America, 1638–1870." At the conclusion of this work, Du Bois offered a "Lesson for Americans." Du Bois's lesson began with the observation that Americans are not known for being a people engaged in self-examination. Rather, Du Bois wrote, Americans tend to deny that any major moral problems exist in their society. If any ills can be found, then Americans seek to find ways to jettison those ills rather than address them and patiently work to answer them. Du Bois wrote that "we have the somewhat inchoate idea that we are not destined to be harassed with great social questions, and that even if we are, and fail to answer them, the fault is with the question and not with us. Consequently, we often congratulate ourselves more on getting rid of a problem than on solving it." Ultimately, Du Bois said, "The riddle of the Sphinx may be postponed, it may be evasively answered now; sometime it must be fully answered."[47]

Du Bois's observation is wise. In the antebellum period, Americans' failure to deal with the sphinx of slavery resulted in the Civil War. Their failure to deal with the sphinx of injustice in their economic system in the post–Civil War industrial period resulted largely in the Great Depression of the 1930s. Their failure to deal with the sphinx of racism during the 1900s continues to bring division, chaos, violence and disruption to American familial, civic, economic, religious and social life. What other sphinxes loom before us as Americans, demanding we answer them before we may pass by safely? Open American exceptionalism is a category of patriotism that acknowledges the reality of flaws, of ills, of problems that need addressing. It is a patriotism that does not shrink back from the duty of dissent. And it is a patriotism that does not idolize the nation or its people. Christianity teaches that no one is innocent; all are guilty of unjust actions. If that is true of individuals, it is certainly true of nations that are made up of individuals. God stands in judgment of human sin, but has provided a way for human sin to be atoned for in the person of Jesus Christ, who paid for sin "once for all" (Hebrews 10:10). Christians who embrace open American exceptionalism can affirm that America is unique, is special and is blessed by God. That means America is responsible for how it uses those many blessings. And American Christians can know, teach and live the great truth that Christ is the last and best hope of humankind—not America.

FOR FURTHER READING

Edwards, Jason A., and David Weiss. *The Rhetoric of American Exceptionalism: Critical Essays.* London: McFarland, 2011.

Glaser, Elisabeth, and Hermann Wellenreuther, eds. *Bridging the Atlantic: The Question of American Exceptionalism in Perspective.* Cambridge: University of Cambridge Press, 2002.

Lieven, Anatol. *America, Right or Wrong: An Anatomy of American Nationalism.* New York: Oxford University Press, 2004.

Niebuhr, Reinhold. *The Irony of American History.* New York: Scribner's, 1952.

Noll, Mark, ed. *Religion and American Politics: From the Colonial Period to the 1980s.* Oxford: Oxford University Press, 1990.

Reagan, Ronald. *The Reagan Diaries.* Edited by Douglas Brinkley. New York: Harper Perennial, 2007.

The Nation and Her Land

Patriotism is not durable in a conquered nation.

ALEXIS DE TOCQUEVILLE, 1835

*How curious a land is this,—how full
of untold story, of tragedy and laughter, and the rich
legacy of human life; shadowed with a tragic past,
and big with future promise!*

W. E. B. DU BOIS, 1903

AT TWELVE MINUTES PAST FIVE in the morning of April 18, 1906, a massive earthquake, which today would likely have registered around 8.3 on the Richter scale, rocked northern California near San Francisco. A huge fire followed the quake and burned for three days, destroying everything within a four-square-mile area. Around 250,000 people were left homeless, and perhaps as many as three thousand people died. In addition to the death toll, the economic damage was about $500 million, a colossal sum in 1906. The San Francisco earthquake and resulting fire was thus one of the worst natural disasters in American history. And in particular, the earthquake revealed a salient urgency of securing a reliable and abundant source of water to the survivors of the city and environs of San Francisco.[1] But where was such a source of water to be found?

The most obvious solution was to dam the Tuolumne River at the narrow western entrance to the Hetch Hetchy Valley just north of the newly formed Yosemite National Park. Civil engineers proposed the construction of a reservoir in Hetch Hetchy as early as 1882, but there was powerful opposition, namely, from Interior Secretary Ethan A. Hitchcock. Because of its transcendent beauty, Hetch Hetchy was designated as a wilderness preserve by the federal government when it created Yosemite in 1890. When the 1906 earthquake destroyed San Francisco, much opposition to the proposed reservoir in Hetch Hetchy evaporated, except among a few of the most committed to preserving the valley's pristine condition. John Muir, among the most prominent conservationists of his time, led a national awareness campaign and urged his friend President Theodore Roosevelt to stand against James R. Garfield, who succeeded Hitchcock as Interior Secretary in 1907, and who supported a federal project constructing a dam and flooding the Hetch Hetchy Valley.[2]

Muir's campaign to save Hetch Hetchy lasted several years, but ultimately failed. Stalwart conservationists like President Roosevelt and Gifford Pinchot, the nation's chief forester, ended up breaking with Muir and supporting the construction of the reservoir for the residents of San Francisco. Roosevelt did not take this position lightly—he was torn between his desire to preserve the natural beauty of Hetch Hetchy and his deep conviction that natural resources must be used for the benefit of the people. The earthquake was a powerful reminder that natural resources, when they could be extracted responsibly, should be used for the people's security and flourishing. Roosevelt wrote in a letter to Robert Underwood Johnson, editor of the *Century*, "As for the Hetch Hetchy matter, it was just one of those cases where I was extremely doubtful; but finally I came to the conclusion that I ought to stand by Garfield and Pinchot's judgment on the matter."[3] After a long debate over the issue in Congress, President Woodrow Wilson signed a bill granting federal money for the Hetch Hetchy reservoir project on December 19, 1913.[4] The O'Shaughnessy dam was completed in 1923.

So ended the first national environmental controversy in American history.[5] But why did such a controversy exist in the first place? Hetch

Hetchy, the strange name of a valley in the middle of nowhere that the vast majority of Americans had never even heard of, became a symbol of a new national interest in preserving wild and beautiful places that seemed to be disappearing from the landscape at the turn of the twentieth century. The short answer to the question is that during this period the beginnings of the American environmental movement were decidedly underway. It was called "conservation" at the time, and perhaps nobody was more important as an impetus for the movement than Theodore Roosevelt, easily the most environmentally activist president in American history.

The longer answer to the question entails how Americans have historically viewed the land of the North American continent that they occupy. If there is one aspect about America that can be truly called exceptional, it is the land itself with its beauty and bounty. The place the colonists encountered did not resemble Europe at all. The entire Western hemisphere was an unbroken wilderness when Europeans first arrived during the fifteenth and sixteenth centuries. North America remained mostly wild until well into the nineteenth century. It was a wilderness occupied by human civilizations, to be sure. But both American continents were primeval, and North America in particular was more thinly populated by indigenous people than Central or South America. The Europeans called the land a *novus mundum*, a "new world." That appellation is no longer accepted in certain circles today, but to the Europeans in the "Age of Discovery" it was a description that was all too obvious. Prior to discovery, the American continents had been unknown to Europeans. The English who settled the Eastern seaboard of North America encountered, from their perspective, an entirely new place.

The stark newness of the continent presented a difficult mental challenge to the English who settled what became the United States. It is easy for us, who live amid the comforts and familiarities of the twenty-first century, to speculate on what attitudes we would have adopted toward the land had we been among the first settlers. But as we think historically about those people who settled here, we have to put aside as best we can our own presuppositions and value judgments. The settlers from the

1600s to the 1800s had no mental category whatsoever for the measureless frontier expanding before them. Most of them were not constitutionally prepared for a place where human communities existed within, and as part of, the vastness and mystery of a limitless wilderness. They were coming from a world where wild places existed in isolated spots outside of, and surrounded by, human activity. Furthermore, these Europeans still possessed a premodern worldview that valued the past over the future, tradition over innovation, the wisdom of antiquity over adaptation to new realities.

Given this fundamental existential challenge, the people who came here were faced with a choice—they could either superimpose their own mental categories upon the new land, or they could invent new categories and adapt accordingly. In other words, they could make the land conform to their worldview, or they could conform to the new world as it presented itself to them. For a civilization that so vitally cherished antiquity, the mental, physical and spiritual challenge of adapting to the newness of America was simply too much for them. As Jack Greene wrote of their situation, Europeans "unavoidably found it almost impossible to assimilate America's many novelties as novelties."[6]

Thus, newcomers in America could have either viewed the land (1) as that which was to be acted upon, much like the indigenous people they encountered and those they enslaved and brought here against their will, or (2) as a divine gift to be nurtured and inhabited with justice in order that all might share in its bounty. Was the land to be taken, conquered and exploited? Were its fruits and splendors to be cornered by some and denied to others? Or was the land to be seen as a heritage to be shared, an endowment bestowed by God with unimaginable potential as well as responsibility? And were the people as a whole to be renewed and cultivated in direct proportion to the renewal and cultivation of the land?

In this chapter, we will see that the *newness* of the land that contained the American nation presented this choice to those in whose hands her destiny was directed between the seventeenth and early twentieth centuries. Too often, those who controlled the wealth and power in the United States looked at the land as something to be conquered, stripped of its wealth, and then left in search of still more land. But not everyone saw the land this way. Many saw the land as a blessing from God that required care and justice. To them, the land possessed moral content just as human beings did, because it was created and given to them by God. If the land was treated with justice, then it would reward its people with its blessings. But if the land suffered from injustice, then the people would also suffer.

Closed American exceptionalism—the brand of exceptionalism marked by exclusion—entails the view that the land is there to be conquered. It is God's country, given to his chosen people to act upon at their will. Open exceptionalism, because it is a view defined by justice and inclusion, entails the view that the land is to be nurtured. How did these two views develop in American history? How does justice apply to the land and its people? And is there a Christian view of the land, and if so, how do we understand it? To these questions we now turn our attention.

The Land and Theology of Place

Places have enormous power over us, both individually and in community. The land is the physical place on which we live. The land is the source of our food and water. It supports our dwelling places. We use its raw materials to manufacture products that make our lives worth living. The land holds our dead ancestors as they rest in their graves. And the land is the repository of our memories. We remember, for example, our childhood experiences on particular places on the landscape. And we as a nation set aside places on the land where defining events took place in our history—the battlefields at Antietam and Little Big Horn, Independence Hall, Selma, Alabama, and Ground Zero, to name a few. These places we set aside as a nation often evoke intense feeling in us. I remember seeing an old man standing alone on Seminary Ridge at the Gettysburg battlefield, looking over the mile-long stretch of grass sloping upward toward Cemetery Hill, where fifteen thousand Confederates marched in Pickett's Charge against the Union forces in 1863. As he stood there looking over the scene, the tears were rolling down his cheeks. His deep, silent and lone response to events that happened long ago on that field testified to the power that that particular place possessed.

The land also often contains religious content for a nation. Anthony Smith wrote that when the land is infused with religious content, it becomes an "ethnoscape" or a "sacred homeland." Smith identified two types of ethnoscapes: "One is the promised land, the land of destination; the other is the ancestral homeland, the land of birth." Americans have assigned both meanings to the land since the colonial period, and Americans are far from being the only nation to consider their land in such terms. Many nations do this to some extent, simply because the power of place over humans is so acute. Perhaps the most famous example of a sacred land is that of Canaan, the Promised Land given by God to his chosen people Israel in the Old Testament.[7]

When the land takes on religious power, it sometimes becomes contested between groups. One group wins out over another, and the winners thus see themselves as the "Chosen," and the losers become the "Others." The Chosen thus belong to the land; the Others become aliens on the land. As Gary Burge wrote, "When *place* is tied to *religion*, suddenly the forces that these two represent become doubly potent. Suddenly I can make claim to a place because my God has given it to me."[8] Americans have frequently seen themselves as God's chosen nation, as we have already seen. The combining of the concept of chosen nation with the concept of sacred land, at least in American history, has often led to unjust actions taken against the land and against whole races and nations, namely, Native Americans, Latinos and African Americans. But when the land is seen by people as a gift of God to be gratefully received, the result has often been beneficial to both the land and the nation.

Puritan conception of the land. The Puritan colonists who settled New England in the seventeenth century sought to interpret the world through a biblical, Calvinistic paradigm. Let's consider three Puritan leaders in particular, specifically their views on possessing the land—Francis Higginson (1586–1630), Edward Johnson (1598–1672) and John Cotton (1584–1652).

Higginson was among the first English colonists to set off for America, arriving in Salem in 1629. He died in August 1630, but before he died, he wrote an essay titled "On the Riches of New England" about the good and bountiful land that the Puritans were colonizing in New England. His purpose was to attract new potential settlers from England, to dispel the idea that Massachusetts was situated in a bleak and howling wilderness, and to assuage fears that existence in America was marked by thinness, poor health and death. "I will endeavor to show you what New England is," Higginson wrote his countrymen, and "report nothing but the naked truth." The four basic elements of fire, earth, water and air produced great bounty in the colony. There was plenty of firewood to be had from the immense forests; the soil was rich and productive, yielding every kind of good crop; the waters of New England provided fish in great quantities; and there was plenty of the purest drinking water imaginable. And the "extraordinary clear and dry air" in New England was such that "many that have been weak and sickly in old England, by coming hither have been thoroughly healed and grown healthful and strong." Higginson stressed that God had blessed the land of New England to be so fruitful, and that those who came to settle there would be exceptionally blessed.[9] The land was yielding its fruit to God's people, and the people were living in harmony with the land and with each other.

Higginson's stress on the special fruitfulness of the land is a bit different from Edward Johnson's descriptions. To be sure, Higginson wrote to encourage Englishmen to come to America and settle it. He promised to give a balanced presentation of New England, but he emphasized that the land as a wilderness was not cursed, but blessed. Johnson's work, *Wonder-Working Providence of Sion's Saviour*, was a history of New England from 1628 to 1652. His purpose was to chronicle the development of the colony from a wilderness to a fruitful land. The land was no paradise when the colonists arrived, but they had to devote themselves to bring the land into cultivation. In particular, Johnson wrote that the colonists worked hard to transform the wilderness into a garden, but as they did so, God was faithful and merciful to bless their efforts. When the colonists first arrived, the land was a "remote, rocky, bushy, wild, woody wilderness" and a "receptacle for Lions, Wolves, Bears, Foxes, Rockoones, Bags, Bevers, Otters and all kind of wild creatures." But as the colonists worked the land diligently and sought the Lord's assistance, "through the mercy of Christ become a second England for fertilness in so short a space that it is indeed the wonder of the world." Johnson wrote that God was to be praised for bringing about this remarkable transformation, and while some had forgotten the goodness of God, others had been faithful to "keep in memory his mercies multitude and declare it to their children's children."[10]

Both Higginson and Johnson stressed God's providence in blessing the land the colonists had settled in New England. Both wrote that while the land was a wilderness, it was not barren, nor was it the home of devils. It was a fruitful and beautiful place. God's hand was on it to sustain and nourish his people whom he planted there. Cotton wrote that this fact was evidence that God had indeed marked this land for his people.

In his "Divine Right to Occupy the Land," Cotton went beyond mere description of God's blessing on the land and pointed out the signs God used to affirm to his people that he had indeed given them title to a particular country. Cotton said that God would either expel his people's enemies through war, or give his people favor with their enemies. God also would clear the land of other nations in the place where his people made their dwellings. Sometimes, the land would be vacant by default. At other times, God's people were to drive out those who occupied it. But they were not allowed to do so "without special commission from Heaven, such as the Israelites had, unless the natives do unjustly wrong them, and will not recompense the wrongs done in a peaceable fort."[11]

Cotton urged the people to consider whether or not they met these divine criteria. It was possible for the colonists to be presumptuous, and take land without God's blessing. They were to ask, "Canst thou say that God spied out this place for thee . . . ? Didst thou find that God made room for thee either by lawful descent, or purchase, or gift, or other warrantable right?" If so, "why, then, this is the place God hath appointed thee; here He hath made room for thee." Once God had given his people title to the land, then they would be in a position to enjoy it as God blessed it and made it bountiful.[12]

Cotton's view then was that New England had been given to the colonists by God, and the evidence for this was to be found in tangible ways. The Puritans seized territory from the Native Americans in the Pequot War (1637) and King Philip's War (1675). Although these wars were fought "without special commission from Heaven," the Puritans nevertheless regarded them as confirmation that God had given them the land. Though the warfare with the Native Americans had wasted the land, God by his mercy would restore both the land and the people when he gave them the final victory. In his poem about King Philip's War titled "New Englands Crisis," Benjamin Tompson (1642–1714) prayed thus:

> Let this dear Lord the sad conclusion be
> Of poor New-Englands dismal tragedy
> Let not the glory of thy former work
> Blasphemed be by pagan Jew or Turk;
> But in its funeral ashes write Thy name
> So fair all Nations may expound the same:
> Out of her ashes let a Phœnix rise
> That may outshine the first and be more wise.[13]

The Puritans did not separate the land from God's providence, but attached theological significance to the land. They believed that God had given it to them, not merely by bringing them to a vacant wilderness, but by actively bestowing it on them by taking it away from the indigenous people. Not all the Puritans accepted this view of the land. Roger Williams is a notable exception, provided we consider him a Puritan figure. But the ideas Cotton expressed were prevalent, and their prevalence continued in the views of white Americans after the Revolution was concluded in 1783.

The plantation system and the land. The largest American acquisition of territory until the Mexican War was the Louisiana Purchase of 1803. The Purchase established important precedents in American land policy that continued throughout the nineteenth and twentieth centuries. First, it established the constitutionality of acquiring foreign land by purchase. Second, it introduced the challenge of assimilating native inhabitants into the United States. Third, it introduced the issue of whether or not slavery would be extended into the newly acquired territories. Prior to the Purchase, slavery had been halted north of the Ohio River in the Northwest Ordinance of 1787, paving the way for small landowners, or what Jefferson called yeoman farmers, to develop the land. After the Louisiana Purchase, land became available in such vast quantities as to encourage the spread of slavery into undeveloped areas of the South and West. The influx of new lands, coupled with the prospect of attractive profits from land speculation and the mass production of staple crops such as cotton, meant that more often than not Americans saw the land in terms of subjugation and economic exploitation.

Short staple cotton became seriously profitable after the invention of the cotton gin in the 1790s. The Louisiana Purchase and the end of the War of 1812 and the Napoleonic Wars in 1815 meant that cotton could be cultivated in new lands, and it could be transported overseas in relative peace. The territory of the future states of Alabama and Mississippi was ideal for cotton production. When Alabama was being settled in the 1810s and '20s, the soil there produced three times the yield in cotton as South Carolina. In 1800, the United States was producing seventy-three thousand bales; by 1820, the yield was ten times that number, and the United States became the leading producer of cotton, passing British India.[14] The upshot of these coinciding realities during the 1810s meant that people often viewed land as cheap. As Daniel Walker Howe wrote, the settlers "gave little thought to preserving the natural environment for future use. . . . They employed profligate methods of agriculture and land-clearing, heedlessly burning of timber and valuable ground cover, leaving precious topsoil to wash or blow away."[15] Because farmers and plantation owners took the short view, it meant that when the land was exhausted, they simply packed up and moved west. Virginia led the nation in population decline, losing a million or so people prior to 1860. More people left Virginia in search of fertile lands in the antebellum period than any other state.[16]

If you asked Thomas Jefferson in the 1780s about this nineteenth-century state of affairs, he likely would have been displeased. Jefferson consistently expressed his vision that the new lands of the western United

States should be peopled and tilled by yeoman farmers, not plantation owners with great numbers of slaves. In 1782, Jefferson wrote,

> Those who labor in the earth are the chosen people of God, if ever he had a chosen people, whose breasts he has made his peculiar deposit for substantial and genuine virtue. . . . Corruption of morals in the mass of cultivators is a phenomenon of which no age nor nation has furnished an example. It is the mark set on those, who not looking up to heaven, to their own soil and industry, as does the husbandman, for their subsistence, depend for it on the casualties and caprice of customers. Dependence begets subservience and suffocates the germ of virtue, and prepares fit tools for the designs of ambition.[17]

In other words, small landowners were the backbone of the republic's virtue. They, more than anyone else according to Jefferson, are the soul of independence, industry and flourishing.

The great plantation owners dependent on slave labor for their production of goods did not embody the spirit of the republic, Jefferson believed early in his career. The institution of slavery, if allowed to expand, threatened the morals of the American people. Slavery undermined industry, both in the master and in the slave. The master became lazy, since his labors were being done by his slaves; the slaves came to hate the land they tilled for the master because his natural-born tendencies to virtue were bottled up in his condition as human property. Jefferson feared the consequences to the republic if slavery were to continue to flourish and expand unabated, given that the institution so undermined the morals of the republic. He famously said,

> Indeed I tremble for my country when I reflect that God is just: that his justice cannot sleep forever: that considering numbers, nature and natural means only, a revolution of the wheel of fortune, an exchange of situation, is among possible events: that it may become probable by supernatural interference! The Almighty has no attribute which can take side with us in such a contest.[18]

Jefferson hoped that slavery would not only cease to expand into the new territories, but that it would also ultimately die of obsolescence.

"The spirit of the master is abating," Jefferson wrote, "that of the slave rising from the dust." Ultimately, Jefferson hoped, there would even be a peaceful and harmonious "total emancipation," rather than a bloodbath resulting in the "extirpation" of plantation owners by their rebellious slaves.[19]

But this was the Jefferson of the early 1780s. Jefferson was among the elite landowners, possessing lands and slaves at his Monticello and Poplar Forest plantations in central and southern Virginia. He was personally and economically invested in preserving slavery. But he was also politically invested. His constituency and his class were the planter elite. Because of these investments in the plantation economy, he lacked the will to do anything to stop the spread of that system over the Appalachians and into the new lands in the Old Southwest. Roger Kennedy wrote that Jefferson in his later years "recoiled from opposing the pursuit of a way of life dominated by great plantations and a reliance upon both slavery and world markets" mainly because he "had his personal economic interests to protect and political ambitions to advance."[20]

It is interesting to note that part of Jefferson's problem with slavery in 1782 was that the slaves came to hate the land they worked for their masters. Thus, the land itself became a curse to the slaves, because the land itself was both the symbol and the reason for their "miserable condition." The slaves' "amor patrie" was destroyed by slavery, according to Jefferson. He said, "If a slave can have a country in this world, it must be any other in preference to that in which he is born to live and labour for another."[21] Thus, the institution of slavery encumbered not just the slaves, but also the land.

Slaves cleared new land of trees to prepare it for mass cultivation of staple crops. They plowed in long, straight rows and sowed their seeds for cotton in those rows under the close supervision of their overseers. When the land became exhausted due to soil erosion and a lack of crop rotation, landowners simply purchased new land rather than improve their existing fields. When a plantation was no longer profitable, the plantation owner simply abandoned it and moved on to new land. For example, the Byrd family's Westover plantation in Virginia was begun in

1730, and was sold in 1814; Carter's Grove was built in 1753 and sold before the end of the century; the Lewis family's Woodlawn plantation, started in 1802, was lost by 1845. The Lee plantation of Stratford, which began in 1725, went about the same time as Monticello was sold out of the Jefferson family.[22] "Migration was *driven* by soil loss and soil sickening and *drawn* by cheap land," wrote Kennedy. "Cheap land was treated as disposable. Cheap things usually are."[23]

Jefferson's vision of a republic of free yeoman landowners, working the land and enjoying its fruits, basing their lives and liberties on their collective virtue, and thereby securing the republic's future prosperity and unity, was a failure. Mark Fiege wrote of Jefferson's thought "that this magical West could 'diffuse' slavery until it experienced its natural demise." Jefferson was wrong.[24] Only the convulsion of the Civil War would bring an end to the injustice of slavery. As we will see below, while the war brought an end to slavery, it did not bring an end to injustice.

Nineteenth-century Romanticism and the land. While the plantation system was spreading into the South in the early nineteenth century, the philosophical system of Romanticism was changing the way many Americans saw the land, wild land in particular. It is important to remember that most of North America was covered over with wilderness, even well into the twentieth century. My grandfather, James Arthur Wilsey, was a geologist in southwest Montana in the 1940s, and even at that late date, much of that region remained wild country and largely unknown. As a PhD student at Princeton University, his doctoral thesis consisted of producing the very first geologic map of southwest Montana.

Nineteenth-century Americans began to see that their land was an extraordinary place because so much of it was wild. Where in Europe did wilderness exist in such primeval purity? Nearly the entire continent of North America was wilderness, whereas Europe was overpopulated—any wild places there were rare, isolated and surrounded by human civilization. Romanticism as a philosophical idea was a direct response to Enlightenment rationalism, the notion that reason was authoritative and could be appealed to for all the answers to human questions. Romanticists, such as Jean-Jacques Rousseau, believed that there were limits to human reason, and that reason could not account for the deep feelings the human person naturally longed to express.[25] Prior to the nineteenth century, Westerners saw wilderness as a void, a waste place, a place inhabited by devils, or a place that must be conquered, subdued and brought under human dominion and cultivation. Many saw forests, swamps, deserts and mountains as barriers, blots on the landscape or the abodes of dark spirits. But by the nineteenth century, largely because of the Romantic movement that assigned value to and emphasis on feeling and mystery, people's view of the natural world changed. They saw God revealing himself and his ways in nature. Many deists of the late eighteenth and early nineteenth century rejected supernatural revelation (the Bible), and believed instead that God spoke through nature and the orderly universe.

Americans of the early nineteenth century, having won their independence, purchased the Louisiana Territory, and possessing a land of supreme beauty and potential, saw the greatest physical evidence of their exceptionalism in the simple and overwhelming fact of the wilderness. No land in the world compared to their land. Writers and painters began to extol the sublimity of America's landscapes, seeing God's excellencies revealed clearly through the wonders he sculpted in its silent, mysterious and awesome places.

Alexander Wilson (1766–1813) wrote a poem titled "The Foresters," in which he described a journey he took through the woods of Pennsylvania and New York to Niagara Falls in 1804. Wilson triumphed in the beauty of the wilderness, and exulted in its majestic timelessness. The wilderness offered an escape from the crowds of the cities, and brought one nearer to the actual moment when God created the world.

> Sons of the city ye whom crowds and noise
> Bereave of peace and Nature's rural joys
> And ye who love through woods and wilds to range
> Who see new charms in each successive change
> Come roam with me Columbia's forests through
> Where scenes sublime shall meet your wandering view.[26]

While in Europe there were, no doubt, places of beauty, nothing could compare to that beauty found in America's forests. There in Europe, the rivers, streams and mountains were well-known to all, and had witnessed the coming and going of European civilization for generation after generation. But here in America, the woods and wilds displayed their splendors in silence as the millennia flowed by unnoticed. Europe had its brilliant poets and artists, but America had its wilderness. Wilson said,

> Our western world with all its matchless floods
> Our vast transparent lakes and boundless woods
> Stamped with the traits of majesty sublime
> Unhonored weep the silent lapse of time
> Spread their wild grandeur to the unconscious sky
> In sweetest seasons pass unheeded by
> While scarce one Muse returns the songs they gave
> Or seeks to snatch their glories from the grave.[27]

Because their land was uniquely blessed with a wilderness untarnished by human civilization, many Americans believed this was a sign of their country's unlimited economic, civilizational and aesthetic potential. Nash wrote that "by the middle of the nineteenth century wilderness was recognized as a cultural and moral resource and a basis for national self-esteem."[28] Frederick Jackson Turner taught that the land defined the American character and American progress. He wrote, "The advance of the frontier has meant a steady movement away from the influence of Europe, the steady growth of independence on American lines."[29] And a school of visual artists arose in the mid-nineteenth century that sought to capture the physical exceptionalism of America on canvas—the Hudson River School of Thomas Cole (1801–1848).

Cole began his career as a portrait painter in Ohio, but he was captivated by the beauty of the forests and wilderness of New York and New Hampshire. Cole, as a Romantic painter, tried to evoke the feelings he had when contemplating the majesty of nature in his artwork. In the 1820s and '30s, he went to the Catskill Mountains in New York, and painted such works as "Falls of the Kaaterskill" (1826), "The Clove, Catskills" (1827), and "View on the Catskill, Early Autumn" (1836–1837). He painted a series of works titled "The Course of Empire" (1834–1836) in which he traced the impact of the rise and fall of civilizations on nature and the landscape. And his famous "Voyage of Life" series (1839–1840) traced the life of a man guided through birth, youth, adulthood and death by his angel.[30]

Figure 6.1. *Voyage of Life: Childhood,* Thomas Cole (1839)

Albert Bierstadt (1830–1902) painted landscapes in the American West, and some of his most famous paintings are of the western national parks at Yosemite, Yellowstone and the Grand Canyon. Bierstadt began his career painting landscapes in Europe. One of his famous early paintings is his work "Lake Lucerne" (1858), but Bierstadt developed his artistic skills in his later career here in America.

Thomas Moran (1834–1926) was another exceptional painter of American landscapes. Mount Moran in the Grand Tetons was named for him. Moran was not only an artist, but also an explorer and outdoorsman. His paintings were influential in Congress setting up Yellowstone as a national park in 1872.[31]

Figure 6.2. *Sunset (California Scenery)*, Albert Bierstadt (1864)

Cole wrote that "the most distinctive, and perhaps the most impressive characteristic of American scenery is its wildness." In America's wilderness, God revealed his "undefiled works, and the mind is cast into the contemplation of eternal things."[32] The Romantic view of American wilderness was not the frontiersman's view, to be certain. The frontiersman still thought of wilderness as that which was to be conquered. This was not a matter of anything less than survival for families carving out a living from the wilderness. The Romantic view of wilderness, however, gained popularity among the urbanite wealthy. To those who had the resources to enjoy the wilderness for its pleasures, preserving it became a primary issue in the late nineteenth and early twentieth centuries.

Conservationist view of the land. No president did more to bring awareness of the importance of preserving America's natural beauty than Theodore Roosevelt (1858–1919). Roosevelt grew up in a wealthy family, and from a young age came to appreciate and love the outdoors. Perhaps the most formative experience in his life was the time he spent in Dakota Territory as a cattle rancher in the 1880s. He wrote extensively about his life as a cowboy, and he learned conservationism while a young man on the frontier. He understood that the sublimity of the wilderness ought to be preserved, but the natural resources of the land should not be left untouched. Conservation meant that the nation could extract natural resources and respect the land at the same time. The resources were there for people to use, and it would be foolish to leave them undeveloped. At the same time, Roosevelt had no use for those who would waste the wild places and wealth that the land offered. He wrote in his autobiography, "The idea that our natural resources were inexhaustible still obtained [when he became president in 1901], and there was as yet no real knowledge of their extent and condition." For this reason, Roosevelt

Figure 6.3. *Lower Yellowstone Range*, Thomas Moran (1875)

wrote, "the first work I took up when I became President was the work of reclamation." His first message to Congress of December 3, 1901, "laid the foundation for the development of irrigation and forestry during the next seven and one-half years. It set forth the new attitude toward the natural resources in the words: 'The Forest and water problems are perhaps the most vital internal problems of the United States.'"[33] Douglas Brinkley wrote that Roosevelt's conservationism was the most consequential and significant presidential achievement between the Civil War and World War I. He wrote, "By reorienting and redirecting Washington, DC bureaucracy toward conservation, Roosevelt's crusade to save the American wilderness can now be viewed as one of the greatest presi-

dential initiatives between Abraham Lincoln's Emancipation Proclamation and Woodrow Wilson's decision to enter World War I."[34]

The development of American views of the land is a complex story,
much more complex than can be captured in the small space of these
pages. But hopefully, as we think about evolving views of the land
through the beginning of the twentieth century, we can see that there
were at least two contrasting views of the land—that it is there to be
conquered, and that it is there to be cultivated and nurtured. The first
view is a closed exceptionalist view; the other is consistent with open
exceptionalism. These two views both acknowledge that God is the giver
of the land. Both of these views can call on the dominion mandate of the
book of Genesis as an authority. But both of these views cannot be sustained at the same time. If we accept the one, then we reject the other.
We will turn now to differentiate closed and open exceptionalist views
of the land.

CLOSED AND OPEN EXCEPTIONALIST ACCOUNTS OF THE LAND

The Bible teaches that God gave human beings the responsibility to
preside over the earth and its animal, vegetable and mineral resources.
This responsibility is recorded in Genesis 1:26-28 and again in Genesis
9:1-7, and theologians call it the dominion mandate. God gave the dominion mandate to humankind at creation, and renewed it after the
flood. The basis of the mandate is that God created humans in his
image. As such, God commanded them to "have dominion over the
fish of the sea and over the birds of the heavens and over the livestock
and over all the earth and over every creeping thing that creeps on the
earth" (Genesis 1:26). As they exercised dominion, God directed
humans to "be fruitful and multiply and fill the earth and subdue it"
(Genesis 1:28). After the flood, God renewed the mandate, adding that
"the fear of you and the dread of you shall be upon every beast of the
earth and upon every bird of the heavens, upon everything that creeps
on the ground and all the fish of the sea" (Genesis 9:2). And whereas
at creation God gave humans freedom to eat only the plants, now they
were allowed to eat meat—"Every moving thing that lives shall be food

for you . . . as I gave you the green plants, I give you everything," God said (Genesis 9:3-4).

Genesis is not the only book of the Bible in which the dominion mandate is found. We also find it in Psalm 8:6-8. Here, the psalmist praised God for having created humans as "a little lower than the heavenly beings and crowned . . . with glory and honor" (Psalm 8:5). Furthermore, the psalmist affirmed that God gave humans "dominion over the works of your hands" and "put all things under [their] feet" (Psalm 8:6).

So Scripture shows that God placed human beings in a specific relationship to the land and its resources. The question, then, is not historically bound up in whether or not humans can or ought to exercise dominion over the land. Rather, the question is about how that dominion is to be exercised in a way reflecting the goodness of God and the inherent goodness God infused into the land when he made it.[35] Was there a particular method of fulfilling the dominion mandate? Who decides what that method is? Does the failure of a culture to fulfill the dominion mandate according to the methods of another culture justify the displacement of that group by the other? And does the dominion mandate give humans the right to "rule" and "subdue" other humans, as well as the land and its resources? These are but some of the many questions surrounding the meaning and application of the dominion mandate. Closed and open exceptionalist accounts of the land in US history generally correspond to how Americans understood and applied the dominion mandate.

Earlier, we saw that in the midst of the 1846 national debate on Oregon Territory—that is, whether the United States should claim all of Oregon ("fifty-four forty or fight") or settle on a negotiated compromise with the British—John Quincy Adams justified his argument to claim all of Oregon in part on the dominion mandate. For Adams, the only people who could claim rightful title to land were those who held and cultivated it. Adams had held the highest offices in the US government by the 1840s, including secretary of state and president. Now he was US representative from Massachusetts, and in that capacity, he supported the termination of the joint occupation of Oregon with Britain and the American acquisition of the whole territory. He asserted that all the British cared to do with Oregon was "to keep it open for navigation, for hunters to hunt the wild beasts . . . for the buffaloes, braves, and savages of the desert."[36] Since this was not a faithful disposal of dominion mandate responsibilities, the British had no legitimate title to the land.

The problem with Adams's view of the dominion mandate is that it assumed there was only one legitimate way to use the land. "Ruling" and "subduing" the land had an almost military sense to Americans of the nineteenth century. Settlers had to conquer and clear the wilderness, and then hold it back from retaking the garden of cultivation they had hacked out. Those who used the land with differing methods than the "Chosen" weren't doing it right. For example, Native Americans often left the largest trees of the forest standing, to give protection to their crops below the leaf canopy from the erosive forces of rainfall. They planted crops among the trees, "poking the earth and planting messily . . . doing less damage to the poultice of leaves and roots and exposing the soil beneath less perilously to erosion."[37] But whites often did not consider this a legitimate means to rule and subdue the land. In contrast, plantation owners came with large companies of slaves to denude the landscape, plow the earth up in straight rows and, ultimately, exhaust the soil till it could no longer sustain crops. Then, they simply moved on to new lands after stripping the old of its nutrients.

The institution of slavery was a great injustice inflicted upon human beings, but it was an injustice inflicted upon the land also. The plantation system entailed both mastery of African Americans and mastery of the land. The system also entailed white mastery of indigenous people, as the US government waged war on Native Americans, particularly in the relocation of the Five Civilized Tribes in the 1830s and in the Indian wars in the West between 1865 and 1890. The land itself suffered from slavery and the destruction of Native Americans. The plantation system left the soil depleted of its nutrients, and the Indian wars resulted in the near extinction of the American buffalo, to name two examples. As the people suffered, the land suffered, too.

W. E. B. Du Bois (1868–1963) wrote of the country surrounding Albany, Georgia, a generation after the Civil War and the emancipation of the slaves. While visiting the farms around Albany, he noted the great contrasts between the richness of the land and the plight of its people who suffered the legacy of slavery. He said that this land was once known as

> the Egypt of the Confederacy,—the rich granary whence potatoes and corn and cotton poured out to the famished and ragged Confederate troops as they battled for a cause lost long before 1861. Sheltered and secure, it became the place of refuge for families, wealth, and slaves. Yet even then the hard ruthless rape of the land began to tell. The red-clay sub-soil already had begun to peer above the loam. The harder the slaves were driven the more careless and fatal was their farming.[38]

These effects took their toll on the land and its people, and the harm the plantation system caused on the land was still being felt in 1903 when Du Bois visited it. African Americans who were working the land as sharecroppers exhibited one of two behavioral traits as a result of the futility of working land that had so little left to yield after years of abuse and degeneracy. One trait was anger; the other was laziness. One man Du Bois met, whom he described as "one big red-eyed black man," had worked for forty-five years on the same farm "beginning with nothing, and still having nothing." The man was dejected, in debt, and showed a seething resentment beneath a thin veneer of amiability. Du Bois and the man were discussing the recent death of an African American boy who had been killed by a policeman simply for talking loudly on the sidewalk in town. Du Bois related that after their discussion, the man "said slowly: 'Let a white man touch me, and he dies; I don't boast this,—I don't say it around loud, or before the children,—but I mean it. I've seen them whip my father and my old mother in them cotton-rows till the blood ran.'"[39]

Another man Du Bois encountered, by the name of Sears, was not angry but lazy. Du Bois met him "lolling under the chubby oak-trees" laughing and telling stories. Sears had worked the same land for twelve years, but had nothing to show for his work. His seven children also worked the land. They could not go to school because there was no money for books or school clothes, and anyway, Sears needed them in the fields. Du Bois characterized the situation in this way: "Careless ignorance and laziness here, fierce hate and vindictiveness there,—these are the extremes of the Negro problem which we met that day, and we scarce knew which we preferred."[40]

Du Bois's descriptions reflect the unique relationship African Americans as a whole had with the land and their resulting approach to conservation. Since African Americans did not emigrate to America by choice, did not work the plantations for their own flourishing and did not have leave to travel or settle at their will or pleasure, their experience of the land has often been different from the free farmers who flowed into the great spaces and carved out lives for themselves. Kimberly Smith wrote that "to black writers working in this tradition, America—not just the political community but the physical terrain—is a land cursed by injustice and in need of redemption."[41]

George Washington Carver (1864–1943), the famous African American botanist at Tuskegee University at the turn of the twentieth century, sought to make right some of the wrongs of slavery to both the land and the people. Like John Quincy Adams, and many before him, he had a keen awareness of the dominion mandate. But his interpretation of Genesis 1:28 was far different than the narrow, arbitrary view taken by Adams and many like him. Smith wrote that Carver "saw humans as 'copartners' with God in the creation—and junior partners at that, whose scientific study of nature is inspired by God and justified by its charitable purpose of relieving human suffering."[42] Carver's biographer, historian Mark Hersey, wrote that "Carver's deep religious sensibilities, which blended Christianity with a profound veneration of the natural world that bordered on mysticism, shaped his work" along with "ideas about how impoverished African American farmers could overcome the obstacles facing them."[43] Thus Carver's brand of conservation possessed a moral dimension informed by the dominion mandate. God's command to humans to fill, rule and subdue the earth was not to be understood in the martial sense of conquest. Rather, it was to be applied in a sense of patient care and nurturing that benefitted the many, rather than the few.

Carver's view of the dominion mandate—that the land is to be cared for, stewarded, husbanded and conserved for the benefit of those who live on it—is an open exceptionalist view of the land. Everyone knew that North America was unique and held immense potential in the years of settlement. But while some who held a closed exceptionalist view of the land meant to conquer and exploit it, all the while denying it to those they deemed outsiders, others had an open exceptionalist view that did not separate the land from its people when it came to justice and flourishing. For example, Alexis de Tocqueville wrote of the close-knit communities of New England, those communities that were tied to the land and to one another through active civic engagement. Tocqueville wrote that the key to the success of democracy in America was "the nature of the territory that the Americans inhabit." He said that New Englanders were devoted to their townships because they were careful to secure the common good, which in turn came from good stewardship of the land and of responsible political action. "The physical causes, independent of the laws, which promote general prosperity are more numerous in America than they ever have been in any other country in the world, at any other period of history. In the United States, not only is legislation democratic, but Nature herself favors the cause of the people."[44]

Tocqueville and Carver had similar views about the close relationship between civic engagement and responsible treatment of the land. Tocqueville observed that New Englanders cared for their own welfare through their just treatment of the land and of each other. Carver sought to teach responsible stewardship of the land to the community around Tuskegee in order that their lives would be enhanced and the wrongs of the past could be forgotten and undone. Carver initiated nature study, especially among the children of African American sharecroppers, in order to teach farmers and their children about the connection between scientific and spiritual study of nature—that the natural world can be manipulated in a responsible way to enrich human beings, but it is also a source of strength and sustenance beyond the mere production of a field. God is the Maker of the land, and he has tied us to the soil in deeply significant ways that are worth exploring for their own sakes. Hersey wrote that, for Carver, "conservation meant preserving the soil, the source of food, and the relationship of farmer and farm."[45]

John Muir (1838–1914) had similar views of the close connection between the land and its people. Muir was not a strict preservationist. He
was not one who thought that wilderness ought to be left in its pristine
condition and its resources left undisturbed in the womb of nature. But
while Muir was vociferous in his defense of pristine wilderness, he was
not a preservationist in this sense. Even Muir believed that the land had
much to offer the advancement of human civilization—provided that its
resources were extracted in a way that did the least harm.

For example, he wrote that the clearing of the forests in the West had
gone far enough, but he did not mean that humans should leave remaining natural resources alone. Rather, he wrote, the remaining forests
"will yield plenty of timber, a perennial harvest for every right use . . . and
will continue to cover the springs of the rivers . . . and give irrigating
waters to the dry valleys . . . and be a blessing to everybody forever."[46]
And in discussing extraction of other natural resources, Muir wrote, "Let
them be as free to pick gold and gems from the hills, to cut and hew, dig
and plant, for homes and bread. . . . The ground will be glad to feed
them."[47] Let them gather the land's riches respectfully and with care.
Muir did not advocate man's expulsion from the wilderness. But in
drawing resources from the land, humans must act justly toward the
land, recognizing that their wasting of the land meant their own destruction, too. "Everybody needs beauty as well as bread," Muir wrote,
"places to play in and pray in, where Nature may heal and cheer and give
strength to body and soul alike."[48] The land was the source of both kinds
of nutrition: physical and spiritual. The land, to Muir, was the indispensable source of humans' needs and wants in their bodies as well as
their souls. It was productive enough to meet both kinds of needs, and
will reward the good steward with its bounty, heedless of race, ethnicity,
creed or other artificial distinction.

CHRISTIANITY AND OPEN AMERICAN EXCEPTIONALIST ACCOUNTING OF THE LAND

Is there a Christian view of the land? If so, what does a Christian view of
the land have to do with open exceptionalist views of the land? Is there

such a thing as "God's country"? Is America "God's country" like Canaan of old? Some of the Puritans thought it was, and many Americans have regarded the land in those terms, as we have seen. The idea of the chosen nation is closely tied to the idea of a sacred land. The land is the physical place the chosen nation occupies, and it lends the nation a measure of authenticity as God's chosen people in a religiously nationalistic paradigm. But such a paradigm is neither consistent with the message of the gospel, nor consistent with the comprehensive message of the Bible.

The orthodox Christian view of God holds that God is omnipresent. He is everywhere at once; there is no place where he is absent. At the same time, God cannot be "located" spatially in any specific place. An instructive passage of Scripture on this great theological truth is in the narrative in the fourth chapter of John's Gospel about Jesus' encounter with the Samaritan woman at the well. The woman said to Jesus that "you say that in Jerusalem is the place where people ought to worship" (John 4:20). Jesus told her that her conception of God was too spatial, too strictly located in one place. He said, "the hour is coming when neither on this mountain [Mt. Gerizim in Samaria] nor in Jerusalem will you worship the Father" (John 4:21). Those who were true worshipers of God, Jesus said, recognized that God was everywhere, but could not be pinpointed in any one place. "But the hour is coming, and is now here, when the true worshipers will worship the Father in spirit and truth. . . . God is spirit, and those who worship him must worship in spirit and truth" (John 4:23-24). Thus, God has not chosen any land as his own, nor has he chosen a land for any particular people since the coming of Jesus Christ.

The coming of Christ is significant to the idea of sacred space in this way—Christ himself is the fulfillment of sacred land theology. In the Old Testament, God chose Israel and planted his people in the Promised Land. The land he gave his people points ahead to union with Christ and the resulting rest we as believers in Christ receive once we have been united to him through faith. Burge insightfully wrote that Christ "is the spatiality, the new locale where God may be met."[49] This is a profound statement, and one that doubtless may be difficult to grasp in its fullness.

In considering how Christ fulfills sacred land theology of the Old Testament, we may relate to the Samaritan woman's apparent exasperation toward the end of her conversation with Jesus: "I know that Messiah is coming. . . . When he comes, he will tell us all things" (John 4:25). Jesus' words in response to her were, as they are to us, simple and yet fathomless. "I who speak to you am he" (John 4:26).

This passage in John, a passage that is pregnant with meaning on a variety of levels, reveals the absurdity of the idea that America is somehow God's country, a sacred place that he has given his chosen people to act upon as they see fit. America as a place is sacred, in that its land is part of the good creation of God. It is a fruitful land, teeming with life and activity. It is a land that contains immeasurable potential for human flourishing, if it is tended justly by its people to the end of general and generous human flourishing. The land in America is indeed a gift from God, blessing bodies, minds and souls. But nothing sets American land apart in any theological sense. This is how *open* American exceptionalism relates to the land. As a gift of God for human flourishing, since humans are created in the image of God, the land is a stewardship and a heritage for all people who come to plant their lives on this soil.

FOR FURTHER READING

Brinkley, Douglas. *The Wilderness Warrior: Theodore Roosevelt and the Crusade for America*. New York: Harper, 2009.

Burge, Gary M. *Jesus and the Land: The New Testament Challenge to "Holy Land" Theology*. Grand Rapids: Baker, 2010.

Fiege, Mark. *The Republic of Nature: An Environmental History of the United States*. Seattle: University of Washington Press, 2012.

Hersey, Mark D. *My Work Is That of Conservation: An Environmental Biography of George Washington Carver*. Athens: University of Georgia Press, 2011.

Kennedy, Roger G. *Mr. Jefferson's Lost Cause: Land, Farmers, Slavery, and the Louisiana Purchase*. Oxford: Oxford University Press, 2003.

Smith, Kimberly K. *African American Environmental Thought: Foundations*. American Political Thought, edited by Wilson Carey McWilliams and Lance Banning. Lawrence: University Press of Kansas, 2007.

7

The Glorious Nation

Friends, this election is about more than who gets what. It is about who we are. It is about what we believe and what we stand for as Americans. There is a religious war going on in this country. It is a cultural war, as critical to the kind of nation we shall be as the Cold War itself. For this war is for the soul of America.

PATRICK J. BUCHANAN, 1992

On MONDAY, AUGUST 17, 1992, I started my first job out of college. That day was my first day as the principal of a small Christian school in rural Virginia. The school was part of an ancient (by American standards) Baptist church, founded in 1773. The school began in 1986 with a vision to educate young people in kindergarten through twelfth grade to think Christianly about the world. I was twenty-three years old, a newly minted graduate of Furman University with a shiny new bachelor's degree in history. I had not an hour of experience in school administration or in teaching. But I was filled with enthusiasm and ready to get started on this new adventure—and leading that school was, in every sense of the word, an adventure.

After a long first day on the job, I remember heading back to my rented room to take in the '92 Republican National Convention being held at the Astrodome in Houston, Texas. I was following the election closely, and was anxious to hear Pat Buchanan give his primetime address to the GOP delegates. The speech he gave that night was the famous "Culture War" speech, in which he observed that the United States had won the Cold War, but now was engaged in a war of identity. Buchanan argued that America had been founded on Judeo-Christian values, and must not succumb to the pressures from social liberals to give in on issues such as abortion, gay marriage, women military-service members in combat and school choice, to name a few. Speaking emotionally about the soldiers who arrived in Los Angeles to pacify the city during the spring 1992 Rodney King riots, Buchanan said, "The mob threatened and cursed, but the mob retreated because it had met the one thing that could stop it: force, rooted in justice, and backed by moral courage." He went on to use the soldiers dispersing the LA riots as a simile for the culture war in America, saying, "As those boys took back the streets of Los Angeles, block by block, my friends, we must take back our cities, and take back our culture, and take back our country."[1]

The notion of "taking back" the country is a familiar one appearing in the rhetoric of the culture wars, especially the rhetoric used by social and religious conservatives. The phrase is ubiquitous, for example, in the literature advocating for the Christian America thesis—the belief that America was founded as a Christian nation.[2] The phrase itself conjures up images of advancing and retreating armies engaged in a shooting war, something like the Korean War of 1950–1953. In that war, the North Koreans advanced into South Korea as far as the Pusan Perimeter. United Nations forces under American leadership intervened, and launched a massive counteroffensive that resulted in the "taking back" of South Korean territory that had been conquered by the North. The culture war rhetoric of "taking back" America is designed to introduce martial images of sacrifice, heroism, victory and conquest in an effort to unite people behind a transcendent cause infused with hopes of future success or dread of imminent and irreversible collapse.

To borrow a martial metaphor from culture war rhetoric, one of the battle fronts in that culture war was education. Many evangelicals since the 1970s have given up on the public education system and formed their own schools in order to train students to adopt a Christian worldview.

Evangelicals have also embraced homeschooling for similar reasons. And a significant part of the "Christian worldview" that has been taught in Christian school and homeschool curriculum is American exceptionalism, frequently of the closed variety. In this chapter, we will consider select Christian school and homeschool curricula as a late-twentieth, early twenty-first-century cultural artifact, to assess its treatment of United States history. The curricula we will consider portray the past in closed exceptionalist terms, with heavy emphasis on a glorious past with little moral reflection. In our critique of the curricula, we will offer a way forward for a more responsible approach for the reading and writing of Christian school and homeschool history curricula, one that avoids the pitfalls of closed exceptionalism, teaches a worldview that is more faithfully Christian and continues to celebrate America consistently with open exceptionalism.

OVERVIEW OF SELECT CHRISTIAN SCHOOL AND HOMESCHOOL HISTORY CURRICULUM

Three of the most popular curricula in Christian school and homeschool use in America are A Beka Book, Bob Jones University Press and Veritas Press. A Beka and Bob Jones have been used since the 1970s, and Veritas has risen in popularity with the classical, Christian educational method since the 1990s. A Beka, Bob Jones and Veritas are used widely throughout the country, and are representative of the evangelical Christian educational paradigm of the last thirty years. That is, emphasis on a Christian worldview defined in terms of the authority of Scripture, young-earth creationism and American exceptionalism is a mark of these three curricula and the general vision of Christian education.

As we consider these three curricula, and the way each text presents America historically, allow me to render a disclaimer at the outset. This is not a scientific survey, nor do I intend to render any judgment one way or the other regarding the value of Christian school or homeschool education in general. What I intend to do in this chapter is analyze history textbooks printed by these three publishers as primary documents representing specific views of history from their particular historical vantage points. From there, I aim to assess their respective methods in how they presented history. The texts I will consider are A Beka's *United States History in Christian Perspective: Heritage of Freedom* (1996), Bob Jones's *United States History* (2001), and Veritas's Omnibus III: *Reformation to the Present* (2006) and Omnibus VI: *The Modern World* (2012). All of these texts were written for high school juniors and seniors, with the exception of the Omnibus III text, which was written for ninth graders.

So, this chapter is an engagement with contemporary history. That is, we will look at these texts as artifacts from a period of US history in which the culture wars played a prominent role in American public discourse. These texts are still in use by millions of students in the present. But we will go beyond mere description of these texts, and will analyze them as historical documents to show that American exceptionalism, and in particular, closed American exceptionalism, has been a "front" in the culture wars in the past twenty years. Each of these three texts sought to use history to advance a particular cause, that is, to view America in exceptionalist terms and to disparage nonexceptionalist views of America.

The A Beka textbook was authored by Michael R. Lowman, George Thompson and Kurt Grussendorf. The text opened with a discussion on "the migration of mankind from the tower of Babel," through the end of the feudal order in Europe, the beginning of the Renaissance and Reformation, to the discovery of America by Christopher Columbus. The authors presented earth history from a young-earth creationist viewpoint, and stated at the beginning that their approach to writing history was providential: "God, in His wisdom, allowed America to remain hidden until the Modern Age had dawned in Europe, bringing with it important changes that would profoundly affect the course of American history."[3]

The first chapter dealt with Spanish and French efforts at colonization, and the second chapter introduced English colonization in Virginia and New England. At this point early in the book, the authors told the story of American development from a distinctly Anglocentric perspective. The book contains thirty chapters in eight units and ends with a treatment of the Clinton Administration in 1995.

In terms of study features, the book contained about sixty maps, along with special topics considered throughout the narrative. The topics were organized into two types, classified respectively as "Highlights of American History" and "Heroes of American History." Some of the "Highlights" included "The Growth of the National Parks System," "Songs of World War I," "Our Native American Heritage," "America Is Great" and "The Moral Values of Capitalism." Some of the biographical sketches of the "Heroes of American History" included Clara Barton, Booker T. Washington, J. P. Morgan, Robert E. Lee, Stonewall Jackson and Alvin York. The Constitution appeared at the back of the book, along with the Declaration of Independence, the Gettysburg Address, and lists of US presidents and the fifty states and capitals.

The authors included a two-page guide to the text titled "How to Use This Book" at the beginning, between the table of contents and prior to the first chapter. In this section, the authors asserted that the way they presented United States history was "a positive, patriotic approach . . . bringing to life events and personalities that have shaped the nation with a special emphasis on our Christian heritage."[4] This statement, along with the opening statement about God's providence in history, revealed much about the authors' agenda in writing the text.

The Bob Jones University (BJU) text was authored by Timothy Keesee and Mark Sidwell. Unlike the A Beka text, the BJU text did not open with any statements on methodology or philosophy. There was no introduction stating the place of God's providence in history. The narrative simply began with a chapter on the first European contact with America, a narrative that was set in the context of the sixteenth-century Reformation. Similar to the A Beka text, only one chapter was devoted to non-English colonization in America. Starting in the second chapter, the text focused on the thirteen British colonies, and the Anglocentric paradigm found in the A Beka text was similar to that found in the BJU text.

Overall, this text was more balanced in its approach to US history than the A Beka text. More attention was given to nonwhite peoples, and while their treatment was still through an Anglocentric paradigm, the authors provided a wider historical development in the BJU text.

Throughout the narrative, there was a distinct flavor of the Christian America thesis, and various events were viewed through the lens of fundamentalism. Still, this text provided a better treatment of the complexity of history, and set events in their context more consistently than the A Beka text in the flow of the narrative.

The text covered material through the 2000 presidential election, and there the narrative stopped. The authors concluded their narrative with an explicit statement on their methodology. In an epilogue titled "Now We See Through a Glass Darkly," the authors provided their closed exceptionalist account of America. In particular, Keesee and Sidwell compared heaven with America in their concluding statements that brought the text to a close. They wrote, "As believers we have a sure destiny as we walk with the Author and Finisher of time to 'a new heaven and new earth.' Our New World discovery, however, unlike Columbus' voyage will not be an accidental landing on a hostile shore. As America was to weary pilgrims long ago, this New World will be a refuge, a welcome shore, a city upon a hill."[5] Thus, while the A Beka text opened with an unambiguous affirmation of an exceptionalist, providential rendering of American history, the BJU text closed with one.

The Veritas Omnibus texts are different than the A Beka and BJU texts. *Omnibus*, a Latin term for "all-encompassing," is a series of texts for seventh through twelfth graders. The Omnibus series treated primary and secondary works from the ancient to modern periods in Western culture. Works of literature, political theory, philosophy, theology and history are part of the Omnibus curriculum, and the students read the textbook's essays as guides to separate primary and secondary texts. So, in Omnibus III and VI, students read individual essays written by individual contributors that are based on works such as *1984*, *The Great Gatsby* and *Uncle Tom's Cabin*. Neither Omnibus III or VI is a history textbook per se; however, they are compendia of essays that set the context for primary and secondary source readings.

The Veritas texts are different from A Beka and BJU in another respect. The Omnibus series was based on the classical Christian model of education. In this model, students are taught within an interdisciplinary framework based on the *trivium*: grammar, dialectic and rhetoric. Omnibus III (edited by Douglas Wilson and G. Tyler Fischer), being a ninth-grade text, was situated as a dialectic text, focused on critical thinking. Omnibus VI (edited by Gene Veith, Douglas Wilson, G. Tyler Fischer and Carl L. Petticoffer), a twelfth-grade text, was situated as a rhetoric text, which focused not only on critical thinking skills, but also on the ability to formulate arguments pertinent to the issues raised in the various readings. Gene Veith, author of the preface for Omnibus VI, wrote, "The Christian worldview is *bigger*—more comprehensive, more complicated, richer—than the humanly-devised secular philosophies, which, by their nature, are limited, reductionistic, and partial. Thus, Christians are freed to respond to what they learn in a more complex way, giving credit where credit is due, while also . . . critiquing what needs to be challenged."[6]

The essays for both primary and secondary source readings in Omnibus were divided up into sections: "Author and Context," "Significance," "Setting" and "Worldview." Overall, the texts represented an attempt to train students how to think critically and Christianly about Western civilization. The Omnibus texts were less explicitly exceptionalist because they addressed Western culture as a whole, but whenever the texts addressed issues in American history, the writers of the essays were decidedly exceptionalist in their treatments.

Toward a Responsible Reading and Writing of History

As we consider these Christian history textbooks, we ask, what exactly is history? What do historians do? Is there a historian's craft, and how does one master that craft? What are the tools used in the craft? Is it possible for us who live in the present to know the past objectively or comprehensively? Is history simply "what happened," devoid of any interpretation? Does history teach lessons? And is it appropriate to make moral judgments concerning events and people of the past?

These questions are fundamental to the study of history. As we consider how to study history responsibly, we ought to first define the term *history*, and distinguish history from *memory* and *the past*. Jacques Le

Goff said that *history*, deriving from the ancient Greek words *istor* (one who sees) and *istorein* (to seek to know), entails the pursuit of knowledge. He wrote, "*Istorie* is thus inquiry. That is the sense of the word at the beginning of Herodotus' 'Histories', which are investigations, inquiries."[7] This conception of history stands in contrast with providential history, or history as "his story." Whereas providentialism presumptuously claims to understand God's particular purposes in the progression of events in the past, critical history aims at evidential analysis of the past with humility. Gordon Wood wrote, "Historians attempt to recover a lost world as accurately as possible and try to show how that different world developed into our own."[8]

Have you ever recounted a story from your own past, perhaps of a vacation you took with your family when you were a child, or about a particularly important person like a grandparent or family friend that has been dead for many years? We all have experiences from our past that we remember, some with profound delight and others with regret. Reminiscing over fond shared experiences in the past with friends and family can be some of the most meaningful times in our lives. Our remembrance of personal past is, for most of us, based on our memories. And our memories are what most of our personal "history" consists of—when we speak about our past experiences, we are usually drawing on memories and not much else in the way of physical evidence or primary documents.

Our memories of the past fade with time, and often we find that our memories of the same events are different from those of others who shared those experiences with us. Recently, a couple of cousins and I were recollecting some details of family history, and we could not agree on the actual dates and other particulars of the experiences we had shared together. Since there was no physical evidence available to us which would settle all dispute, we had to agree to disagree.

The point is that there is a difference between memory and history. All too frequently, that which is nothing more than a nation's collective memory of its past passes off as its history. The difference between memory and history is that history is an interpretation of the past based on documentation and records left behind, like letters, pictures, diaries, periodicals, minutes and so forth. Memories are often based on feelings and mental pictures from the past rather than reliable documentary evidence, and are often idealized versions of events and people long gone. Memories can be altered by our nostalgia, purged of their less attractive aspects and cherry-picked based on their utility in the present. Robert Tracy McKenzie characterized collective memory this way: "Typically, only a portion of popular perception of the past is firmly grounded in historical evidence. The other part—often the more entertaining part— consists of stuff somebody made up."[9]

What about *the past*? Are *the past* and *history* the same thing? We often use the terms synonymously, but they are not the same. The past consists of all the events that have taken place, and all the people who have ever lived prior to the present moment. The past includes every-thing—the things with which there is corroborating physical evidence, and the things of which nothing is left. The more distant a particular past episode is to the present, the more strange and different it is to us who live in the here and now. But history is the attempt to make sense of the past. It is written (and read) by people who have presuppositions, biases and personal backgrounds of their own. Historians write history using whatever evidence remains from a past event, and often the evidence that is left represents but a paltry remnant. John Fea observed that "history is a discipline—the art of reconstructing the past."[10] It is a discipline that requires scrupulous attention to detail, an awareness of the enormity of the task and the resulting meekness that comes from the realization that the more diligent our analysis of the past is, the more we recognize how much we do not, and perhaps can never, know.

Memory and history often merge into what historians call a *usable past*. A usable past is a past mined by ideologues for particular infor-mation that they can marshal in support of a political, social, philo-sophical or religious cause. It can also be used for nationalist causes. For example, Smith observed that *ethnohistory* is "the selective, shared memories of successive generations of the members of communities, and the ways in which the generations represent and hand down the tales of the community's past to each other. . . . '[T]he ethnic past' (or pasts) that they reinterpret and reproduce is at once a usable and sacred past."[11] Thus, ethnohistory is a usable past that is laden with transcendence by and for a particular community. Closed exceptionalist civil religion is a form of ethnohistory.

Smith wrote that ethnohistory is powerful because it draws on a belief in a past golden age, a glorious past in which a nation appears in its most authentic form (recall Smith's term, the "cult of authenticity"). A nation's golden age represents a time in which the people were at their height of moral purity. The leaders of the nation were the most wise. And golden ages also represent nations as being at the pinnacle of their prestige, peace and prosperity. Ethnohistory minimizes change over time and seeks continuity between the past golden age and a nation's present age of decline, in order to recover the purity of its past. Smith wrote, "Golden ages provide essential blueprints for realizing the national self and for encouraging the process of collective regeneration. This is what nationalists have in mind when they use the familiar metaphors of 'national awakening,' 'rebirth,' and 'regeneration.'"[12] Thus, ethnohistory is largely concerned with "taking back" the nation and restoring it to its former glory, for which Pat Buchanan—a politician, not a historian—so strongly advocated in August 1992.

History, as an art of reconstructing the past, is at its heart an interpretation of primary resources—artifacts that are contemporary to the particular period the historian considers. Those primary resources are the tools that historians use to reconstruct the past, to make sense of it for us who live in the present. But is history useful for us? Many use history to forward a political agenda, or critique contemporary culture. But historians hesitate to draw useful tidbits from the historical record for advancing an agenda. They are not necessarily looking to "make history relevant." This does not mean that history offers nothing to us in the here and now. Wood said that while history does not offer us specifically applied lessons to any present situation, "history is like experience and old age: wisdom is what one learns from it."[13] McKenzie wrote that studying history is like peering into the night sky and considering one's place under the vast mantle of innumerable stars—"our natural response should be one of wonder and awe and a humbling awareness of our own limitations."[14] And Fea wrote of the historian's task in terms of extending grace to the people of the past who are dead, to extend them "intellectual hospitality." He said, "We need to study history not because it can win us political points or help us push our social and cultural agendas forward, but because it has the amazing potential to transform our lives."[15]

When it comes to drawing wisdom from the past, we must be careful to discern between making normative moral judgments based on history, and reflecting morally on history. McKenzie emphasized the importance of this distinction, especially for a Christian. Moral judgments based on history are problematic, he said, because they require obedience to history where no divine mandate to do so exists. History is not authoritative, so drawing normative moral lessons from a past golden age of national history is not only unwise; it undermines the authority of Scripture by neglecting it and replacing it with another authority. It also places the person making the moral judgment in an artificially privileged position, so that with the Pharisee he demands others be subject to an extrabiblical source of authority arising from his own selfish motivations. Moral reflection, however, is directed selfward. McKenzie wrote that moral judgment "renders a verdict but requires nothing of the knowing heart. Moral reflection is deeply introspective and never leaves the heart untouched."[16]

What then are some general rules for historical thinking? Citing historians Thomas Andrews and Flannery Burke, Fea wrote that historians think about history using five principles, each beginning with the letter C: change over time, context, causality, contingency and complexity. *Change over time* seems obvious, but the principle reminds us that the past is foreign to us who live in the present. Past people lived and thought in vastly different ways, and the deeper the past, the more foreign it is to us. The principle of *context* aids the historian in situating a particular past event in relation to other events in its time. Remembering that events are products of *causality* helps us to consider why events happened the way they did. It also helps us to see events in the larger whole. Understanding that events in history are *contingent* means that there are no inevitabilities in history. Things in the past could have happened differently—nothing occurring in the past was predetermined. Finally, the people and events of the past are stunningly *complex*, more complex than we sometimes recognize. Human nature, free will, ideas, unforeseen consequences, cause-and-effect relationships and a host of other realities converge in time. Furthermore, the historian is left with at best a partial record in the form of primary sources, and her task of reconstructing the past for a present audience can be exceedingly difficult.[17]

Thinking historically does not happen automatically. Not everyone who talks about the past is a historian. The past is not a gold mine to be excavated for valuable nuggets validating a political, social, religious or nationalist agenda. And historians interpret past events and people using evidence and guided by intellectual standards to pursue accuracy and equity in their treatment of the past. Wise historians allow moral principles to rise implicitly from the historical narrative itself, rather than explicitly preaching those moral principles using history as their basis.[18]

How, then, may we evaluate the history texts published by A Beka, Bob Jones and Veritas? Did these widely read Christian school and homeschool curricula engage in thoughtful and responsible Christian historical thinking? Let us turn now to consider these texts, and how they presented history.

EXCEPTIONALISM AND CHRISTIAN SCHOOL HISTORY TEXTS

A primary goal of the A Beka, BJU and Veritas texts was to train students to think Christianly, specifically about the past. This is not only a worthy goal for Christian publishers and writers; it is a vital one. As a faith system, Christianity is necessarily historical. God's revelation to humans is progressive in and through time. His revelation culminated in the person of Jesus Christ. Hebrews 1:1-2 explains the progressive nature of God's revelation like this: "Long ago, at many times and in many ways, God spoke to our fathers by the prophets, but in these last days he has spoken to us by his Son." The life and work of Christ occurred in a specific time span, and his death and resurrection occurred on identifiable dates on the calendar.[19] Christianity as a faith system is not ethnohistorical, not memorial, not legendary and not mythical. It is historical, and as a historical faith, its proponents hold the study of history in the highest esteem. And Christianity provides a firm basis for the study of history, namely, that God created the space-time-matter continuum in which history takes place. And Christianity teaches that, as Creator, God is bringing history to a point in which all things will culminate in the eternal glory and reign of Christ. While humans cannot point specifically to God's purposes in particular historical events (and should not try, absent direct revelation), God has spoken definitively to the fact that he has ultimate purposes to achieve in history, even as he hides many of these purposes from human sight.

So these textbooks not only affirmed a Christian view of history; they each set out to inculcate this perspective in the minds of the students who read them. But in aiming for this goal of training students to think Christianly about the past, they have not pursued the goal of training Christian students to think historically. There is no false choice between thinking Christianly and thinking historically. Since Christianity is a historical faith, it follows that thinking Christianly and thinking historically are eminently compatible. More than that, thinking historically is entailed in thinking Christianly. However, if American exceptionalism is considered an essential aspect of the Christian worldview—essential enough to structure the American historical narrative around it—then a person ceases to think either Christianly or historically.

Each of the three texts presented American history in closed exceptionalist terms. To varying extents, each text was ethnohistorical, morally censorious (rather than morally reflective) and lacking in critical historical thinking. They were ethnohistorical in that closed American exceptionalism was their operating paradigm. Each was morally censorious, because they idealized the past and viewed the present state of America as being in moral and spiritual decline. And they lacked historical thinking in that they failed to account consistently for change over time, complexity and contingency when explaining historical events and trends.

Ethnohistorical (closed exceptionalist).

A Beka text. The text was explicit about its methodology from the beginning—the authors stated, "*United States History* takes a positive, patriotic approach to American history, bringing to life events and personalities that have shaped the nation with a special emphasis on our Christian heritage."[20] Thus, from the outset, the authors bent American history along a religious exceptionalist trajectory, and this trajectory was plain throughout the text. For example, in the section on the drafting and ratification of the Constitution, the authors cast "America's heritage" in classic Christian America thesis terms. "*The secret to America's success is the influence of Biblical Christianity*," the authors emphasized. "'Righteousness exalteth a nation: but sin is a reproach to any people' (Prov. 14:34). . . . Without the moral character rooted in Biblical Christianity, all of the other circumstances with which America has been blessed would be insufficient to maintain a longlasting democratic republic."[21] And in comparing the American Revolution with the French Revolution, the authors argued that America's Revolution was a success and that of the French a failure because America's revolution was Christian and the French was atheistic. In fact, the only analysis of the French Revolution the authors gave was in one paragraph, in which they observed that the French had no "heritage of Biblical Christianity" to serve as a moral guide.[22]

In the section on the Mexican War, the authors treated the settling of Texas in the 1820s and '30s, the tensions between the Texans and the Mexican government over slavery, and the Texas Revolution. When the authors discussed the war between the United States and Mexico, they laid all the fault for the war at the feet of the Mexicans, stressing that President Polk had gone to tremendous lengths to keep the peace, offering $30 million for the purchase of New Mexico and California. The conclusion the authors reached concerning the commencement of hostilities was that Mexico should have acquiesced to American demands. "[Mexico] would have been wise to seriously consider Slidell's offer. It certainly could have used the money, and the New Mexico and California territories . . . seemed likely to be soon swallowed up by Americans anyway, just as Texas had been. But the Mexican government stubbornly claimed all of Texas."[23]

PLUCKED :

THE MEXICAN EAGLE BEFORE THE WAR! °R; THE MEXICAN EAGLE AFTER THE WAR!

Figure 7.1. "Plucked" (1847). This cartoon depicts the American humiliation of Mexico in the Mexican-American War. This brand of sentiment regarding America's war with Mexico is evident in the A Beka text.

Casting America and American foreign policies in righteous terms continued throughout the text's treatment of the nineteenth- and twentieth-century conflicts. As the authors developed their narrative on America's recent past, they gave Presidents Ronald Reagan and George H. W. Bush credit for restoring pride in America after a long period of collective self-doubt during the 1960s and '70s. Reagan built up America's military and overawed the Soviet Union until it collapsed. Bush saw to it that "the legacy of the Reagan years bore fruit" and "America proudly led UN forces in Operation Desert Storm, defending the people of the Middle East."[24] Throughout the text, the authors presented America as morally innocent and more righteous than any other nation in human history.

BJU text. The BJU text was less explicit in its exceptionalist treatment of US history—there were no declarations about exceptionalist methodologies like there were in the A Beka text, at least until the end. Still, the authors' closed exceptionalism was clear at various points in its narrative. For example, in the first chapter, Keesee and Sidwell offered an extended special section on the eastern indigenous tribes that focused on their cultures at the time of English colonization in the seventeenth century. But their treatment was plainly Eurocentric. The authors stressed that "contrary to popular conception, American Indians were not backward savages; they built societies of surprising complexity." Later however, the authors cautioned their readers not to be overly enthusiastic about their sophistication. They wrote, "Too much can be made of Iroquois government and civilization. It was not a democratic republic by any means. Also the Iroquois could be some of the most savage of the American Indians when attacked."[25] These statements naturally raise the questions—What was surprising about the Native Americans' ability to produce complex civilizations? Who doesn't have the capacity to fight savagely when defending themselves? And did the authors grasp the racist undertones to the term *savage* when they wrote the text? Further, why compare the Iroquois confederacy of the seventeenth century to postrevolutionary American-style democracy? And why back off from being too enthusiastic about admiring the richness of native culture and contribution to human civilization? To do so perhaps seemed unfitting to the authors, as they were writing an exceptionalist history of the United States.

By far the most striking exceptionalist language came at the end of the text. As stated above, while the A Beka text laid its exceptionalist cards on the table at the beginning of the book, the BJU authors waited until the end to do so. Amazingly, the authors made a comparison between America and heaven in their statement that "as America was to weary pilgrims long ago, this New World [that is, heaven] will be a refuge, a welcome shore, a city upon a hill."[26] If the reader had any suspicions at all about the authors' use of a closed exceptionalist framework before this statement, then she would have to sweep away any doubts after this statement.

Veritas Texts. The Omnibus III and VI texts, as stated above, are different than their A Beka and BJU counterparts in that they did not treat American history narratively. Instead, when the texts addressed American history, they did so in a focused way using primary and secondary sources. Thus, exceptionalism was not structural in the texts, but it did appear explicitly in some of the essays pertinent to American history. For example, George Grant authored the essay titled "Foundational American Documents" in Omnibus III. Grant presented the Constitution in glowing terms in this essay. He compared the American Constitution with those of other countries and argued that no other political document can compare with the strength and endurance of the American Constitution. Of all the "social contracts, manifestos, national charters and constitutions" appearing in Europe and Latin America, only the US Constitution still exists, according to Grant. Not only that, "there is little doubt that the same fate yet awaits the emerging democracies that have begun dotting the maps of Europe, Asia, and Africa following the collapse of communism." Grant asserted at the close of his essay that the US Constitution is "a creed. It is the very quintessence of American exceptionalism."[27]

Interestingly enough, all three texts compared the American and French Revolutions and concluded that the American Revolution was a Christian-theistically centered and morally superior expression of rebellion than that of the French Revolution. We have already seen how the A Beka text handled the comparison. The BJU text handled it in similar fashion. But the Omnibus texts developed the comparison further than the A Beka or BJU texts in two complete essays: in the Omnibus III essay introducing Edmund Burke's *Reflections on the Revolution in France* and in an Omnibus VI essay titled "The American and French Revolutions Compared," both written by Douglas Wilson, one of the most significant figures in classical Christian education. In both of these essays, Wilson asserted that the term *revolution* was problematic when applied to the American War of Independence. For Wilson, what happened in America was simply a change of government, and this change was wrought by the colonists in an effort to be true to the tradition of self-government that existed in England for centuries. But, Wilson stressed, the chaos in France is rightly called a revolution, because the French overturned every unifying structure in their society. Thus, Wilson could describe the French Revolution as "illegal," "unconstitutional," "radical" and "unrighteous." In contrast, Wilson described the American

Revolution as "legal," "constitutional," "conservative" and "*righteous.*"[28] Thus, the American Revolution was unique and categorically superior to the French Revolution, according to Wilson.

Each text presented American history through the lens of closed exceptionalism. At times, closed exceptionalism was explicit, and at other times, implicit. Nevertheless, closed exceptionalism was a central intellectual paradigm defining their presentations of the past. The result of these texts' slavish devotion to closed exceptionalism was that the authors engaged in moral judgments, came short in moral reflection and failed to think historically.

Morally censorious or lacking in moral reflection.

A Beka text. Sweeping moral judgments appeared in many places in the text, but little moral reflection. This was clear especially in the authors' treatment of nonwhite peoples—Native Americans, African Americans and Latinos. It was also clear in the authors' treatment of recent history, as they looked from their late twentieth-century perspective to the future with a mixture of hope of spiritual recovery and dread of moral collapse.

Particularly in regard to their treatment of slavery in the nineteenth century, the authors' lack of moral reflection is apparent. In the chapter "Slavery and Secession: 1831–1860," the authors included a section titled "The Problem of Slavery." In this page-length section, the authors discussed the problems slavery as an institution presented to Americans in terms of immigration, class divisions and economic hardships. Immigrants had a more difficult time finding work in the South than in the North due to slavery; the upper class accumulated more wealth than any other class in the years leading up to the Civil War; and the planters were burdened with the economic hardship of having to take care of elderly slaves when they could no longer work. According to Lowman, Thompson and Grussendorf, these factors comprised all the problems slavery presented to Americans. The authors failed to include any discussions on contemporary debates on slavery from Scripture; nothing on the abolitionist argument about the inconsistency of slavery in a free society; nothing from a Christian perspective on the ethics of American slavery in general; and nothing on how slavery contributed to the failures of the Constitution. The problems of slavery simply were social and economic, not moral, according to the text.[29]

But the authors were quick to point out moral problems of late twentieth-century America. The authors treated gambling, pornography, homosexuality, crime, greed, abortion and other moral plagues in the final chapter covering the 1990s. According to the authors, the policies of "liberal" politicians were to blame for these blights on American society. The election of Bill Clinton in 1992 occurred mainly because Americans were duped into thinking that the American economy was about to collapse, and the authors expressed their concerns about America's future. After Clinton's election, "traditional values, limited government, and free enterprise economics of the Reagan era came under heavy attack. Yet despite the liberal trends in American society, many Americans committed to the family, the sanctity of life, free enterprise, and other traditional values." Ultimately, the authors insisted, "only a nationwide, spiritual revival can preserve America's heritage of freedom."[30]

BJU text. Keesee and Sidwell failed to offer any historical moral perspective on slavery, like their A Beka counterparts. They offered scant attention to the institution at all until they arrived in their narrative at the nineteenth century and their discussion on the Civil War. They downplayed slavery's significance as a cause of the Civil War, and also minimized Lincoln's moral abhorrence to slavery. In their discussion of the causes of the Civil War, Keesee and Sidwell wrote that "the central issue that sparked the Civil War concerned the nature of the Union"—in other words, state rights was the central issue of the war. And slavery? "Slavery was another issue over which the sections parted company. While the institution of slavery was not the primary cause of the war it was a highly charged, emotionally divisive issue among certain influential groups in the North and South."[31] Just another issue, nothing to see here—and one that was more of an emotional dispute, devoid of substance and limited merely to particular "groups." Not only is this characterization not historically accurate; it fails to account for the immensely complex moral, theological and economic problem of slavery, especially as it was articulated from the 1830s to the 1860s.

In fact, the BJU text had an element of the Southern Lost Cause in its treatment of the end of the war and the start of Reconstruction. The problem the authors found with the assassination of Lincoln was that "the hateful and vindictive men [the Radical Republicans in the Senate] would have their way in the South."[32] And as they brought their presentation of the Civil War to a close, they called on Jefferson Davis to give the Civil War chapter's final word through his last presidential address from Danville: "Let us not then despond, my countrymen . . . let us meet the foe with fresh defiance, with unconquered and unconquerable hearts." The South, according to Keesee and Sidwell, "was an impoverished land of widows and orphans where the wounds of war were nursed in bitterness until the scars became badges of pride."[33] Aside from the question of historical equity in casting the war in these terms, the lack of moral discernment in the authors' treatment of slavery, the Civil War and its aftermath is perplexing.

In like fashion with the A Beka text, while there was little historical moral discussion on the institution of slavery or Jim Crow, it was abundant when the BJU authors discussed the period of the 1970s to 1990s. The Clinton years, Keesee and Sidwell wrote, were a time when moral decline was at its steepest. The authors depicted late twentieth-century American moral decline mainly through the lens of the gay rights movement and the Lewinsky scandal. And like the authors of the A Beka text, the BJU authors were both hopeful and fearful of the future. "In a humanistic and often hostile society that has drifted far from its spiritual moorings, perhaps the opposition to such Christian leadership has never been greater, but then neither has the opportunity for Christian service been greater."[34]

Veritas Texts. Omnibus III included an essay introducing some of the slave narratives that were compiled through New Deal legislation during the 1930s. The inclusion of these narratives is both original and helpful for a high school audience, making Omnibus III a unique secondary-school textbook. The essay, "Slave Narratives," was written by Douglas Wilson and G. Tyler Fischer. The authors' characterization of slavery in this essay is problematic from a historical and moral perspective—they argued that slavery per se was not necessarily ethically wrong in part because Jesus did not preach against it. They urged that if masters had treated their slaves ethically, and slaves had submitted humbly according to biblical standards laid down in Ephesians 6, Colossians 3 and 1 Timothy 6, then American slavery could have survived. So, Wilson and Fischer asserted, "the believing slave ought to work even more gladly, because the recipient of his efforts [the master] is a faithful and beloved brother."[35]

Aside from the fact that (1) this was a simply terrible way to characterize the plight of American slaves and (2) this argument situated Wilson and Fischer squarely within the antebellum proslavery intellectual tradition, Wilson failed to apply the same standards he used in his characterization of slavery to the American colonists fighting the Revolution. Ultimately, for Wilson, the gospel of Christ must settle all injustice and animosity in human relationships. He argued this point in his treatment of the French Revolution as well as in the essay he wrote with Fischer on the slave narratives. "For us as Christians, we have to realize that the solution to political turmoil and revolution has to be the gospel. . . . *Unbelief had to be seen as the deepest cause of all the cultural troubles, and the gospel was the only answer.*"[36]

Indeed, it is hard for a Christian to disagree. But for Wilson to come along later in a separate essay comparing the American and French Revolutions and declare the American Revolution as "righteous" is inconsistent with his earlier call to trust in the gospel for the correction of all injustice. Wilson applied Ephesians 6, Colossians 3 and 1 Timothy 6 to say that slaves should have graciously submitted to their masters as their brothers in Christ and "work as unto the Lord." But he neglected to apply Romans 13:1-5 or 1 Peter 2:13-17 to the American colonists in 1775–1783, both passages that admonish believers to submit to the ruling authorities.[37] If injustice is rooted in unbelief in the gospel, and if belief in the gospel rights all wrongs, and following the New Testament is an act of belief in the gospel—then why did Wilson characterize the American Revolution, a bloody "change in government,"[38] as "righteous"? Why would Wilson call for slaves to submit, but not call for the colonists to do the same? This inconsistency between the essays that Wilson authored and coauthored in the two Omnibus texts (both texts of which he served as one of the general editors) reveals a stunning lack of moral reflection on slavery and the American Revolution, and instead, the presence of a closed exceptionalist agenda in his attempt at writing history.

Lacking in historical thinking. All three texts have significant blind spots in the ways their authors wrote about the past. Considering the five Cs of historical thinking, the A Beka, BJU and Veritas texts consistently failed to account for change over time, complexity and contingency of past events. This is partly due to the fact that the texts' authors closely observed the paradigm of closed American exceptionalism in their writing of history. Each in their unique ways, the authors of these texts accepted the Christian America thesis, the assertion that America was founded on biblical principles and that this biblical founding is the basis of special and unique divine favor. In particular, in the way each text treated the success of the Revolution, their comparisons of the American and French Revolutions, and their minimizing the moral evil of slavery and its primary importance to the failure of the Constitution and the resulting Civil War, they situated America in a divinely privileged and sacrosanct position in relation to other nations.

They also cast America's past as a sort of golden age—in Smith's ethno-historical terms, an age in which America enjoyed its most authentic form, in contrast with the moral decline of the late twentieth century. Seeking continuity with this golden age, each text called for a national recovery of perceived past moral and spiritual purity. The A Beka and BJU texts stressed the need for Christian leaders to rise up and lead the way back to this golden age. Lowman, Thompson and Grussendorf wrote that "America's future rests in the hands of her people, and God's people bear the greatest responsibility. As salt and light, Christians must strive to hold back the evil and preserve the good in America."[39] Keesee and Sidwell, reflecting on the spiritual greatness of the veteran soldiers suffering at Valley Forge and the towering faithfulness of Stonewall Jackson, wrote, "At no time in America's history has there been a greater need for such spiritual leaders driven by the compelling demands of Calvary."[40] And O. Woelke Leithart, in his Omnibus VI essay, "Foundational American Documents," argued for a hermeneutical framework for the Constitution similar to that which Christians use to interpret the Bible. Leithart suggested that the Constitution should be interpreted as a fixed document, as if it were transcendent and eternal like the Bible, without accounting for human fallibility, the historical context of its production or the change over time since the eighteenth century. He wrote that, in the past, "we treated words—laws and contracts—as words that were binding and permanent." Since the words of both the Constitution and Scripture were both "binding and permanent," the Supreme Court "would have a firm foundation concerning the meaning of words and how those meanings are connected to the meaning of the words when they were penned." Furthermore, and most importantly, Leithart lamented, "had the Supreme Court been following biblical principles . . . it would not have sanctioned activities like abortion, because the Constitution does not speak to them explicitly."[41] This longing for continuity over time, rather than acknowledging the reality of change over time, presents a problem for closed exceptionalist history writing. Acknowledging change over time undermines the concept of the golden age, first by questioning the validity of such a concept, and second by rendering the aspects of such an age as nonbinding on the present.

CONCLUSION

To echo the apostle Paul, "What then shall we say to these things?" Is there a way to celebrate American uniqueness, American glories and American contributions to human flourishing without the triumphalism and ethnohistory of closed exceptionalism? I believe that it is hard to argue that America is not a special and unique place. As a Christian, I also believe it is hard to argue that America has not been divinely blessed as a haven of freedom, opportunity and material bounty. And it is fair to say that America has played a major role in helping the cause of justice where injustice has made human life wretched in the world. So in these respects, yes, America is an exceptional place and has an exceptional history. Also, students of every religious faith commitment can and should be taught to be thankful and proud of America, and that patriotic fervor is, on the whole, a desirable and wholly appropriate thing.

Open American exceptionalism affirms that America has been a force for justice, as well as a force for injustice. Historically, open exceptionalism allows for the complexity of American history. American history is not simply a narrative of a nation's journey from "strength to strength," or one righteous triumph to another. American history reveals ambiguity in Americans' behavior and faithfulness to the principles on which the nation was founded. Americans have been true, false and indifferent to their stated ideals over time. There is no golden age to go back to, no glorious past to recover or to "take back." America consists of Americans, who are flawed and fallible human beings. Americans have set themselves on a pursuit of justice, of equality, of opportunity and of natural rights and freedoms. But Americans of every generation have continually struggled to understand what those things mean, how they are to be applied and who gets to enjoy them to their fullest extent. Religious people have always been influential in these issues, but even religious people who are dedicated to divine principles sometimes fail to see clearly and act faithfully. All people, including Christians, succumb to selfishness, shortsightedness, violence and vice. The human condition is complex, thus the American condition is complex. American history is therefore complex. Open exceptionalism, as a concept, allows for the historical realities of change over time, context, causality, complexity and contingency.

Most importantly, if our goal as Christians is to teach younger generations how to think Christianly, then we who teach and write history and theology must both think historically and think Christianly. It will not do to equate patriotic fervor with Christian spirituality. It is not appropriate to consider American exceptionalism—closed or open—as an essential aspect of the Christian worldview. America is not God's chosen nation; it does not exist in some specially privileged position with God. And whatever God's sovereign plan is for America in his overall program for human history, no man, no woman, no child can know it because

God has not spoken it. The Christian worldview is animated by the person and work of Jesus Christ, and no person, no nation, no power can add or detract from who he is and what he has done—America included.

McKenzie spoke about C. S. Lewis's observation that humans are tempted to "link our commitment to Christ too closely with one or more of our other group attachments."[42] As American Christians, this often occurs when we associate patriotism with spirituality. Evangelical churches are guilty of this all the time, especially around Memorial Day and Independence Day. Pledges to the flag, singing patriotic hymns, extolling the glorious dead and their sacrifices on our behalf for the cause of freedom—these are all things we Christians often do alongside the worship of Christ during the time we set aside for our sacred corporate gathering around prayer, the Scriptures and the sacred ordinances. Does it not seem strange and contradictory that we who affirm the sole supremacy of Christ exult over American glory at the same time and place we gather to confess that "Jesus is Lord"? Patriotic expressions of gratitude to those who have given their lives for our country *are* important and necessary. But for us Christians, those expressions should be vitally separate from expressions of our unique and (truly) sacred devotion to Christ. McKenzie wrote, "When the boundaries between [patriotism and spirituality] become blurred, we fall prey to what Lewis called 'Christianity And,' a state of confusion in which it becomes easy to mix up means and ends and increasingly difficult to think clearly about the world around us."[43] May it not be so for American Christians.

FOR FURTHER READING

Cheng, Eileen Ka-May. *The Plain and Noble Garb of Truth: Nationalism and Impartiality in American Historical Writing, 1784–1860*. Athens: University of Georgia Press, 2011.

Fea, John. *Why Study History? Reflecting on the Importance of the Past*. Grand Rapids: Baker, 2013.

McKenzie, Robert Tracy. *The First Thanksgiving: What the Real Story Tells Us About Loving God and Learning from History*. Downers Grove, IL: IVP Academic, 2013.

Molho, Anthony, and Gordon S. Wood, eds. *Imagined Histories: American Historians Interpret the Past*. Princeton: Princeton University Press, 1998.

Wilsey, John D. *One Nation Under God? An Evangelical Critique of Christian America*. Eugene, OR: Pickwick, 2011.

Wood, Gordon S. *Revolutionary Characters: What Made the Founders Different*. New York: Penguin, 2006.

Open Exceptionalism and Civic Engagement

The scars and foibles and contradictions of the Great do not diminish but enhance the worth and meaning of their upward struggle.

W. E. B. Du Bois, 1922

In 1922, when W. E. B. Du Bois wrote in *The Crisis* that Abraham Lincoln was "of illegitimate birth, poorly educated and unusually ugly, awkward, ill-dressed," and that he was a man of profound inconsistency, "[both] despising Negroes and letting them fight and vote; protecting slavery and freeing slaves," many of his readers took offense.[1] His African American audience rightly remembered Lincoln as their great liberator, and many of Du Bois's readers could not add nuance to their conceptions of him. A few months later, Du Bois addressed those concerned readers, calling them to seek the whole truth of the matter and not merely an imagined ideal picture of the truth. He wrote of Lincoln, "I love him not because he was perfect but because he was not and yet triumphed."[2]

Open exceptionalism is an expression of patriotism like Du Bois's expression of love for Lincoln. At the heart of what it means to be an American is the act of calling America back to faithfulness to its first principles motivated by authentic patriotism. In an open exceptionalist account of America, we affirm that America is different because it is a nation in which dissent is not only allowed; it is a virtue. Dissenting colonists in the eighteenth century, after all, birthed the nation. Open exceptionalism opens the door for citizens to acknowledge, to address and to rectify real American flaws because, in so doing, citizens express true love for country.

We witness a clash between open and closed exceptionalism in a 1957 letter from Du Bois to Secretary of State John Foster Dulles. The State Department refused to issue Du Bois and his wife passports to travel to

Figure 8.1. William Edward Burghardt Du Bois

Ghana to attend its celebrations as a newly independent nation. This was despite the fact that the Ghanian people, led by Kwame Nkrumah, had invited the Du Boises. Not only that, Du Bois had been instrumental in establishing the Pan-African congresses that stood against European colonial rule. Du Bois wrote to Dulles to protest the situation, stating that he had committed no crimes to warrant the government's limiting of his freedom to travel. True, Du Bois wrote, he had criticized the United States on a number of occasions. But he also gave it credit when credit was due. Du Bois challenged Dulles to be true to the American ideals of personal liberty, human dignity and self-determination. These were, in fact, ideals on which the two of them agreed when they personally met during the formation of the United Nations. Du Bois reminded Dulles,

When, Sir, in 1945 in San Francisco, I had an interview with you, we discussed the trustee provisions of the United Nations charter then in process of formation. I got from that talk an impression of your sympathy with Africa and hostility towards the colonial system. If I was right, I trust this was still your attitude and that you realize that Africa is starting forward and is asking not simply for investment in South Africa and the Belgian Congo, but recognition of black folk as human beings and citizens of a modern state. I therefore write to ask permission to visit Ghana on this occasion in response to their repeated requests, on the first day of the ninetieth year of my life.[3]

In this letter, we see a member of a socially rejected and persecuted minority appealing to a member of the dominant group, one who was a high-ranking officer of the American government, for justice in the name of the ideals upon which the United States was founded. Du Bois's letter represents an act of civic engagement in the spirit of open exceptionalism— a citizen explicitly addressing a problem in American society in order to help rectify it. In this act of civic engagement, Du Bois expressed some of the highest American ideals—both in the act of writing and in the content of his writing.

We have come to the close of this book on American exceptionalism as an aspect of civil religion. In this concluding chapter, we will consider why exceptionalism as a civil religious belief matters. In short, open exceptionalist civil religion provides a basis for unity in the midst of diversity. Because of this, open exceptionalism fosters positive civic engagement by holding forth the ideals expressed in the American civil religious canon, recognizing that those ideals are always among the worthiest of goals for Americans to continually pursue within their national community.

Beyond mere national "team spirit," American exceptionalism matters because it generates powerful assumptions in citizens' minds about their national identity. Exceptionalist assumptions—unstated reasons people hold to justify their words and actions in the public square—entail ramifications affecting how they engage society. Furthermore, Christian people in particular have a long history of civic engagement going back to the early centuries of the church in the Roman Empire. Specifically, Christian Americans have always been engaged in culture, and indeed, Christian ideas were deeply influential (but not exclusive) in the nation's founding.[4]

Many Christians assume that God chose America to be his special people to do his work in the world. Many uncritically accept patriotic expressions as a part of church worship services. Christians often sing songs linking patriotic devotion with love for God and think little about what the words mean and how those words fit into their overall theological matrix of beliefs. For many Christian people, patriotism equals spirituality because their assumption is that America is God's country. Anyone who stands with America is, therefore, holy, good and just. Anyone who stands against America is scandalous, immoral—perhaps even demonic.

By linking the American nation with God in the ways we have seen in this book, closed American exceptionalism produces harmful assumptions leading to a form of civic engagement that divides people into groups, namely, the Chosen and the Inferior Other. Closed exceptionalism takes the ideals like federal democracy, individual freedom, equality, natural rights and government by consent and spiritualizes them, so that they become normative and binding in their uniquely American expression for all people at all times regardless of contingent factors. Closed exceptionalism breeds injustice.

Open exceptionalism is an intellectual framework that situates American ideals in history and experience. It accounts for flaws and imperfections in the American nation. Open exceptionalism does not envision a nation divided into groups, but one united around commonly held ideals applied to all and places enjoyed by all. And open exceptionalism does not conflict with Christian teaching by idealizing or idolizing the nation.

An open exceptionalist civil religion potentially brings unity out of a diverse populace. One of the ways it promotes unity is through symbols and practices. For example, Arlington National Cemetery is a powerful civil religious symbol. Arlington is a hallowed place Americans set aside for those who gave the full measure of devotion to their country, that they may rest in their graves. As you enter the grounds of the cemetery, you see signs admonishing all visitors to observe "silence and respect." The signs are everywhere, but most visitors do not need reminding.

During the height of the tourist season, you will find people from a wide variety of ethnic, linguistic, (presumably) religious and national backgrounds. You will find children, teenagers, young adults and elderly people. Many are visiting graves of loved ones, but most of them are there to see John F. Kennedy's tomb, the Tomb of the Unknowns, and the rows of neatly laid out plots and headstones. The majority of the visitors exhibit unity through their respectful behavior, as well as their observance of the civil religious practice of visiting the cemetery. There are a host of symbols and practices in American civil religion, and vast majorities of Americans generally know and understand them and demonstrate solidarity when practicing them. Peter Gardella referred to the displays of the Declaration of Independence and the Constitution at the National Archives in Washington, DC—two documents of the American "Old Testament" canon—saying that "every day, people from around the world line up—many with an attitude that resembles that of pilgrims—to visit these documents."[5] Gardella identified four values that bring coherence to civil religion: "Personal freedom . . . , political democracy, world peace, and cultural . . . tolerance."[6] While more values could be added to the list, and while not everyone agrees on the exact definitions for these values, Gardella insisted that these values "are denied by no one who claims to speak in the tradition of the United States."[7]

Open exceptionalist civil religion focuses on these liberal ideas. But they are more accurately understood as values more than they are hard and fast doctrines. They are ideals that Americans perennially pursue, and often fail to attain. Nevertheless, Americans have shown themselves to be a uniquely self-examining people, with a remarkable ability to reflect on past mistakes and work to avoid repeating them. This does not mean Americans are always successful. But a strong reforming tradition historically exists among Americans, and American history can be read largely as a series of often logically connected, social, political, economic and religious reforms in the direction of human flourishing and freedom.

Gardella wrote that most Americans come to accept the open exceptionalist values of civil religion not through reason but through symbols. "They have learned to value liberty, democracy, peace, and tolerance

through the monuments, texts, and images of American civil religion."[8]
If Gardella is right, and I believe he is, then an open exceptionalist account of civil religion shows that Americans have much more in common than they may think—during a national election cycle, for example, or while waiting for a controversial Supreme Court decision. And such a civil religion allows religious people to practice their faith untainted by a militant, closed exceptionalist Americanism that effectually diverts attention away from the truly sacred and toward national glory, which is merely fleeting.

An Open Exceptionalist Model for Civic Engagement

Perhaps the first task before Christian people, when considering what open exceptionalist civic engagement looks like, is to differentiate the church from the nation while situating the church within the national community. By doing this, Christians understand that patriotism does not equate to spirituality. By simultaneously distancing the church from the nation and placing it within the nation, Christians need not sacrifice their unique confession of faith, their loyalty to the nation or their prophetic voice when the nation acts unjustly.

One of the earliest Christian voices to situate the church in relation to the nation was the second-century apologist Justin Martyr (ca. 114–165). Justin addressed his *First Apology* directly to the Roman emperor Antoninus Pius (r. 138–161), to the Senate and to the Roman people. In the *Apology*, he sought justice for the Christians—a socially rejected and persecuted minority in the Roman Empire. Appealing to reason and good faith, Justin sought to clarify what Christians believed, dispel evil rumors about them and demonstrate their unmatched loyalty to the nation. Justin's *Apology* is helpful for Christians today who confuse America with the kingdom of heaven. America is not the kingdom, and American patriotism does not equate to godly devotion. But sacrificial loyalty to the nation is not incompatible with the faith, provided that Christians follow Christ's admonition in Mark 12:17 to "render to Caesar the things that are Caesar's, and to God the things that are God's."

Justin wrote that the Christians were not seeking after an earthly kingdom, but a heavenly kingdom. In this, they were following Christ's statement to Pontius Pilate while he stood trial prior to being crucified: "My kingdom is not of this world" (John 18:36). Justin said, "If we looked for a human kingdom, we should also deny our Christ, that we might not be slain. . . . But since our thoughts are not fixed on the present, we are not concerned when men cut us off."[9] Nevertheless, Justin wrote, it was impossible for the emperor to find more loyal subjects among the Romans than the Christians. "And more than all other men are we your helpers and allies in promoting peace, seeing that we hold this view that it is alike impossible for the wicked . . . to escape the notice of God," Justin wrote.[10] In other words, Christians were the most loyal subjects of the empire, because in their subjection to the emperor they were demonstrating their subjection to God. Christians' love for God, the greatest of duties, moved them to bow before Caesar, the civil authority established over them by God.

Christians' loyalty to Rome, according to Justin, reached even to absurd levels, at least to human eyes. Again, love for God and obedience to Christ's specific commands motivated this absurd loyalty. "And concerning our being patient of injuries, and ready to serve all, and free from anger, this is what [Christ] said: 'To him that smiteth thee on the one cheek, offer also the other; and him that taketh away thy cloak or coat, forbid not. . . . And let your good works shine before men, that they, seeing them, may glorify your Father which is in heaven.'" Justin quoted Luke 6:29 and Matthew 5:16 to demonstrate the lengths Christians would go to show their loyalty to Rome. In fact, Justin told the emperor and Senate, Christians even paid the tax collectors every penny they were assessed, even when the collectors raised those taxes by extortion. "And everywhere we, more readily than all men, endeavor to pay to those appointed by you the taxes both ordinary and extraordinary as we have been taught by Him." Still, even while the Christians went to these great extents to demonstrate their submission and loyalty to Rome, there were limits. Justin wrote, "Whence to God alone we render worship, but in other things we gladly serve you, acknowledging you as kings and rulers of men, and praying that with your kingly power you be found to possess also sound judgment."[11] In other words, God alone was due worship and first-order love and obedience; yet Caesar was God's established ruler over all things of a civil nature for the Christians.

Thus, Justin situated the church within the Roman imperial order. No one was more devoted to the flourishing of Roman society than the Christians. No one served the emperor more faithfully and with more subservience than the Christians. The Christians even paid extorted tax monies in the spirit of Christ's teaching: "Him that taketh away thy cloak forbid not to take thy coat also" (Luke 6:29 KJV). And even though the Romans persecuted the Christians, Justin wrote, the Christians were committed to love their persecutors. "And of our love to all, [Christ] taught thus: 'If ye love them that love you, what new thing do ye? for even fornicators do this. But I say unto you, Pray for your enemies, and love them that hate you, and bless them that curse you, and pray for them that despitefully use you.'"[12] And yet, Justin reminded his hearers, Christians worshiped neither Rome nor its emperor, but God alone. "But just so much power have rulers who esteem opinion more than truth, as robbers have in a desert. And that you will not succeed is declared by the Word, than whom, after God who begat [Christ], we know there is no ruler more kingly and just," wrote Justin.[13] Here he insisted that Rome's persecution of the Christians would not succeed in blotting them out. Rome's rulers, in unjustly pursuing the Christians, were destined by God to fail in their attempts because they were also under the rule of God. Justin said, "If you pay no regard to our prayers and frank explanations, we shall suffer no loss, since we believe . . . that every man will suffer punishment in eternal fire according to the merit of his deed, and will render account according to the power he has received from God."[14]

An open exceptionalist civil religion affirms how Justin situated the church within the nation. The church and the nation are distinct. While the civil leaders are established by God (see Romans 13:1-5), they are not flawless. While the nation is devoted to high ideals like religious freedom, the nation is not morally regenerate. This conception of the nation cannot be styled, "America, right or wrong" or "America, love it or leave it." Authentic patriotism—taking the form of sacrificial devotion and love for the national community—is entirely appropriate. But when the nation offends justice, then the church must find its prophetic voice and call the nation to amend its ways. Martin Luther King Jr. was such a prophet. So was W. E. B. Du Bois.

Du Bois was one of the most prolific writers and profound thinkers in American history. His thought and writings cover a multitude of topics, and he conducted his ideas through a variety of literary genres such as history, fiction and poetry. I like to refer to Du Bois as a black Aristotle, because like the ancient tutor of Alexander, his thought and writings are so ample, innovative and profound. He lived into his nineties, and few lived a richer, more productive life. His voice rang through the America of Jim Crow and inspired millions of blacks to stand against the innumerable limitations, injuries and indignities placed upon them by official American persecution. In fact, Du Bois's voice is, in many ways, like Justin's. Like Justin, Du Bois was a member of a persecuted minority. Like Justin, Du Bois appealed to a Christian ethic in his plea for justice. Like Justin, Du Bois warned a racist American society that God would not abide wickedness forever. And like Justin, Du Bois exposed false Christianity and explained true Christianity to those hypocritical ones professing the faith but refusing to live by the faith. Just as Justin wrote to Emperor Antoninus Pius, Du Bois wrote to President Woodrow Wilson in 1913, "We want to be treated as men. . . . We want lynching stopped. We want no longer to be herded as cattle on street cars and railroads." Further, he appealed to the best of American ideals in his letter to Wilson in behalf of African Americans chafing under institutional racism: "In the name of that common country for which your fathers and ours have bled and toiled, be not untrue, President Wilson, to the highest ideals of American Democracy."[15] Note that Du Bois emphasized that it was not whites alone who sacrificed all for the nation. African Americans had borne the burden for liberty alongside whites; they had earned their rightful place as equally valuable and acknowledged citizens in American polity and society.

Du Bois has been characterized by many historians as irreligious, or even anti-Christian. Nothing could be further from the truth. Edward J.

Blum demonstrated this fact in his religious biography of Du Bois, sub-titled *American Prophet*. Describing the presence of religion in Du Bois's life and writings, Blum said it was "ubiquitous." Blum wrote, "Du Bois was an American prophet; he was a moral historian, a visionary sociol-ogist, a literary theologian, and a mythological hero with a black face." By the end of his life in 1963, Blum said, "Du Bois became a rogue saint and a dark monk to preach the good news of racial brotherhood, eco-nomic cooperation, and peace on earth."[16]

But Du Bois was not a Christian according to the pattern of early to mid-twentieth-century Christianity, defined as it was in America by a white culture that systematically oppressed him and his race. Christi-anity, as defined by whites, was a perversion of true Christianity because it was built on racial hubris. Du Bois said that "white Christianity is a miserable failure" because, in its racial superiority over African Amer-icans, whites "denied Christ" by "claiming super-humanity" and consis-tently "scoff endlessly at our shortcomings."[17] In contrast, African Amer-icans embodied the truest form of Christian ethics as they bore up under institutionalized racism. Concerning faithfulness to the teachings of Christ and the Golden Rule, Du Bois said, "In these matters the American black man occupies a singular place . . . [in that] he himself as a group exemplifies Christian ethics to an astonishing degree; he represents the meek and the lowly; he has been 'slow to wrath and plenteous in mercy.' He has attempted . . . to forgive his enemies and turn the other cheek."[18] In holding out African Americans' faithfulness to Christ's ethical stan-dards to the persecuting majority, Du Bois reads much like Justin, who advocated for the Christians in Rome during the second century in similar ways.

Du Bois eloquently described some of his most cherished convic-tions at the beginning of his work *Darkwater*, published in 1920. In his "Credo," Du Bois explained his vision of justice and brotherhood of all humanity, regardless of artificial racial distinctions. He wrote, "I believe in God who made of one blood all nations that on earth do dwell. I believe that all men, black and brown and white, are brothers, varying through time and opportunity, in form and gift and feature, but differing in no essential particular, and alike in soul and the possibility of infinite development."[19]

This belief animated his belief in the sinfulness of racist America in the early and mid-twentieth century. In *Dusk of Dawn*, Du Bois inserted a fictional character to illustrate and explain this racism. Du Bois's character is a white man of stature in American society—an Episcopalian, a Republican, an opera enthusiast, a member of the American Legion, with a host of other associations. And he is middle-aged, married, making an income of $10,000 per year. His pastor, the Reverend J. Simpson Stodges, DD,

> preaches to him Sundays (except July, August, and September) a doctrine that sounds like this . . . : Peace on Earth is the message of Christ, the Divine leader of men; that this means Good Will to all human beings; that it means Freedom, Toleration of the mistakes, sins, and shortcomings of not only your friends but of your enemies. That the Golden Rule of Christianity is to treat others as you want to be treated, and that finally you should be willing to sacrifice your comfort, your convenience, your wealth, and even your life for mankind.[20]

Rev. Stodges's preaching sounds good, until he tells the man that, since "we can't always attain the heights, much less live in their rarefied atmosphere," then the thing to do was to "at least live like a Gentleman with the 'G' capitalized."[21]

Since the preacher taught that the Christian moral system was entirely unattainable, and thus futile, the logic brought the upstanding man from "Christian" to "Gentleman." As a "Gentleman," he is concerned about his country's standing on the international scene, especially during the conflagration of World War I in Europe. Concern for America logically entails a further progression from "Gentleman" to "American." As an "American," the man believes he is to support the country no matter what, "thick and thin," and that America "must sit among the great powers of the earth." America should be considered by other nations "as a sort of super-power, umpire of humanity, tremendous, irresistible."[22] From these hyperpatriotic sentiments, logic brought the man to the final stage of "White Man." As "White Man," he realized that "his whiteness was fraught with tremendous responsibilities" and that "colored folks were a threat to the world. They were going to overthrow white folk by sheer weight of numbers, destroy their homes and marry their daughters."[23] As "White Man," the man's attitudes toward the world were defined by "War, Hate, Suspicion and Exploitation."[24]

Each stage of mental, spiritual and emotional development in this man—Christian, Gentleman, American and White Man—was defined by a set of codes. In table 8.1 we see how the progression of stages logically took shape along with their corresponding codes.

Table 8.1. Character development in Du Bois's *Dusk of Dawn*

Christian	Gentleman	American	White Man
Peace	Justice	Defense	War
Good Will	Manners	Caste	Hate
Golden Rule	Exclusiveness	Propaganda	Suspicion
Liberty	Policy	Patriotism	Exploitation
Poverty	Wealth	Power	Empire

In Du Bois's fictional story of the white man's progression from Christianity to militant white supremacy, we see a progression from Christianity to closed American exceptionalism. But we must understand Du Bois's warning. First, it is important to note carefully that Du Bois was *not* saying that Christianity per se leads to closed exceptionalism. Recall that Rev. Stodges preached a good message, but divorced his message from reality in his conversation with the man. The Christian message, for Stodges, was an impossible ideal, a futile aspiration. The best anyone could hope for, according to Stodges, was to live like a gentleman. So, the white supremacy of closed American exceptionalism logically flowed *not* from the Christian ethic but from the denial of its truth and power in favor of something counterfeit. Thus, from this *counterfeit* ethic logically flowed the white supremacy of closed exceptionalism.

Many Christians today, in their conflation of the Christian message with Americanism resulting in closed exceptionalism, exhibit similar patterns of thought. They hear Christianity taught and preached. They read the gospel in their Bibles. But many professing Christians wave off the Christian ethic with sayings like, "Christians aren't perfect, just forgiven." Or, they envision God as an American, who continually reminds his chosen nation that "if my people who are called by name humble themselves, and pray and seek my face and turn from their wicked ways, then I will hear from heaven and will forgive their sin and heal their land" (2 Chronicles 7:14). And they take Christ's words to his disciples, which he gave to them in the upper room the night of his betrayal to explain the meaning of his impending death—"Greater love has no one than this, that someone lay down his life for his friends" (John 15:13)—and apply them particularly to American soldiers dying in battle.

The problem with these, and many other Americanized distortions of the gospel, is not that they are patently false. There is some truth to each of these platitudes. But if we honestly evaluate them biblically, these platitudes amount to a counterfeit, Americanized Christianity. They lead well-meaning Christian people down a path to closed American exceptionalism, and to potential for wrong in the name of right.

Du Bois, in the style of a prophet, warned Americans of this downward progression in *Dusk of Dawn* and a host of other writings. While the rock bottom of this progression was militant white supremacy, a key step was closed exceptionalism, the idea that America was always right and must be defended and justified at all costs. The irony of Du Bois was that even though he was not, strictly speaking, an orthodox evangelical Protestant, he had a better understanding of the disconnect between the Christian gospel and exceptionalist religious nationalism than many, if not most, church people of his day. Blum put it this way: "The supposedly irreligious Du Bois seemed to have more faith in the social power of Christianity than many of its proclaimed believers."[25]

Juxtaposing Justin and Du Bois in an attempt to build an open American exceptionalist model for civic engagement may seem strange. They lived seventeen centuries apart and in vastly different historical situations. But both were members of a persecuted minority. Both voiced messages of justice, brotherhood and freedom. Both sought to capture the meaning of the Christian ethic and apply that ethic to the public square. And both Justin and Du Bois registered dissenting voices from the respective majorities of their times. In these ways, they model an open exceptionalist civic engagement that was edifying and enduring. Dissent in the direction of just reform is squarely within the American civic tradition. Many of the most dedicated American patriots were those who raised their voices to call their country back to the liberal ideals at the basis of the nation's founding. Many of those patriots were professing Christians, although they represented a variety of denominational, confessional and practical differences. But the open exceptionalist model for civic engagement tends toward justice—where every person receives their due, and where each is afforded the dignity they deserve as being created in the image of God.

Ronald Reagan, when he spoke to the National Association of Evangelicals in Orlando, Florida, in 1983, was best remembered for calling the Soviet Union an "evil empire." In fact, most people may not remember anything about that speech except that particular reference. In reality, Reagan spoke about a variety of issues, and he did not get to the Soviet "evil empire" until close to the conclusion of the speech. For instance, he spoke about the injustice of abortion, saying "until it can be proven that the unborn child is not a living entity, then its right to life, liberty, and the pursuit of happiness must be protected."[26] He also spoke about the injustice of racism, particularly in the churches. He urged the gathered clergy in attendance to "use the mighty voice of your pulpits and the powerful standing of your churches to denounce and isolate these hate groups in our midst. The commandment given us is clear and simple: 'Thou shalt love thy neighbor as thyself.'"[27] Interestingly, Reagan used a line from a document in the American civil religious canon and a reference from the Bible to extol not just an American, but a human, ideal: the dignity of every human soul. Du Bois often used the same method to emphasize the same ideal. In this way, perhaps Reagan and Du Bois—two figures not often associated together—are alike in important ways. To be sure, Reagan and Du Bois would have parted ways on many, if not most, social, economic and political issues. But on the broad values of American civil religion, especially as Gardella identified them—liberty, democracy, world peace and cultural tolerance—there is likely more common ground between them than not. As Du Bois would likely have heartily agreed with Reagan's words on basic human dignity for the defenseless and oppressed, Reagan would likely have resonated with this prayer on humility from Du Bois. May it be so for each of us.

> May the Lord give us both the honesty and strength to look our own faults squarely in the face and not ever continue to excuse or minimize them, while they grow. Grant us that wide view of ourselves which our neighbors possess, or better the highest view of infinite justice and goodness and efficiency. In that great white light let us see the littleness and narrowness of our souls and the deeds of our days, and then forthwith begin their betterment. Only thus shall we broaden out of the vicious circle of our own admiration into the greater commendation of God. Amen.[28]

FOR FURTHER READING

Blum, Edward J. *W. E. B. Du Bois: American Prophet.* Philadelphia: University of Pennsylvania Press, 2007.

Du Bois, W. E. B. *W. E. B. Du Bois: Writings.* Edited by Nathan Huggins. New York: Library of America, 1986.

Hawkins, J. Russell, and Phillip Luke Sinitiere. *Christians and the Color Line: Race and Religion After "Divided by Faith."* Oxford: Oxford University Press, 2014.

Sommer, Carl J. *We Look for a Kingdom: The Everyday Lives of the Early Christians.* San Francisco: Ignatius Press, 2007.

Tocqueville, Alexis de. *Democracy in America.* With an introduction by Alan Ryan. New York: Knopf, 1994.

Notes

INTRODUCTION

[1]Theodore Roosevelt, "True Americanism," in *Theodore Roosevelt: An American Mind; Selected Writings*, ed. Mario R. DiNunzio (New York: Penguin, 1994), 167.

[2]Ibid., 168.

[3]Ibid.

[4]CNN Political Unit, "Polls: Is America Exceptional?," *CNN Politics Political Ticker*, September 12, 2013, http://politicalticker.blogs.cnn.com/2013/09/12/polls-is-america-exceptional/.

[5]Vladimir V. Putin, "A Plea for Caution From Russia," *The New York Times*, September 11, 2013, www.nytimes.com/2013/09/12/opinion/putin-plea-for-caution-from-russia-on-syria.html?_r=0.

[6]Jim DeMint, president of The Heritage Foundation, wrote a letter to Putin shortly after his op-ed appeared in the *New York Times*, clarifying for the Russian president the meaning of American exceptionalism. Scribd, "Letter from Jim DeMint to President Vladimir Putin on American Exceptionalism," September 13, 2013, www.scribd.com/doc/167987463/Letter-from-Jim-DeMint-to-President-Vladimir-Putin-on-American-Exceptionalism.

[7]John Winthrop, "A Modell of Christian Charity," in *God's New Israel: Religious Interpretations of American Destiny*, ed. Conrad Cherry, rev. ed. (1971; repr., Chapel Hill: University of North Carolina Press, 1998), 40.

[8]Peter Gardella, *American Civil Religion: What Americans Hold Sacred* (Oxford: Oxford University Press, 2014), 5.

[9]See Jean Jacques Rousseau, *The Social Contract*, The Great Books of the Western World, ed. Robert Maynard Hutchins, no. 38 (Chicago: Encyclopedia Britannica, 1952).

[10]Robert N. Bellah, "Civil Religion in America," in *Beyond Belief: Essays on Religion in a Post-Traditional World* (New York: Harper and Row, 1970), 170-71.

[11]Ibid.

[12]See Richard V. Pierard and Robert D. Linder, *Civil Religion and the Presidency* (Grand Rapids: Academie, 1988), and Raymond Haberski Jr., *God and War: American Civil Religion Since 1945* (New Brunswick: Rutgers University Press, 2012).

[13]Haberski, *God and War*, 5.

[14]Gardella, *American Civil Religion*, 7.

[15]Gordon S. Wood, *The Idea of America: Reflections on the Birth of the United States* (New York: Penguin, 2011), 320.

[16]Bellah, "Civil Religion," 175.

[17]Robert N. Bellah, "Religion and the Legitimation of the American Republic," in *Varieties of Civil Religion*, ed. Robert N. Bellah and Phillip E. Hammond (San Francisco: Harper and Row, 1980), 15.

[18]Bellah, "Civil Religion," 178.

[19]Cherry, *God's New Israel*, 3.

[20]Alexis de Tocqueville, *Democracy in America*, intro. by Alan Ryan (New York: Knopf, 1994), I.xvii.302.

[21]Bellah, "Civil Religion," 181.

[22]Cherry, *God's New Israel*, 12.

[23]See Rodney Stark, *America's Blessings: How Religion Benefits Everyone, Including Atheists* (West Conshohocken, PA: Templeton, 2012).

[24]Tocqueville, *Democracy in America*, I.xvii.306.

[25]Bellah, "Legitimation," 12.

[26]Seymour Martin Lipset, *American Exceptionalism: A Double-Edged Sword* (New York: Norton, 1996), 19.

[27]Ibid.

[28]See Richard Hughes, *Myths America Lives By* (Chicago: University of Illinois Press, 2003).

[29]Gardella, *American Civil Religion*, 3.

[30]Tocqueville, *Democracy in America*, II.ix.36-37. Emphasis added.

[31]Daniel T. Rodgers, "Exceptionalism," in *Imagined Histories: American Historians Interpret the Past*, ed. Anthony Molho and Gordon S. Wood (Princeton: Princeton University Press, 1998), 23.

[32]Abraham Lincoln, "Annual Message to Congress," in *Selected Speeches and Writings*, ed. Don E. Fehrenbacher (New York: Library of America, 2009), 364.

[33]James W. Ceaser, "The Origins and Character of American Exceptionalism," in *American Exceptionalism: The Origins, History, and Future of the Nation's Greatest Strength*, ed. Charles W. Dunn (Lanham, MD: Rowman and Littlefield, 2013), 11.

[34]Hugh Heclo, "Varieties of American Exceptionalism," in Dunn, *American Exceptionalism*, 28. Heclo produced a chart tracking the appearance of the terms *American exceptionalism* and *American patriotism* in Google Books from the years

1800 to 2000. The highest spike, reaching .00001%, occurs in the appearance of *American patriotism* in books published in 1918 and 1919. While the appearance of the term *American exceptionalism* is barely noticeable before about 1940, by 1985, the term's appearance spikes to the prominent levels that *American patriotism* reached in 1919.

[35]Ceaser, "Origins and Character," 16.

[36]Ibid.

[37]Ibid., 17.

[38]Heclo, "Varieties," 29.

[39]Ibid., 34. Emphasis added.

[40]Ibid.

[41]Martin Luther King Jr., "I See the Promised Land," in *A Testament of Hope: The Essential Writings and Speeches of Martin Luther King, Jr.*, ed. James Melvin Washington (New York: HarperOne, 1986), 282.

[42]Lipset, *American Exceptionalism*, 26.

[43]Ibid.

[44]See John D. Wilsey, *One Nation Under God? An Evangelical Critique of Christian America* (Eugene, OR: Pickwick, 2011) for a full discussion of this assertion.

[45]Sidney E. Mead, "Nation with the Soul of a Church," *Church History* 36, no. 3 (September 1967): 283.

CHAPTER 1: THE ORIGINS OF AMERICAN EXCEPTIONALISM

[1]David M. Potter, *The Impending Crisis: America Before the Civil War: 1848–1861*, ed. Don E. Fehrenbacher (1976; repr., New York: Harper Perennial, 2011), 193.

[2]Alexis de Tocqueville, *Democracy in America*, intro. by Alan Ryan (New York: Knopf, 1994), I.xvii.290.

[3]George McKenna, *The Puritan Origins of American Patriotism* (New Haven: Yale University Press, 2007), 51.

[4]The seventeenth-century Puritan colonies included Massachusetts, Connecticut, Plymouth, New Haven, New Hampshire and Rhode Island. Rhode Island was viewed as somewhat of a maverick colony by Puritans elsewhere in New England, due to the circumstances surrounding its founding by Massachusetts exile Roger Williams. To give an idea of Rhode Island's pariah status, the colony was not invited to join a coalition of other Puritan colonies against the Indians or the French in the colonial wars of the seventeenth and eighteenth centuries.

[5]John Winthrop, "A Modell of Christian Charity," in *God's New Israel: Religious Interpretations of American Destiny*, ed. Conrad Cherry, rev. ed. (1971; repr., Chapel Hill: University of North Carolina Press, 1998), 39.

[6]Ibid., 40.

[7]Larry Witham, *A City upon a Hill: How Sermons Changed the Course of American History* (New York: HarperOne, 2007), 39.

[8]Ibid.

[9]Ibid.

[10]Sacvan Bercovitch, *The American Jeremiad* (Madison: University of Wisconsin Press, 1978), 93-94.

[11]Sacvan Bercovitch, *The Puritan Origins of the American Self* (1975; repr., New Haven: Yale University Press, 2011), 36.

[12]Samuel Danforth, "A Brief Recognition of New-England's Errand into the Wilderness: An Online Electronic Text Edition (1670)," ed. and transcribed Paul Royster, Faculty Publications, University of Nebraska-Lincoln Libraries, paper 35, 5; http://digitalcommons.unl.edu/libraryscience/35.

[13]Ibid., 19.

[14]Bercovitch, *Puritan Origins*, 100-101.

[15]Ernest Lee Tuveson, *Redeemer Nation: The Idea of America's Millennial Role* (Chicago: University of Chicago Press, 1968), x.

[16]See Augustine, *Concerning the City of God Against the Pagans*, trans. Henry Bettenson (New York: Penguin, 2003), books 20–22, for Augustine's arguments laying out the meaning of the millennium and the eternal fate of the two cities—the city of man to be judged and condemned to everlasting, conscious torment, and the city of God to eternal bliss in heaven.

[17]Tuveson, *Redeemer Nation*, 19.

[18]Not progress in the Enlightenment sense; millennial progress was guided by divine providence, effected by human effort, and directed toward the goal of the second advent of Christ. The inevitable progress of the nineteenth-century Enlightenment lacked the theistic foundation of millennial progress.

[19]Mark A. Noll, *America's God: From Jonathan Edwards to Abraham Lincoln* (Oxford: Oxford University Press, 2002), 78.

[20]Will and Ariel Durant, *The Age of Reason Begins: A History of European Civilization in the Period of Shakespeare, Bacon, Montaigne, Rembrandt, Galileo, and Descartes; 1558–1648*, vol. 7 of *The Story of Civilization* (New York: Simon & Schuster, 1961), 220.

[21]John Locke, *Second Treatise on Civil Government*, ed. Peter Laslett, Cambridge Texts in the History of Political Thought, ed. Raymond Geuss and Quentin Skinner (1960; repr., Cambridge: Cambridge University Press, 2008), XV.171, 15-19. Emphasis added. Note Locke's definition of natural rights in terms of life, liberty and property. Locke used the general term *property* to encapsulate all natural rights, that is, rights with which each individual is born.

[22]Pauline Maier, *From Resistance to Revolution: Colonial Radicals and the Development of American Opposition to Britain, 1765–1776* (New York: W. W. Norton, 1991), xx.

[23]See Noll, *America's God*, 53-72.

[24]Jonathan Mayhew, "A Discourse Concerning Unlimited Submission," in *The Puritans: A Sourcebook of Their Writings*, ed. Perry Miller and Thomas H. Johnson (1963; repr., Mineola, NY: Dover, 2001), 1:280.

[25]See Noll, *America's God*, 53-72. Noll pointed out that many Americans saw republicanism as incompatible with the Christian view of human sinfulness and the necessity for the substitutionary atonement of Christ until about the 1740s in America. After that time, republicanism was largely embraced and merged with Christian theology by Protestants in a way that was unique in America.

[26]Witham, *City upon a Hill*, 3.

[27]Michael Wigglesworth, "God's Controversy with New England," in *The American Puritans: Their Prose and Poetry*, ed. Perry Miller (New York: Columbia University Press, 1956), 295-300.

[28]Nicholas Street, "The American States Acting over the Part of the Children of Israel in the Wilderness and Thereby Impeding Their Entrance into Canaan's Rest," in Cherry, *God's New Israel*, 69.

[29]Ibid., 81.

[30]Jonathan Edwards, "The Latter-Day Glory Is Probably to Begin in America," in Cherry, *God's New Israel*, 55.

[31]Abraham Keteltas, "God Arising and Pleading His People's Cause," in *Political Sermons of the American Founding Era, 1730–1805*, ed. Ellis Sandoz (Indianapolis: Liberty Fund, 1991), 603.

[32]"And to the woman were given two wings of a great eagle, that she might fly into the wilderness, into her place, where she is nourished for a time, and times, and half a time, from the face of the serpent. And the serpent cast out of his mouth water as a flood after the woman, that he might cause her to be carried away of the flood. And the earth helped the woman, and the earth opened her mouth, and swallowed up the flood which the dragon cast out of his mouth. And the dragon was wroth with the woman, and went to make war with the remnant of her seed, which keep the commandments of God, and have the testimony of Jesus Christ" (KJV).

[33]Samuel Sherwood, "The Church's Flight into The Wilderness," in Sandoz, *Political Sermons of the American Founding Era*, 522.

[34]Ibid., 520.

[35]John Fea, *Why Study History? Reflecting on the Importance of the Past* (Grand Rapids: Baker, 2013), 20.

[36]Eileen Ka-May Cheng, *The Plain and Noble Garb of Truth: Nationalism and Impartiality in American Historical Writing, 1784–1860* (2008; repr., Athens: University of Georgia Press, 2011), 17.

[37]Everett is known for having preceded Abraham Lincoln on the stage dedicating the national cemetery at Gettysburg on November 19, 1863. Everett spoke for over

two hours, while Lincoln famously spoke for about two minutes.

[38]Jack Greene, *The Intellectual Construction of America: Exceptionalism and Identity from 1492 to 1800* (Chapel Hill: University of North Carolina Press, 1993), 208.

[39]Jonathan Boyd, "This Holy Hieroglyph: Providence and Historical Consciousness in George Bancroft's Historiography" (PhD diss., Johns Hopkins University, 1999), 187.

[40]Ibid., 188.

[41]Ibid., 202.

CHAPTER 2: EXPANSION, SLAVERY AND TWO AMERICAN EXCEPTIONALISMS

[1]David A. Clary, *Eagles and Empire: The United States, Mexico, and the Struggle for a Continent* (New York: Bantam, 2009), 40-41, and Ray Allen Billington, *Westward Expansion: A History of the American Frontier* (1960; repr., New York: Macmillan, 1963), 577-78.

[2]James K. Polk, "To the Senate and House of Representatives, May 11, 1846," in *A Compilation of the Messages and Papers of the Presidents*, vol. 5 (New York: Bureau of National Literature, 1897), 2292.

[3]Billington, *Westward Expansion*, 587.

[4]Richard Kluger, *Seizing Destiny: How America Grew from Sea to Shining Sea* (New York: Knopf, 2007), 299.

[5]Roger G. Kennedy, *Mr. Jefferson's Lost Cause: Land, Farmers, Slavery, and the Louisiana Purchase* (New York: Oxford University Press, 2003), 27.

[6]George Brown Tindall and David Emory Shi, *America: A Narrative History* (1984; repr., New York: Norton, 2000), 509.

[7]Edward W. Emerson and Waldo E. Forbes, eds., *Journals of Ralph Waldo Emerson*, 10 vols. (Boston, 1909–14), 7:206, quoted in James M. McPherson, *Battle Cry of Freedom: The Civil War Era* (1988; repr., New York: Oxford University Press, 2003), 51.

[8]McPherson, *Battle Cry of Freedom*, 51.

[9]James Oliver Horton and Lois E. Horton, *Slavery and the Making of America* (New York: Oxford University Press, 2005), 148. Solomon Northup's book was produced as a movie titled *Twelve Years a Slave* in 2013.

[10]Solomon Northup, *Twelve Years a Slave*, ed. Sue Eakin and Joseph Logsdon (Baton Rouge: Louisiana State University Press, 1968), 172.

[11]Horton and Horton, *Slavery*, 130.

[12]Lincoln Mullen, "The Spread of U. S. Slavery, 1790–1860," *Lincoln Mullen: Historian of American Religions*, interactive map, http://lincolnmullen.com/projects/slavery.

[13]Walter Ehrlich, "*Scott v. Sandford*," in *The Oxford Companion to the Supreme Court*

of the United States, ed. Kermit L. Hall, James W. Ely Jr. and Joel B. Grossman (1992; repr., New York: Oxford University Press, 2005), 888.

[14]Ibid., 889.

[15]Frederick Douglass, "'Men of Color! To Arms!' Broadside, Rochester, March 21, 1863," *University of Rochester Frederick Douglass Project*, https://www.lib.rochester.edu/index.cfm?PAGE=4372.

[16]Anders Stephanson, *Manifest Destiny: American Expansion and the Empire of Right* (1995; repr., New York: Hill and Wang, 1996), 6. Emphasis original.

[17]Frederick Merk, *Manifest Destiny and Mission in American History* (Cambridge: Harvard University Press, 1995), 27-28.

[18]John L. O'Sullivan, "Annexation," *United States Magazine and Democratic Review* 17, no. 85 (July 1845): 5.

[19]Ibid.

[20]John L. O'Sullivan, "The True Title," *New York Morning News*, December 27, 1845, quoted in Merk, *Manifest Destiny*, 31-32. It is possible that Jane Storm wrote "The True Title" under the pseudonym C. Montgomery, and thus was the actual coiner of the term *manifest destiny*. See Daniel Walker Howe, *What Hath God Wrought: The Transformation of America, 1815–1848* (Oxford: Oxford University Press, 2009), 703, for some details on that debate.

[21]O'Sullivan, "Annexation," 7.

[22]John L. O'Sullivan, "The Course of Civilization," *United States Magazine and Democratic Review* 6, no. 21 (September 1839): 208-11.

[23]Ibid., 211.

[24]John L. O'Sullivan, "European Views of American Democracy—No. II," *The United States Magazine and Democratic Review* 2, no. 8 (July 1838): 352-53.

[25]Ibid.

[26]John L. O'Sullivan, "Territorial Aggrandizement," *The United States Magazine and Democratic Review* 17, no. 88 (October 1845): 245.

[27]Ibid., 247.

[28]Thomas R. Hietala, *Manifest Design: American Exceptionalism and Empire* (1985; repr., Ithaca, NY: Cornell University Press, 2003), 194.

[29]Kluger, *Seizing Destiny*, 429.

[30]John L. O'Sullivan, "Democracy," *The United States Magazine and Democratic Review* 7, no. 27 (March 1840): 228-29.

[31]James M. McPherson, "Lincoln Off His Pedestal," *New York Review of Books*, September 24, 2009, http://www.nybooks.com/articles/archives/2009/sep/24/lincoln-off-his-pedestal/.

[32]William Wolf, *The Almost Chosen People: A Study of the Religion of Abraham Lincoln* (New York: Doubleday, 1959), 24.

[33]Abraham Lincoln, "From Sixth Lincoln-Douglas Debate, Quincy, Illinois, October

13, 1858," in *Selected Speeches and Writings*, ed. Don E. Fehrenbacher (New York: Library of America, 2009), 184.

[34]Allen C. Guelzo, *Abraham Lincoln: Redeemer President* (Grand Rapids: Eerdmans, 1999), 195.

[35]Abraham Lincoln, "From Fifth Lincoln-Douglas Debate, Galesburg, Illinois, October 7, 1858," in Fehrenbacher, *Selected Speeches and Writings*, 177.

[36]At the same time, we must acknowledge that in justifying the use of force to compel the Southern states back into the Union, Lincoln's thought was more in line with Thomas Hobbes's political philosophy than Locke's.

[37]Abraham Lincoln, "Address to Young Men's Lyceum, January 27, 1838," in Fehrenbacher, *Selected Speeches and Writings*, 18.

[38]Abraham Lincoln, "Meditation on the Divine Will, Early September, 1862," in Fehrenbacher, *Selected Speeches and Writings*, 344.

[39]Richard V. Pierard and Robert D. Linder, *Civil Religion and the Presidency* (Grand Rapids: Academie, 1988), 105.

[40]Abraham Lincoln, "Second Inaugural Address, March 4, 1865," in Fehrenbacher, *Selected Speeches and Writings*, 450.

[41]John L. O'Sullivan, "Introduction," *The United States Magazine and Democratic Review* 1, no. 1 (October 1837): 7.

[42]Lincoln, "Annual Message to Congress, December 1, 1862," in Fehrenbacher, *Selected Speeches and Writings*, 364.

[43]Abraham Lincoln, "Speech to the 166th Ohio Regiment, Washington, DC, August 22, 1864," in Fehrenbacher, *Selected Speeches and Writings*, 431.

[44]Abraham Lincoln, "From First Lincoln-Douglas Debate, Ottawa, Illinois, August 21, 1858," in Fehrenbacher, *Selected Speeches and Writings*, 149.

[45]Jean H. Baker, "Lincoln's Narrative of American Exceptionalism," in *We Cannot Escape History: Lincoln and the Last Best Hope of Earth*, ed. James M. McPherson (Urbana, IL: University of Illinois Press, 2001), 39. In Lincoln's December 1, 1862, message to Congress, he proposed a constitutional amendment that abolished slavery by January 1, 1900, and encouraged Congress to assist in settling freed slaves in Africa, Central America and the Caribbean islands.

[46]John L. O'Sullivan, "On the Intelligence of the People," *The United States Magazine and Democratic Review* 8, no. 34 (October 1840): 364.

[47]Sidney Mead, "Abraham Lincoln's 'Last, Best Hope of Earth': The American Dream of Destiny and Democracy," *Church History* 23, no. 1 (March 1954): 33.

CHAPTER 3: THE CHOSEN NATION

[1]Will Durant, *The Reformation: A History of European Civilization from Wyclif to Calvin: 1300–1564*, vol. 6 of *The Story of Civilization* (New York: Simon and Schuster, 1957), 586. As I have indicated earlier, I love Durant's style as a tremendously de-

scriptive storyteller. His eleven-volume *Story of Civilization* is a beautifully readable, thorough and integrative survey for the general reader of Western civilization from prehistory to the fall of Napoleon.

[2]Tyndale was burned at the stake after being strangled in 1536.

[3]Richard Hughes, *Myths America Lives By* (Chicago: University of Illinois Press, 2003), 23.

[4]Anthony Smith, *Chosen Peoples: Sacred Sources of National Identity* (Oxford: Oxford University Press, 2003), 37.

[5]Ibid., 38-39.

[6]Ibid., 40.

[7]John Fea, *Was America Founded as a Christian Nation? A Historical Introduction* (Louisville: Westminster John Knox, 2011), 3-75.

[8]George McKenna, *The Puritan Origins of American Patriotism* (New Haven: Yale University Press, 2007), 49.

[9]Nicholas Guyatt, *Providence and the Invention of the United States, 1607–1876* (Cambridge: Cambridge University Press, 2007), 174.

[10]See Nathan O. Hatch, *The Democratization of American Christianity* (New Haven: Yale University Press, 1989).

[11]Eran Shalev, *American Zion: The Old Testament as a Political Text from the Revolution to the Civil War* (New Haven: Yale University Press, 2013), 4.

[12]Abigail and John Adams, *The Book of Abigail and John: Selected Letters of the Adams Family, 1762–1784*, ed. Lyman Henry Butterfield, Marc Friedlaender and Mary-Jo Kline (Boston: Northeastern University Press, 2002), 155-56, quoted in James P. Byrd, *Sacred Scripture, Sacred War: The Bible and the American Revolution* (New York: Oxford University Press, 2013), 47.

[13]Ibid.

[14]Thomas Jefferson, "Second Inaugural Address," in *A Compilation of the Messages and Papers of the Presidents*, vol. 1 (New York: Bureau of National Literature, 1897), 370.

[15]John Fea, *Why Study History? Reflecting on the Importance of the Past* (Grand Rapids: Baker, 2013), 58.

[16]Jack Greene, *The Intellectual Construction of America: Exceptionalism and Identity from 1492 to 1800* (Chapel Hill: University of North Carolina Press, 1993), 16.

[17]Ibid., 54-55.

[18]Alan Heimert, *Religion and the American Mind: From the Great Awakening to the Revolution*, Jonathan Edwards Classic Studies Series, vol. 5 (1966; repr., Eugene, OR: Wipf and Stock, 2006), 94.

[19]Shalev, *American Zion*, 153.

[20]Fea, *Was America Founded*, 4.

[21]Ibid., 8. See also Daniel Walker Howe, *What Hath God Wrought: The Transfor-*

242   *Notes to Pages 103–110*

mation of America, 1815–1848, Oxford History of the United States, ed. David M. Kennedy (New York: Oxford University Press, 2007).

[22]Byrd, *Sacred Scripture, Sacred War*, 10.

[23]Mark Noll, *The Civil War as a Theological Crisis* (Chapel Hill: University of North Carolina Press, 2006), 75.

[24]Fea, *Was America Founded*, 20. The preamble to the Confederate Constitution said, "We, the people of the Confederate States, each State acting in its sovereign and independent character, in order to form a permanent and federal government, establish justice, insure domestic tranquility, and secure the blessings of liberty to ourselves and to our posterity—invoking the favor and guidance of Almighty God—do ordain and establish this Constitution for the Confederate States of America."

[25]Noll, *Theological Crisis*, 81.

[26]See John Eliot, "Puritan Missions to the Indians," in *Discovering a New World*, vol. 1, The Annals of America, ed. Mortimer J. Adler and Charles Van Doren (Chicago: Encyclopaedia Britannica, 1968), 180-83; Benjamin Franklin, "The Futility of Educating the Indians," in Adler and Van Doren, *Discovering a New World*, 1:497-98; Cotton Mather, *Magnalia Christi Americana* (Boston: Belknap, 1977).

[27]Nicole Guétin, *Religious Ideology and American Politics: A History* (London: McFarland, 2009), 146.

[28]Reginald Horsman, *Race and Manifest Destiny: The Origins of American Racial Anglo-Saxonism* (Cambridge: Harvard University Press, 1981), 192.

[29]Ibid., 100.

[30]Charles Anderson, *An Address on Anglo-Saxon Destiny: Delivered Before the Philomathesian Society of Kenyon College, Ohio, August 8, 1849 and Repeated Before the New England Society of Cincinnati; December 20, 1849* (Cincinnati, 1850), 3-4, and Albert Gallatin, "Peace with Mexico" (1847), in *The Writings of Albert Gallatin*, ed. Henry Adams, 3 vols. (1879; repr., New York: Antiquarian Press, 1960), 3:581-86; quoted in Horsman, *Race and Manifest Destiny*, 266-71.

[31]David Brion Davis, *Inhuman Bondage: The Rise and Fall of Slavery in the New World* (New York: Oxford University Press, 2006), 50.

[32]Thomas R. Dew, *Review of the Debate in the Virginia Legislature of 1831 and 1832* (Richmond, 1832), 103; quoted in Horsman, *Race and Manifest Destiny*, 123.

[33]*Richmond Palladium*, March 8, 1848; quoted in Horsman, *Race and Manifest Destiny*, 245.

[34]Horsman, *Race and Manifest Destiny*, 245.

[35]John W. Blassingame, *The Slave Community: Plantation Life in the Antebellum South* (1972; repr., New York: Oxford University Press, 1979), 97-98.

[36]Davis, *Inhuman Bondage*, 203.

[37]James Cone, "Black Spirituals: A Theological Interpretation," in *African American*

Religious Thought: An Anthology, ed. Cornel West and Eddie S. Glaude Jr. (Louisville: Westminster John Knox, 2003), 780.

[38]Hughes, *Myths America Lives By*, 39.

[39]Martin Luther King Jr., "Letter from a Birmingham City Jail," in *A Testament of Hope: The Essential Writings and Speeches of Martin Luther King, Jr.*, ed. James M. Washington (1986; repr., New York: HarperOne, 1991), 293.

[40]Malcolm X, "The Ballot or the Bullet," in *The Portable Malcolm X Reader*, ed. Manning Marable and Garrett Felber (New York: Penguin, 2013), 324.

[41]Cone, "Black Spirituals," 787.

[42]King, "Letter," 293.

[43]Malcolm X, "Ballot or the Bullet," 323.

[44]David T. Koyzis, *Political Visions and Illusions: A Survey and Christian Critique of Contemporary Ideologies* (Downers Grove, IL: IVP Academic, 2003), 118.

[45]Smith, *Chosen Peoples*, 50.

[46]Koyzis, *Political Visions and Illusions*, 117-18.

[47]McKenna, *Puritan Origins*, 202.

[48]Noll, *Theological Crisis*, 94.

CHAPTER 4: THE COMMISSIONED NATION

[1]William Inboden, *Religion and American Foreign Policy, 1945–1960: The Soul of Containment* (2008; repr., New York: Cambridge University Press, 2010), 227.

[2]Carol Burnett, interview by Diane Rehm, *National Public Radio*, April 10, 2013, http://thedianerehmshow.org/shows/2013-04-10/carol-burnett-carrie-and-me-mother-daughter-love-story/transcript.

[3]Anthony Smith, *Chosen Peoples: Sacred Sources of National Identity* (Oxford: Oxford University Press, 2003), 49.

[4]Richard M. Gamble, *The War for Righteousness: Progressive Christianity, the Great War, and the Rise of the Messianic Nation* (Wilmington, DE: ISI, 2003), 23.

[5]Stephen Kinzer, *The Brothers: John Foster Dulles, Allen Dulles, and Their Secret World War* (New York: Henry Holt, 2013), 323.

[6]Frederick Jackson Turner, "The Significance of the Frontier in American History," in *Does the Frontier Experience Make America Exceptional?*, ed. Richard W. Etulain, Historians at Work (Boston: Bedford/St. Martin's, 1999), 19.

[7]Ibid., 40.

[8]Theodore Roosevelt, "America's Part of the World's Work," in *Theodore Roosevelt: An American Mind: Selected Readings*, ed. Mario R. DiNunzio (New York: Penguin, 1994), 183.

[9]Woodrow Wilson, "Eighth Annual Message to Congress, December 7, 1920," in *A Compilation of the Messages and Papers of the Presidents*, vol. 17 (New York: Bureau of National Literature, 1897), 8882.

[10]Milan Babík, *Statecraft and Salvation: Wilsonian Liberal Internationalism as Secularized Eschatology* (Waco, TX: Baylor University Press, 2013), 198.

[11]Ibid., 202.

[12]Franklin D. Roosevelt, "Annual Message to Congress, January 6, 1941," in *The Second World War and After, 1940–1949*, vol. 16, The Annals of America, ed. Mortimer J. Adler and Charles Van Doren (Chicago: Encyclopaedia Britannica, 1968), 45.

[13]Andrew Preston, *Sword of the Spirit, Shield of Faith* (New York: Anchor, 2012), 317.

[14]Kinzer, *The Brothers*, 115.

[15]Harry S. Truman, "Inaugural Address, January 20, 1949," in Adler and Van Doren, *The Second World War and After*, 562.

[16]Henry P. Van Dusen, ed., *The Spiritual Legacy of John Foster Dulles: Selections from His Articles and Addresses* (Philadelphia: Westminster, 1960), xiii.

[17]Preston, *Sword of the Spirit, Shield of Faith*, 386.

[18]Ibid., 406.

[19]Inboden, *Religion and American Foreign Policy*, 227.

[20]Preston, *Sword of the Spirit, Shield of Faith*, 451.

[21]John Quincy Adams, "Speech to the United States House of Representatives, July 4, 1821," *Presidential Rhetoric.com*, www.presidentialrhetoric.com/historicspeeches /adams_jq/foreignpolicy.html.

[22]Kinzer, *The Brothers*, 115.

[23]John Foster Dulles, *War or Peace* (New York: Macmillan, 1950), 5.

[24]Ibid., 8.

[25]Ibid., 9.

[26]Ibid., 9-10.

[27]Ibid., 13.

[28]Ibid., 15.

[29]John Foster Dulles, "Christian Responsibility for Peace, May 4, 1948," in Van Dusen, *Spiritual Legacy of John Foster Dulles*, 153.

[30]Conrad Cherry, ed., *God's New Israel: Religious Interpretations of American Destiny*, rev. ed. (1971; repr., Chapel Hill: University of North Carolina Press, 1998), 304.

[31]Quoted in Raymond Haberski Jr., *God and War: American Civil Religion Since 1945* (New Brunswick: Rutgers University Press, 2012), 38.

[32]John Foster Dulles, "A Policy of Instant Retaliation, May 9, 1952," in *Cold War in the Nuclear Age, 1950–1959*, vol. 17, The Annals of America, ed. Mortimer Adler and Charles Van Doren (Chicago: Encyclopaedia Britannica, 1968), 125.

[33]John Foster Dulles, "The Strategy of Massive Retaliation, January 12, 1954," in Adler and Van Doren, *Cold War in the Nuclear Age*, 252.

[34]John Foster Dulles, "Our Spiritual Heritage, October 21, 1947," in Van Dusen, *Spiritual Legacy of John Foster Dulles*, 64.

[35]John Foster Dulles, "Patriotism and the American Tradition, June 12, 1955," in Van Dusen, *Spiritual Legacy of John Foster Dulles*, 39-40.

[36]John Foster Dulles, "The Power of Moral Forces, October 11, 1953," in Van Dusen, *Spiritual Legacy of John Foster Dulles*, 223.

[37]Ibid., 224-25.

[38]John Foster Dulles, "Containment or Liberation, January 15, 1953," in Adler and Van Doren, *Cold War in the Nuclear Age*, 204-5.

[39]John Foster Dulles, "Peace Through Law, January 31, 1959," in Adler and Van Doren, *Cold War in the Nuclear Age*, 530.

[40]Haberski, *God and War*, 109.

[41]Ronald Reagan, "Evil Empire Speech, March 8, 1983," *Miller Center, University of Virginia*, http://millercenter.org/president/speeches/detail/3409.

[42]Charles Krauthammer, "The Hundred Days," *Time*, December 31, 2001, http://content.time.com/time/magazine/article/0,9171,1001544,00.html.

[43]Quoted in Niall Ferguson, *Colossus: The Rise and Fall of the American Empire* (New York: Penguin, 2004), ix.

[44]Andrew J. Bacevich, *The Limits of Power: The End of American Exceptionalism* (New York: Metropolitan, 2008), 11.

[45]J. William Fulbright, "Old Myths and New Realities, March 25, 1964," in *The Burdens of World Power, 1961–1968*, vol. 18, The Annals of America, ed. Mortimer Adler and Charles Van Doren (Chicago: Encyclopaedia Britannica, 1968), 228.

[46]*Memorandum of the Subcommittee on National Security and International Operations of the Committee on Government Operations*, US Senate, 89th Congress, 1st session, 1965, 2-3; quoted in Ronald Steel, *Pax Americana* (New York: Viking, 1967), 9.

[47]Martin Luther King Jr., "A Time to Break Silence," in *A Testament of Hope: The Essential Writings and Speeches of Martin Luther King, Jr.*, ed. James Melvin Washington (New York: HarperOne, 1986), 240-41.

[48]Henry Steele Commager, "Who Is Loyal to America?," in Adler and Van Doren, *The Second World War and After*, 459.

[49]Ibid., 462.

[50]George W. Bush, "America and Africa: Remarks at the Leon H. Sullivan Foundation, February 26, 2008," *Presidential Rhetoric.com*, www.presidentialrhetoric.com/speeches/02.26.08.html.

CHAPTER 5: THE INNOCENT NATION

[1]Ronald Reagan, "The Long Goodbye, November 4, 1994," in *The Speeches of Ronald Reagan*, ed. Maureen Harrison and Steve Gilbert (n.p.: Excellent Books, 2004), 163.

[2]Ronald Reagan, "Farewell Address to the Nation, January 11, 1989," in *Speaking My Mind: Selected Speeches* (New York: Simon and Schuster, 1989), 416.

[3] Will Durant, *The Reformation: A History of European Civilization from Wyclif to Calvin: 1300–1564*, vol. 6 of *The Story of Civilization* (New York: Simon and Schuster, 1957), 552.

[4] Thomas More, *The Utopia of Thomas More* (Roslyn, NY: Walter J. Black, 1947), 18.

[5] Jack Greene, *The Intellectual Construction of America: Exceptionalism and Identity from 1492 to 1800* (Chapel Hill: University of North Carolina Press, 1993), 28.

[6] See Richard M. Gamble, *In Search of the City on a Hill: The Making and Unmaking of an American Myth* (London: Continuum, 2012), for an excellent historical treatment of Winthrop's metaphor and what it reveals about how Americans have self-identified over the generations.

[7] John Winthrop, "A Model of Christian Charity," in *God's New Israel: Religious Interpretations of American Destiny*, ed. Conrad Cherry, rev. ed. (1971; repr., Chapel Hill: University of North Carolina Press, 1998), 40.

[8] Richard Hughes, *Myths America Lives By* (Chicago: University of Illinois Press, 2003), 153-89.

[9] Ari Hoogenboom, "American Exceptionalism: Republicanism as Ideology," in *Bridging the Atlantic: The Question of American Exceptionalism in Perspective*, German Historical Institute, ed. Elisabeth Glaser and Hermann Wellenreuther (Cambridge, UK: University of Cambridge Press, 2002), 44.

[10] Thomas Paine, *Common Sense* (New York: Peter Eckler, 1918), 57-58.

[11] Reinhold Niebuhr, *The Irony of American History* (New York: Scribner's, 1952), 24.

[12] Ronald Reagan, "Remarks at the Annual Convention of the National Association of Evangelicals, Orlando, Florida, March 7, 1983," in *Speaking My Mind*, 178.

[13] Ronald Reagan, *The Reagan Diaries*, ed. Douglas Brinkley (New York: Harper Perennial, 2007), 135.

[14] Hughes, *Myths*, 172.

[15] John L. O'Sullivan, "The Great Nation of Futurity," *United States Democratic Review* 6, no. 23 (November 1839): 427.

[16] Ibid., 430.

[17] Albert J. Beveridge, "The Star of Empire," in Cherry, *God's New Israel*, 158.

[18] Ibid., 159.

[19] J. William Fulbright, "The Arrogance of Power," in *The Burdens of World Power, 1961–1968*, vol. 18, The Annals of America, ed. Mortimer Adler and Charles Van Doren (Chicago: Encyclopaedia Britannica, 1968), 363.

[20] "President Johnson Says Vietnam Policy Is Not an Arrogance of Power," *NBC Nightly News*, New York, November 5, 1966, https://archives.nbclearn.com/portal /site/k-12/browse/?cuecard=60098.

[21] Jimmy Carter, "Crisis of Confidence, July 15, 1979," *American Experience*, www.pbs .org/wgbh/americanexperience/features/primary-resources/carter-crisis/.

[22]Richard V. Pierard and Robert D. Linder, *Civil Religion and the Presidency* (Grand Rapids: Academie, 1988), 258.

[23]Ronald Reagan, "We Will Be as a City upon a Hill: Governor Reagan's Speech to the Conservative Political Action Committee, January 25, 1974," in Harrison and Gilbert, *Speeches of Ronald Reagan*, 21.

[24]Ibid., 23.

[25]Ronald Reagan, "An Empire of Ideals: Republican National Convention Address, August 17, 1992," in Harrison and Gilbert, *Speeches of Ronald Reagan*, 158.

[26]Ronald Reagan, "This Last Best Hope: State of the Union Address, January 27, 1982," in Harrison and Gilbert, *Speeches of Ronald Reagan*, 48.

[27]Ronald Reagan, "Address to the Nation on the U.S. Air Strike Against Libya, April 14, 1986," in *Speaking My Mind*, 288.

[28]Ronald Reagan, "The Making of a President: 1980 RNC Nomination Acceptance Speech, July 17, 1980," in Harrison and Gilbert, *Speeches of Ronald Reagan*, 35.

[29]Ronald Reagan, "Remarks and Question-and-Answer Session with Students at Moscow State University, May 31, 1988," in *Speaking My Mind*, 383.

[30]Reagan, "We Will Be as a City," 21.

[31]Ronald Reagan, "Remarks at the Statue of Liberty Centennial Ceremonies, July 3, 1986," in *Speaking My Mind*, 300.

[32]In his 1974 speech to the Conservative Political Action Committee and his 1982 State of the Union Address, to name two.

[33]Ronald Reagan, "Letters to the Editor, June 1975," in *Reagan in His Own Hand: The Writings of Ronald Reagan That Reveal His Revolutionary Vision for America*, ed. Kiron K. Skinner, Annelise Anderson and Martin Anderson (New York: Touchstone, 2001), 16.

[34]Ronald Reagan, "Remarks at the Memorial Service for Members of the 101st Airborne Division, December 16, 1985," in *Speaking My Mind*, 282.

[35]Ronald Reagan, "Remarks on the Anniversary of Martin Luther King, Jr.'s, Birth, January 15, 1983," *Speaking My Mind*, 163.

[36]Ibid.

[37]Ibid.

[38]Ronald Reagan, "Address to the Nation on the Tower Commission Report, March 4, 1987," in *Speaking My Mind*, 335.

[39]Ibid., 337.

[40]Ibid., 336.

[41]Ibid., 339.

[42]David Gelernter, *Americanism: The Fourth Great Western Religion* (New York: Doubleday, 2007), 2.

[43]Niebuhr, *Irony*, 39.

[44]Ibid., 5-6.

[45]Martin Luther King Jr., "The American Dream," in *A Testament of Hope: The Essential Writings and Speeches of Martin Luther King, Jr.*, ed. James M. Washington (1986; repr., New York: HarperCollins, 1991), 208.

[46]Fulbright, "Arrogance of Power," 362.

[47]W. E. B. Du Bois, *The Suppression of the African Slave Trade to the United States of America, 1638–1870*, in *W. E. B. Du Bois: Writings*, ed. Nathan Huggins (New York: Library of America, 1986), 197.

CHAPTER 6: THE NATION AND HER LAND

[1]James L. Mallery, "San Francisco Earthquake and Fire," in *The Oxford Companion to United States History*, ed. Paul S. Boyer (New York: Oxford University Press, 2001), 682-83.

[2]Roderick Nash, *Wilderness and the American Mind* (New Haven: Yale University Press, 1967), 161.

[3]Theodore Roosevelt, letter to Robert Underwood Johnson, December 17, 1908; quoted in Douglas Brinkley, *The Wilderness Warrior: Theodore Roosevelt and the Crusade for America* (New York: Harper, 2009), 790.

[4]Nash, *Wilderness*, 179.

[5]See Robert W. Righter, *The Battle over Hetch Hetchy: America's Most Controversial Dam and the Birth of Modern Environmentalism* (New York: Oxford University Press, 2006), for a full-length academic treatment of the Hetch Hetchy debate.

[6]Jack Greene, *The Intellectual Construction of America: Exceptionalism and Identity from 1492 to 1800* (Chapel Hill: University of North Carolina Press, 1993), 13.

[7]Anthony Smith, *Chosen Peoples: Sacred Sources of National Identity* (Oxford: Oxford University Press, 2003), 137.

[8]Gary M. Burge, *Jesus and the Land: The New Testament Challenge to Holy Land Theology* (Grand Rapids: Baker, 2010), ix.

[9]Francis Higginson, "On the Riches of New England," in *Discovering a New World*, vol. 1, The Annals of America, ed. Mortimer J. Adler and Charles Van Doren (Chicago: Encyclopaedia Britannica, 1968), 95-98.

[10]Edward Johnson, *Wonder-Working Providence of Sion's Saviour in New England*, ed. J. Franklin Jameson (New York: Scribner's, 1910), 210.

[11]John Cotton, "The Divine Right to Occupy the Land," in Adler and Van Doren, *Discovering a New World*, 107.

[12]Ibid.

[13]Benjamin Tompson, "New Englands Crisis," in *The Puritans: A Sourcebook of Their Writings*, ed. Perry Miller and Thomas H. Johnson (1963; repr., Mineola, NY: Dover, 2001), 640.

[14]Daniel Walker Howe, *What Hath God Wrought: The Transformation of America*,

1815–1848, Oxford History of the United States, ed. David M. Kennedy (New York: Oxford University Press, 2007), 128.

[15]Ibid., 140.

[16]Ibid., 158.

[17]Thomas Jefferson, *Notes on the State of Virginia*, in *Thomas Jefferson, Writings* (New York: Library of America, 1984), 290-91; quoted in Roger G. Kennedy, *Mr. Jefferson's Lost Cause: Land, Farmers, Slavery, and the Louisiana Purchase* (New York: Oxford University Press, 2003), 26.

[18]Thomas Jefferson, *Notes on the State of Virginia*, query 17 and 18, in *The Sacred Rights of Conscience: Selected Readings on Religious Liberty and Church-State Relations in the American Founding*, ed. Daniel L. Dreisbach and Mark David Hall (Indianapolis: Liberty Fund, 2009), 294.

[19]Ibid.

[20]Kennedy, *Mr. Jefferson's Lost Cause*, 16.

[21]Jefferson, *Notes*, in Dreisbach and Hall, *Sacred Rights*, 293.

[22]Ibid., 16.

[23]Ibid., 14.

[24]Mark Fiege, *The Republic of Nature: An Environmental History of the United States* (Seattle: University of Washington Press, 2012), 94.

[25]See Jean-Jacques Rousseau, *Emile: Or, on Education* (Amherst, NY: Prometheus, 2003).

[26]Alexander Wilson, *The Foresters: A Poem Descriptive of a Pedestrian Journey to the Falls of Niagara in the Autumn of 1804* (West Chester, PA: Joseph Painter, 1838), 5.

[27]Ibid., 6.

[28]Nash, *Wilderness*, 67.

[29]Frederick Jackson Turner, "The Significance of the Frontier in American History," in *Does the Frontier Experience Make America Exceptional?*, ed. Richard W. Etulain, Historians at Work (Boston: Bedford/St. Martin's, 1999), 20.

[30]See *Explore Thomas Cole*, http://explorethomascole.org/, for an interactive tour through some of Cole's famous works.

[31]Nash, *Wilderness*, 83.

[32]Thomas Cole, "Essay on American Scenery," *American Monthly Magazine* 1 (1836): 4-5; quoted in Nash, *Wilderness*, 81.

[33]Theodore Roosevelt, *Theodore Roosevelt: An Autobiography* (1913; repr., New York: Da Capo, 1985), 409-10.

[34]Brinkley, *Wilderness Warrior*, 21.

[35]In Genesis 1, the creation appeared "good" to God in six places: "And God saw that it was good" (Genesis 1:10); "And God saw that it was good" (Genesis 1:12); "And God saw that it was good" (Genesis 1:18); "And God saw that it was good" (Genesis 1:21); "And God saw that it was good" (Genesis 1:25); "And God saw everything that he had made, and behold, it was very good" (Genesis 1:31).

[36]Quoted in Richard Kluger, *Seizing Destiny: How America Grew from Sea to Shining Sea* (New York: Knopf, 2007), 429.

[37]Kennedy, *Mr. Jefferson's Lost Cause*, 9.

[38]W. E. B. Du Bois, *The Souls of Black Folk*, in *W. E. B. Du Bois: Writings*, ed. Nathan Huggins (New York: Library of America, 1986), 449.

[39]Ibid., 452.

[40]Ibid.

[41]Kimberly K. Smith, *African American Environmental Thought: Foundations*, American Political Thought, ed. Wilson Carey McWilliams and Lance Banning (Lawrence: University Press of Kansas, 2007), 8.

[42]Ibid., 97.

[43]Mark D. Hersey, *My Work Is That of Conservation: An Environmental Biography of George Washington Carver* (Athens: University of Georgia Press, 2011), 5.

[44]Alexis de Tocqueville, *Democracy in America*, intro. by Alan Ryan (New York: Knopf, 1994), I.xvii.290-91.

[45]Hersey, *My Work*, 220.

[46]John Muir, *Our National Parks*, in *The Eight Wilderness Discovery Books* (London: Diadem, 1992), 593.

[47]Ibid., 604.

[48]John Muir, *The Yosemite*, in *The Eight Wilderness Discovery Books*, 714.

[49]Burge, *Jesus and the Land*, 130.

Chapter 7: The Glorious Nation

[1]Patrick J. Buchanan, "Address to the Republican National Convention, August 17, 1992," *American Rhetoric Online Speech Bank*, www.americanrhetoric.com /speeches/patrickbuchanan1992rnc.htm.

[2]See John D. Wilsey, *One Nation Under God? An Evangelical Critique of Christian America* (Eugene, OR: Pickwick, 2011), 43-94, for a treatment of the assertions made by Christian America authors from 1977 to 2007.

[3]Michael R. Lowman, George Thompson and Kurt Grussendorf, *United States History in Christian Perspective: Heritage of Freedom* (1982; repr., Pensacola, FL: A Beka, 1996), 5.

[4]Ibid., x.

[5]Timothy Keesee and Mark Sidwell, *United States History* (1982; repr., Greenville, SC: Bob Jones University Press, 2001), 656.

[6]Gene Edward Veith, Douglas Wilson and G. Tyler Fischer, Omnibus VI: *The Modern World* (Lancaster: Veritas Press, 2012), xiii. In the interest of full disclosure, I should mention that I contributed a piece to this textbook. I wrote the essay guiding the students through David McCullough's *John Adams*. Given the fact that I had recently completed my PhD dissertation critiquing the Christian America

thesis, I sought to avoid treating my topic using an exceptionalist or presentist framework.

[7]Jacques Le Goff, *History and Memory*, trans. Steven Rendall and Elizabeth Claman, European Perspectives (New York: Columbia University Press, 1992), 101-2.

[8]Gordon S. Wood, *The Purpose of the Past: Reflections on the Uses of History* (New York: Penguin, 2008), 161.

[9]Robert Tracy McKenzie, *The First Thanksgiving: What the Real Story Tells Us About Loving God and Learning from History* (Downers Grove, IL: IVP Academic, 2013), 124.

[10]John Fea, *Was America Founded as a Christian Nation? A Historical Introduction* (Louisville: Westminster John Knox, 2011), xxv.

[11]Anthony Smith, *Chosen Peoples: Sacred Sources of National Identity* (Oxford: Oxford University Press, 2003), 169.

[12]Ibid., 215-16.

[13]Wood, *Purpose of the Past*, 71.

[14]McKenzie, *First Thanksgiving*, 18.

[15]John Fea, *Why Study History? Reflecting on the Importance of the Past* (Grand Rapids: Baker, 2003), 131, 140.

[16]McKenzie, *First Thanksgiving*, 182.

[17]Fea cited Thomas Andrews and Flannery Burke when he wrote about the five Cs of historical thinking in *Was America Founded*, xxiv-xxv, and *Why Study History?*, 6-15. See Thomas Andrews and Flannery Burke, "What Does It Mean to Think Historically?," *AHA Perspectives* 45, no. 1 (January 2007), www.historians .org/Perspectives/issues/2007/0701/0701tea2.cfm, for the original concept of the five Cs of historical thinking.

[18]Fea, *Why Study History?*, 106.

[19]See Andreas J. Köstenberger and Justin Taylor, *The Final Days of Jesus: The Most Important Week of the Most Important Person Who Ever Lived* (Wheaton: Crossway, 2014), for a detailed chronological analysis of Christ's passion week that, according to the authors, began on March 29, AD 33.

[20]Lowman, Thompson and Grussendorf, *United States History*, x.

[21]Ibid., 132-33. Emphasis original.

[22]Ibid., 149.

[23]Ibid., 265.

[24]Ibid., 677.

[25]Keesee and Sidwell, *United States History*, 39, 43.

[26]Ibid., 656.

[27]George Grant, "Foundational American Documents," in Omnibus III: *Reformation to the Present*, ed. Douglas Wilson and G. Tyler Fischer (2006; repr., Lancaster: Veritas, 2010), 91.

[28]Douglas Wilson, "The American and French Revolutions Compared," in Omnibus VI: *The Modern World*, 137. Emphasis added.

[29]Lowman, Thompson and Grussendorf, *United States History*, 273.

[30]Ibid., 677-78.

[31]Keesee and Sidwell, *United States History*, 286-87.

[32]Ibid., 315.

[33]Ibid.

[34]Ibid., 656.

[35]Douglas Wilson and G. Tyler Fischer, "Slave Narratives," in Omnibus III: *Reformation to the Present*, 201.

[36]Douglas Wilson, "Reflections on the Revolution in France," in Omnibus III: *Reformation to the Present*, 159. Emphasis added.

[37]There was, of course, a lively biblical argument before and during the revolutionary period over the meaning of Romans 13, 1 Peter 2 and other similar passages. For instance, Jonathan Mayhew preached a sermon on Romans 13 titled "A Discourse Concerning Unlimited Submission and Non-Resistance to Higher Powers" in January 1750 in which he proposed that resistance to an unjust government is not prohibited. Samuel West made a similar argument from Titus 3:1 in May 1776. But John Wesley urged rebellious American colonists to submit to the British government on the basis of 1 Peter 2:17 in his 1775 "Calm Address to Our American Colonies." Wilson did not reference this historical debate in any of his writings on the American Revolution or slavery, thus failing to account for the historical complexity of submission to the British government.

[38]Wilson, "Reflections on the Revolution in France," 158.

[39]Lowman, Thompson and Grussendorf, *United States History*, 678.

[40]Keesee and Sidwell, *United States History*, 656.

[41]O. Woelke Leithart, "Foundational American Documents," in Omnibus VI: *The Modern World*, 114.

[42]McKenzie, *First Thanksgiving*, 20.

[43]Ibid.

CHAPTER 8: OPEN EXCEPTIONALISM AND CIVIC ENGAGEMENT

[1]W. E. B. Du Bois, "Abraham Lincoln, May 1922," in *W. E. B. Du Bois: Writings*, ed. Nathan Huggins (New York: Library of America, 1986), 1197. *The Crisis* is the journal of the NAACP, which Du Bois helped found in 1909.

[2]W. E. B. Du Bois, "Again, Lincoln, September 1922," in Huggins, *W. E. B. Du Bois: Writings*, 1198.

[3]Letter from W. E. B. Du Bois to John Foster Dulles, February 22, 1957, James Aronson-W. E. B. Du Bois Collection (MS 292), Special Collections and University

Archives, University of Massachusetts Amherst Libraries, http://credo.library
.umass.edu/view/full/mums292-b001-i021.

[4]See John D. Wilsey, *One Nation Under God: An Evangelical Critique of Christian
America* (Eugene, OR: Pickwick, 2011). In this book, I argued that America was not
specifically founded on Christianity, but on religious freedom. See John Fea, *Was
America Founded as a Christian Nation? An Historical Introduction* (Louisville:
Westminster John Knox, 2011), for a historical treatment of the question of Amer-
ica's religious origins.

[5]Peter Gardella, *American Civil Religion: What Americans Hold Sacred* (Oxford:
Oxford University Press, 2014), 2.

[6]Ibid., 3.

[7]Ibid.

[8]Ibid., 5-6.

[9]Justin Martyr, *The First Apology of Justin*, in *The Apostolic Fathers, Justin Martyr,
Irenaeus*, vol. 1, Ante-Nicene Fathers (1885; repr., Peabody, MA: Hendrickson,
1999), 166.

[10]Ibid.

[11]Ibid., 168.

[12]Ibid., 167. Justin quoted Luke 6:28.

[13]Ibid., 166.

[14]Ibid., 168.

[15]W. E. B. Du Bois, "An Open Letter to Woodrow Wilson, March 1913," in Huggins,
W. E. B. Du Bois: Writings, 1144.

[16]Edward J. Blum, *W. E. B. Du Bois: American Prophet* (Philadelphia: University of
Pennsylvania Press, 2007), 221.

[17]W. E. B. Du Bois, "The Souls of White Folk," in Huggins, *W. E. B. Du Bois: Writings*, 927.

[18]W. E. B. Du Bois, "The Negro as a National Asset," *Homiletic Review* 86 (July 1923):
52-58. Quoted in Blum, *American Prophet*, 119.

[19]W. E. B. Du Bois, *Darkwater: Voices from Within the Veil* (New York: Harcourt,
Brace, and Howe, 1920), 3.

[20]W. E. B. Du Bois, *Dusk of Dawn: An Essay Toward an Autobiography of a Race
Concept*, in Huggins, *W. E. B. Du Bois: Writings*, 666-67.

[21]Ibid., 667.

[22]Ibid., 670.

[23]Ibid., 671.

[24]Ibid., 673.

[25]Blum, *American Prophet*, 115.

[26]Ronald Reagan, "Remarks at the Annual Convention of the National Association
of Evangelicals," in *Speaking My Mind: Selected Speeches* (New York: Simon and
Schuster, 1989), 175.

[27]Ibid., 176.

[28]W. E. B. Du Bois, *Prayers for Dark People*, ed. Herbert Aptheker (Amherst: University of Massachusetts Press, 1980), 19.

List of Illustrations
and Credits

I.1. Theodore Roosevelt. Rockwood, George Gardner, photographer. "[Colonel Theodore Roosevelt, in uniform, full-length portrait, standing, facing slightly left]." New York, 1898. From Library of Congress Prints and Photographs Division. http://lccn.loc.gov/96522761.

1.1. William Walker. Brady, Mathew B., photographer. "[William Walker, three-quarter length studio portrait, standing, left arm resting on pedestal, facing slightly right]." Between 1855 and 1860. From Library of Congress Prints and Photographs Division. www.loc.gov/pictures/item/2003663046.

2.1. Dred Scott. Century Company. "Dred Scott." Published in *Century* magazine, June 1887. From Library of Congress Prints and Photographs Division. http://hdl.loc.gov/loc.pnp/pp.print.

2.2. "The Political Quadrille." "The political quadrille. Music by Dred Scott." [Cincinnati?: s.n.], 1860. From Library of Congress Prints and Photographs Division. http://hdl.loc.gov/loc.pnp/pp.print.

2.3. John Gast's *American Progress*. Crofutt, George A. *American Progress*. Print. 1873. After 1872 painting of the same title by John Gast. From Library of Congress Prints and Photographs Division. http://hdl.loc.pnp/pp.print.

3.1. President Andrew Jackson. Carter, Dennis Malone, artist, and Alexander Hay Ritchie, engraver. "Andrew Jackson." New York: Ritchie & Co., 1860. From Library of Congress Prints and Photographs Division. http://lccn.loc.gov/96521663.

3.2. Malcolm X. Hiller, Herman, photographer. "Malcolm X at Queens Court."

New York World-Telegram and the Sun, 1964. From Library of Congress Prints and Photographs Division. www.loc.gov/pictures/item/97519439.

4.1. **Secretary of State John Foster Dulles.** Leffler, Warren K., photographer. "[John Foster Dulles speaking at a podium]." 1958. From Library of Congress Prints and Photographs Division. www.loc.gov/pictures/item/2011660831.

5.1. **The announcement of the lying in state of Ronald Reagan.** Author's personal collection.

5.2. **President Lyndon B. Johnson.** "[Lyndon B. Johnson, head-and-shoulders portrait, facing left]." The White House. 1964. From Library of Congress Prints and Photographs Division. www.loc.gov/pictures/item/96522661.

5.3. **President Ronald Reagan.** "[Ronald Reagan, head-and-shoulders portrait, facing front]." Official White House photograph. 1981. From Library of Congress Prints and Photographs Division. www.loc.gov/pictures/item/96522678.

6.1. *Voyage of Life: Childhood.* Cole, Thomas, artist, and James Smillie, engraver. "*Voyage of Life—Childhood,* From the original painting by Thomas Cole, in the possession of Rev'd Gorham D. Abbott, Spingler Institute, New York." [New York?]: Printed by R. Holdgate, [between 1848 and 1850]. From Library of Congress Prints and Photographs Division. http://hdl.loc.gov/loc.pnp /pp.print.

6.2. *Sunset (California Scenery).* Bierstadt, Albert, artist. *Sunset (California Scenery).* L. Prang & Co., 1864. From Library of Congress Prints and Photographs Division. www.loc.gov/pictures/item/95514513.

6.3. *Lower Yellowstone Range.* Moran, Thomas, artist. *Lower Yellowstone Range.* L. Prang & Co., 1874, c1875. From Library of Congress Prints and Photographs Division. www.loc.gov/pictures/item/93500961.

7.1. **"Plucked."** "Plucked or, The Mexican eagle before the war! The Mexican eagle after the war!" *Yankee Doodle* 2, no. 32 (1847): 55. From Library of Congress Prints and Photographs Division. www.loc.gov/pictures /item/2002695264.

8.1. **William Edward Burghardt Du Bois.** Battey, Cornelius Marion, photographer. "W. E. B. (William Edward Burghardt) Du Bois." 1918. From Library of Congress Prints and Photographs Division. www.loc.gov/pictures /item/2003681451.

Author Index

Subject Index

Finding the Textbook You Need

The IVP Academic Textbook Selector
is an online tool for instantly finding the IVP books
suitable for over 250 courses across 24 disciplines.

ivpacademic.com